More
Process Patterns

Managing Object Technology Series

Additional Volumes in Preparation

More Process Patterns

Delivering Large-Scale Systems Using Object Technology

Scott W. Ambler

PUBLISHED BY THE PRESS SYNDICATE OF THE UNIVERSITY OF CAMBRIDGE
The Pitt Building, Trumpington Street, Cambridge CB2 1RP, United Kingdom

CAMBRIDGE UNIVERSITY PRESS
The Edinburgh Building, Cambridge CB2 2RU, UK
http://www.cup.cam.ac.uk
40 West 20th Street, New York, NY 10011-4211, USA
http:www.cup.org
10 Stamford Road, Oakleigh, Melbourne 3166, Australia

Published in association with SIGS Books

First published in 1999

Design and composition by Kevin Callahan/BNGO Books
Cover design by Yin Moy and Tom Jezek

Printed in the United States of America

A catalog record for this book is available from the British Library.

Library of Congress Cataloging-in-Publication Data is on record with the publisher.

ISBN 0-521-65262-6 hardback

To my parents, Bill and Loreen.

About the Author

scottAmbler is an instance of an SeniorOOConsultant with ambySoftInc based in Sharon, Ontario (http://www.ambysoft.com). Messages can be sent to him via the electronic mail contact point scott@ambysoft.com.

scottAmbler is a very versatile object that will change type in order to meet the needs of his clients. For example, he often takes on the role of OOMentor, OOTrainer, OOProcessExpert, or OODeveloper, and columnist with computingCanada (plesmanPublications). Scott has been an instance of an OOConsultant since 1991. scottAmbler has instantiated the book *The Object Primer* (sigsBooksCambridgeUniversityPress, nyCity, 1995), *Building Object Applications That Work* (sigsBooksCambridgeUniversityPress, nyCity, 1998), and *Process Patterns* (sigsBooksCambridgeUniversityPress, nyCity, 1998). He holds the roles of contributing-Editor with softwareDevelopment (millerFreemanPress), columnist with objectMagazine (sigsPublications). scottAmbler is an avid watcher of StarTrekEpisodes, and intends to one day do his doctorate degree at starFleetAcademy.

scottAmbler used to be a MasterStudent object, having received an InformationScienceDegree from universityOfToronto. As a MasterStudent, scottAmbler did a lot of work in OO CASE and instantiated a ThesisPaper object in computer-supported co-operative work (an academic alias for groupWare). Before becoming a MastersStudent, he was an instance of a TechnicalSystemAnalyst at royalBankOfCanada where he originally became interested in object-orientation.

Contents

Contents

Part 1 Deliver   *41*

Chapter 2
The Deliver Phase   43

Chapter 9

The Identify Defects and Enhancements Stage   **185**

Contents

xviii

Illustrations

Abbreviations

4GL	Fourth-generation language
ACD	Automatic call distribution
BDE	Business domain expert
C/S	Client/server
CASE	Computer-aided system engineering
CBT	Computer-based training
CCB	Configuration control board
CI	Configuration item
CM	Configuration management
CMM	Capability Maturity Model
CORBA	Common Object Request Broker Architecture
COTS	Commercial-off-the-shelf
CPU	Central processing unit
CR	Change request

CRC	Class responsibility collaborator
CRUD	Create, read, update, delete
DB	Database
DBA	Database administrator
DFD	Data-flow diagram
ER	Entity-relationship
FLOOT	Full life cycle object-oriented testing
GUI	Graphical user interface
HFE	Human factors engineer
^{SM}**IDEAL**[1]	Initiating, Diagnosing, Establishing, Acting, and Leveraging
IRR	Internal rate of return
IS	Information system
ISO	International Standards Organization
IT	Information technology
JAD	Joint application development
JIT	Just in time
JRP	Joint requirements planning
KISS	Keep it simple, silly
KPA	Key process area
MIS	Management information system
NCSS	Non-comment source statement
NIH	Not invented here
OODBMS	Object-oriented database management system
OID	Object identifier
OMG	Object Management Group

---

[1] ^{SM}IDEAL is a service mark of Carnegie Mellon University.

OML	OPEN modeling language
OO	Object-oriented
OO	Object-orientation
OOA	Object-oriented analysis
OOD	Object-oriented design
OOP	Object-oriented programming
OOSP	Object-Oriented Software Process
OOUI	Object-oriented user interface
OPEN	Object-Oriented, Process, Environment, and Notation
OTC	Object technology center
PAT	Process action team
PERT	Program Evaluation and Review Technique
PMI	Project Management Institute
QA	Quality assurance
RAD	Rapid application development
RAM	Requirements allocation matrix
RDB	Relational database
SCM	Software configuration management
SCR	Software change request
SCRB	Software configuration review board
SDLC	System development life cycle
SEI	Software Engineering Institute
SEPG	Software Engineering Process Group
SME	Subject-matter expert
SPICE	Software Process Improvement and Capability dEtermination

SPR	Software problem report
SQA	Software quality assurance
SQL	Structured query language
SRS	System requirement specification
T&E	Training and education
UAT	User-acceptance testing
UI	User interface
UML	Unified Modeling Language
V&V	Verification & Validation
VDD	Version description document
WBS	Work breakdown structure
Y2K	Year 2000

Foreword

THIS book continues a new approach to understanding the key development issues that constantly distract important software projects from delivering effective software, because they aren't documented in most organizations. It has been known for many years that an effective software development lifecycle will deliver good software with fewer defects than the uncontrolled random iteration of code and requirement. The initial book defined the core development stages and lifecycle. The second volume provides the management, testing, and delivery phases of development.

The world of software and system development is changing. Tools and languages are starting to gain de facto standards that are allowing projects to develop the more complex systems being demanded by the business and end users. As more people join the software industry, experience is being stretched and it is becoming more difficult to find senior developers with more than three strong projects behind them. Communicating experience is becoming one of the most important success factors to most development teams. Quality systems are fine for defining the letter of the law and rules that must be obeyed to keep a project on track, but they often miss the guidance and explanation of why it is important to follow the steps outlined in their often hundreds of pages. These can make quality systems very unapproachable by the average developer.

Scott's book provides an intuitive and clearly written guide to the key issues, concepts, deliverables and processes needed to deliver a successful project. He writes as if he is your own personal mentor, sitting next to you, answering the questions that face every project, team, manager, and developer.

The book uses the new and evolving form of patterns to structure and communicate a wide range of personal experience and best practiceóthe things those most seasoned system and software professionals all know, but progressively forget to communicate to the teams and developers they work with. "It's common knowledge" is often the excuse, but the pace of software development and the constantly changing faces in many companies means that it becomes common to only a few. This book and it predecessor provides a wealth of real practical knowledge that every developer needs but often misses out on.

With this book Scott has set a foundation of a next generation of process and pattern development that will evolve, I believe, toward a standard way of describing, documenting, and structuring experience and knowledge about software and system development processes. There is still much work to be done in this arena, but this book (and its companion) will provide an invaluable reference of concepts and processes that will allow many projects to recognize and formalize their own development process.

I would expect that many IT professionals will recognize much of the advice within the book, but will gain considerably for being able to read and relate the knowledge with a development lifecycle. By following the patterns presented in the book and balancing the forces and drivers of their own project, they will improve not only their own personal performance and effectiveness, but will start to raise the process maturity of the team and project they apply the process patterns to.

Don Kavanagh,
Principal Methodologist, SSA Object Technology

Preface

ORGANIZATIONS have moved beyond the pilot project stage and are now using object technology to build large-scale, mission-critical business applications. Unfortunately they are finding that the processes that proved so successful on small, proof-of-concept projects do not scale very well for real-world development. Today's organization needs a collection of proven techniques for managing the complexities of large-scale, object-oriented software development projects: a collection of process patterns. A process pattern describes a collection of general techniques, actions, and/or tasks for developing object-oriented software. In many ways process patterns are the reusable building blocks from which your organization can tailor a mature software process. To be fair, however, it isn't enough to just have a collection of process patterns, you must have a pattern language of process patterns that fit together as a consistent whole, that form a complete software process. That is what *Process Patterns* and its sister book *More Process Patterns* provide.

The object-oriented software process (OOSP) presented in these two volumes is a collection of process patterns that are geared toward medium to large-size organizations that need to develop software to support their main line of business. Although the OOSP could easily be modified for the development of shrink-wrapped software, I would rather point you in the direction of the Unified software process. The Unified software process was created by a leading maker of shrink-wrapped development tools. There is no such thing as a one-size-fits-all process, and the OOSP is just one of several approaches to developing object-oriented (OO) software.

I have chosen to describe the OOSP as a collection of process patterns that have been proven in practice: they are not the theoretical musings of an ivory-tower academic who has never built software. The OOSP provides a framework which addresses issues such as how to:

- successfully deliver large applications using object technology

- develop applications that are truly easy to maintain and enhance

- manage these projects

- ensure that your development efforts are of high quality.

Dispelling Industry Myths

These two books actively attack several myths of the object industry. First, the belief that object development is a purely iterative process is questionable at best. Although this might appear to be true for small pilot projects using OO technology, the reality for large-scale, mission-critical applications is that the OO development process is serial in the large and iterative in the small, delivering incremental releases over time. At the time of this writing, the interesting thing is that the Unified software process is in fact based on this concept, although they still claim that they have an incremental process. Oh well; old myths die hard, I guess.

Second, these books also disprove the myth that you can do less testing when you use OO technology. The reality is that the exact opposite is true: you need to do more. One of my fundamental beliefs, a belief shared by the vast majority of professional software engineers, is that testing and quality assurance should be performed throughout the entire development process, not just at the end of it. Furthermore, the reality of incremental development is that you need to perform more regression testing than with single-shot, "big-bang" development.

Third, these two books disprove the myth that we only need to be concerned with development issues while building an application. The reality is that the concerns of maintenance and support are just as important, if not more so, than those of development. The OOSP explicitly includes both maintenance and support as part of the project life cycle, so as to put it in the face of everyone involved in the development process. There is a saying in the computer industry: A good developer knows that there is more to development than programming; a great developer knows that there is more to development than development.

Fourth, I hope that these books disprove the myth that processes only result in needless paperwork. My experience has been that process patterns, when applied intelligently, increase the productivity of developers. My experience has also been that when process patterns are applied less than intelligently — that when the paper pushers have too much influence in an organization — they can decrease your productivity. The process patterns of the OOSP pattern language have been proven to work in practice — how you choose to implement them will determine how successful you are. Organizations that keep the end goal in mind — that of developing, maintaining, and supporting software that fulfills the needs of their user community — will be successful with process patterns. Those that follow processes simply for the sake of following processes are likely to fail.

The Object-Oriented Software Process (OOSP)

So what do these books cover? First of all, they are organized by the four serial phases of OO development: Initiate, Construct, Deliver, and Maintain and Support. Second, each phase is then divided further into its iterative stages. As a result, the two books are organized into the following chapters:

Process Patterns:

- Introduction to the OOSP
- The Initiate phase
- Define and validate initial requirements
- Define the initial management documents
- Justify the project
- Define the project infrastructure
- The Construct phase
- Model
- Program
- Generalize
- Test in the small
- Concluding Remarks

More Process Patterns:

- Where we've been: *Process Patterns*
- The Deliver phase
- Test in the large
- Rework
- Release the application
- Assess the project
- The Maintain and Support phase
- Support the application
- Identify bugs and enhancements
- The project and cross-project tasks of the OOSP
- Introducing the OOSP into your organization

As I describe each serial phase and iterative stage throughout the books I address a series of project and cross-project tasks that are crucial to your success. These tasks are:

- Project management

- People management

- Quality assurance

- Risk management

- Reuse management

- Training and education

- Deliverable management

- Infrastructure management

Yet Another Silver Bullet?

A silver bullet is a single process or technology that you can purchase and introduce into your organization that will magically slay the lycanthropes of missed project deadlines, over-budget projects, and applications that don't meet the needs of their users. Process patterns are definitely not silver bullets; nothing is. Implementing the process patterns presented in these books will prove to be a difficult task that will take several years to accomplish. If you are looking for a quick fix to your problems then this is not it — nothing is.

These books describe a collection of process patterns, presenting them at a level of detail that describes the issues and potential pitfalls that you may face, but does not dictate detailed specifics for implementing the given processes. For example, the chapter for the Model stage covers object-oriented modeling, explaining the main modeling techniques and how they fit together as well as providing a proven strategy for organizing the modeling effort. What it does not do is tell you how to model in detail — if you want to learn how to draw class diagrams or data models then you need to pick up one or more of the excellent books referred to in that chapter. Process patterns are conceptually similar to design patterns and analysis patterns which model a solution to a common problem but leave the implementation details up to you.

When you intelligently apply process patterns of the OOSP pattern language you can greatly improve the quality of the applications that you build and increase their chance of success. These patterns are proven in practice. They work. Developing software is a complex task, and you need development processes that reflect this fact, processes that support and enhance the efforts of software professionals. These volumes describe how to develop large-scale, mission-critical applications using object technology, explaining how the process patterns all fit together. I believe the OOSP presented in these books is complete and provides sufficient material from which your organization can tailor a mature software process that meets its unique needs.

The History of This Book

When I began writing this book series — *The Object Primer, Building Object Applications That Work, Process Patterns,* and *More Process Patterns* — my original intention was that the third book would be an "OO for managers" book. Although my intention was good, during the time that I wrote the first two books, several very good books geared specifically for managers came onto the market. I needed to rethink my strategy, and my recent experiences on projects indicated to me that there is a desperate need for a book about the OO development process; hence *Process Patterns* and *More Process Patterns*.

At about the same time, the object technology consulting firm that I worked for was doing some serious soul-searching. We had been very successful implementing applications using object technology, having worked on both small and large projects for a multitude of clients in a wide range of industries. Several of our projects had even been nominated for OO industry awards, resulting in two runners-up and one first prize. Our crisis came when we experienced our first failed project (also my first failed project), the first time we had ever been subcontracted and the first time we were not in complete control. I was the lead architect on the project, so I saw first-hand everything that went wrong — an incredibly valuable learning experience. I have read articles in business journals that state that the best potential new hire is someone who has failed, learned from their experience, and then bounced back. Now I know where they were coming from, and you know what? They were right.

Once the dust settled from the inevitable finger-pointing, we came to the conclusion that although we knew what we were doing going in, had even planned to do the "right things" on the project, we had allowed the prime contractor and the client to steer us off track into failure. This happened because we did not have our software process adequately documented. We knew what we were doing, we effectively understood and had been applying a collection of process patterns for software for several clients, we worked well together, everyone knew how to do their part, but what we did not have was a fully documented software process that showed how we did what we did. When the project ran into trouble, we did not have a completely documented process to fall back on, to warn us that something was going wrong.

Because it was clear that we needed to complete the documentation of our development process, and in part because I was already working on it anyway for these two books, I was put in charge of managing the documentation of the company's software process — an internal project whose purpose was to finish defining how it is that we build systems.

Time passed, the company successfully followed their software process on several projects, and I moved on to greener pastures to help other organizations define and implement software development processes that met their specific needs. *Process Patterns* and *More Process Patterns* summarize my experiences developing large-scale, mission-critical software for a wide variety of organizations, as well as my experiences helping these organizations understand how to effectively and efficiently develop object-oriented software. I believe that these two books will provide an excellent starting point from which your organization can define an OOSP that meets your specific needs.

How to Read These Books

I would like to begin by saying that everyone should read the first chapter of *Process Patterns*, which describes what process patterns are and overviews both the ⊖OSP and the Capability Maturity

Model (CMM). Everyone should also read Chapter 10 of *More Process Patterns*, which summarizes and expands on the project and cross-project tasks described throughout the two volumes; these tasks are the glue that hold projects together. Fundamentally, however, you need to read the entirety of both books at some point so that you gain an understanding of how software is developed, maintained, and supported. Yes, it is critical to have a detailed understanding of your job, but at the same time it is important to understand the "big picture" and how you fit into it. My experience is that the best software developers understand the entire OOSP and then concentrate on the portion of it that they enjoy most.

Senior Management

You also need to read Chapter 11 of *More Process Patterns*, which discusses the issues involved with introducing process patterns into an organization. Yes, buying every member of your staff a copy of these books is a good start (although, from my point of view, buying each of them several copies would be a better start), but the fact remains that process improvement is a multi-year effort that must be actively supported and nurtured. I have provided you with a very good basis from which to begin your efforts; now the hard part is up to you.

Project Managers

Sorry, but you need to read both books, from front to back. A good start would be to read the first chapter and then follow with the phase summary chapters (2 and 7 of *Process Patterns*, and 2 and 7 of *More Process Patterns*), and then Chapter 10 of *More Process Patterns* for a discussion of the project and cross-project tasks. This would provide you with a good overview of how the entire development process works, but you would still want to go back and read the book from cover to cover to gain a detailed understanding of the OOSP and of the process patterns that you will use on your projects.

Modelers and Programmers

You will want to read the Construct phase chapters (7 through 11 of *Process Patterns*) to understand what your roles in the development process are and how you will work together with the test community.

You should also read the Initiate phase chapter (Chapter 2 of *Process Patterns*) and the Define and Validate Initial Requirements stage chapter (Chapter 3 of *Process Patterns*) to understand how the inputs into the Construct phase are created, and the Delivery phase chapter (Chapter 2 of *More Process Patterns*) to understand the needs of your immediate customers. You will also need to understand the Rework stage, covered in Chapter 5 of *More Process Patterns*, to understand the issues involved with addressing defects discovered during testing in the large.

Testers

You need to read the two testing chapters (Chapter 11 of *Process Patterns* and Chapter 3 of *More Process Patterns*). Testers who are involved with testing during construction (testing in the small) need to read the Define and Validate Initial Requirements chapter and the Construct phase chapters. Testers who are involved in testing after construction (testing in the large) need to read the Deliver phase chapter and the Test in the Large chapter.

Quality Assurance Engineers

You should start by reading the introductory chapter of *Process Patterns* and the quality assurance section in Chapter 10 of *More Process Patterns*. Then, depending on the portions of the OOSP that you are involved with you will need to read the appropriate chapters to understand the processes that you are supporting.

Process Managers

Like project managers, you need to read both books from cover to cover. A good start would be to read chapters 1 of *Process Patterns* and 10 and 11 of *More Process Patterns*. You should focus on Chapter 11 because it describes a strategy for introducing and managing software process improvement within an organization, the main focus of your job. You should then follow by reading both volumes from front to back so that you understand the OOSP in its entirety.

Reuse Engineers

Because reuse can be achieved throughout the entire OOSP, you will need to read the portions of the books that describe the

One of the things you will notice is that I have reused some of the text describing the various types of reuse in several places throughout the book; not only do I preach reuse, I live it.

processes that you support. A good place to start would be to read the Model stage chapter and the Generalize stage chapter (Chapter 10 of *Process Patterns*), which describe techniques that support systematic and opportunistic reuse respectively. As you would expect, Chapter 10 of *More Process Patterns* summarizes the reuse techniques and opportunities presented throughout both books.

Software Configuration Management (SCM) Engineers

You will want to read The Construct phase chapter (Chapter 7 of *Process Patterns*) which describes in detail the SCM procedures that should be followed throughout the OOSP. The other Construct phase chapters are also important because they describe the main development processes that SCM must support. Chapter 9 of *More Process Patterns* is also important for you because it describes the Identify Defects and Enhancements stage, which focuses on allocating maintenance changes to existing software, an important process that SCM enables.

Risk Assessors

You will need to read the chapters corresponding to the processes that you are assessing, and you will be happy to note that each stage chapter includes a section describing potential risks for that stage. These risks are also summarized in Chapter 10 of *More Process Patterns*.

Training Managers

You will find that Chapter 10 of *More Process Patterns* summarizes the training needs for teaching the OOSP to your organization's information professionals, needs that were first identified in the appropriate project phase and stage chapters. Chapter 5 of *More Process Patterns*, which describes the Release stage, includes a section describing the training needs for your organization's user, support, and operations communities when a new application, or a new version, is to be released.

Support and Operations Engineers

You will want to read the Release stage chapter as well as the Maintain and Support phase chapters (Chapters 7 to 9 of *More Process Patterns*) as these chapters focus on issues pertinent to the operation and support of applications.

Professors and Students

I believe that *Process Patterns* and *More Process Patterns* would be ideal texts for a second- or third-year university/college course about the software process. These books should be taught and read cover to cover in the order presented.

Online Process Patterns Resources

I have developed, and continue to maintain, The Process Patterns Resource Page

http://www.ambysoft.com/processPatternsPage.html

which contains links to key web sites on the Internet that deal with process patterns, organizational patterns, patterns in general, antipatterns, the software process, and software process improvement. I also make it a habit to post white papers about important topics in object-oriented development, including new patterns, and I hope that you find this page (and my entire site) useful.

Sharing My Thoughts and Experiences With You

In *The Object Primer* I explicitly pointed out useful techniques with specific "Tips" boxes. In *Building Object Applications That Work* I added "Scott's Soapbox" boxes that I used to identify my personal, and sometimes controversial, views on problems faced when developing object-oriented applications. In these books I add "War Story" boxes where I describe real-world experiences that I have had to help explain the importance of a concept or technique and to show that it works in practice and not just in theory.

Acknowledgments

I would like to recognize the following people for their input into the development of *Process Patterns* and *More Process Patterns*, and/or for their feedback regarding my published papers/articles which in turn made it into this book.

Susan Ambler, Little Su-Su Literature Services
Brad Appleton, Motorola AIEG
Jennifer Barzso, GE Capital (Canada)
Michael A. Beedle, FTI Consulting
Kevin Callahan, BNGO Books
Steve Cohen, Abstract Solutions
Amy S. Gause, Northern Telecom
Lothlórien Homet, SIGS Books
Lou Hawn, Insight Technology Group
Matthew Lusher, copy editor
John Nalbone, Insight Technology Group
Craig Ostrom, Boeing Information Services
Mark Peterson, Insight Technology Group
Chris Roffler, Insight Technology Group
Jeanette Snover, Insight Technology Group
Walter Thiem, Mark Winter & Associates
Robert White, RJW Consulting

Chapter 1

Introduction to
More Process Patterns

WHEN we left off in *Process Patterns* (Ambler, 1998b) I had taken you to the point where your software was written. Now in *More Process Patterns* I'll show you how to deliver, and then maintain and support applications built using object-oriented (OO) technology. Sadly, these are two topics that have been generally overlooked by the object community, until now. There is a lot more to OO development than writing code. There is also a lot more to it than creating use cases, CRC models, and class diagrams. OO development is about creating applications that solve the needs of your users. It's about doing this in such a way that the applications that are built are timely, accurate, and of high quality. This book is about helping you to accomplish these worthy goals.

In this chapter I summarize key concepts presented in *Process Patterns*. I explore common myths about object-oriented development; describe what process patterns are all about; discuss the object-oriented software process (OOSP) focusing on the serial phases, iterative stages, and the project and cross-project tasks that are vital to the success of your software efforts; and overview the Software Engineering Institute (SEI)'s Capability Maturity Model (CMM).

1.1 Exploring Object-Oriented Myths

One thing that you have likely read is that OO development by its very nature is iterative. As you saw in *Process Patterns* this is only partly true. The main components of OO development—modeling, programming, and testing in the small (formerly known as unit testing)—are in fact performed iteratively. Professional software development, however, is comprised of far more than just these three things. We have several aspects of project initiation to contend with, all of which should be done long before development begins. We eventually have a code freeze, perhaps several over time, after which we perform testing in the large (formerly known as system testing) and hopefully deliver the application. After the application is up and running in the field we need to track change requests, including both enhancements and problem reports, so that the application may be updated in the future. The fact of the matter is that although OO development is iterative in the small, it is by its very nature serial in the large. I will explore this issue in detail throughout this book.

The fact that OO development is iterative is a myth.

You have probably also heard that OO development is incremental; in other words, applications are built and released a portion at a time. This can also be true, but does not necessarily have to be so. I have been involved in many OO projects over the years, some of which took an incremental approach and some of which didn't.

OO development is often incremental, but not always.

1.2 What Is a Process Pattern?

To define what a process pattern is, I would first like to explore its two root words: process and pattern. A process is defined as a series of actions in which one or more inputs are used to produce one or more outputs. Defining a pattern is a little more difficult. Alexander (1979) hints at the definition of a pattern by pointing out that the same broad features keep recurring over and over again, although in their detailed appearance these broad features are never the same. Alexander shows that although every building is unique, each may be created by following a collection of general patterns. In other words, a pattern is a general solution to a common problem or issue, one from which a specific solution may be derived.

The repetition of patterns is quite a different thing than the repetition of parts. Indeed, the different parts will be unique because the patterns are the same.
—Christopher Alexander

Coplien (1995), in his paper *A Generative Development-Process Pattern Language,* hints at the definition for the term *process pattern* in his statement that *the patterns of activity within an organization (and hence within its project) are called a process.* For the purposes of this book, I define a process pattern to be a collection of general techniques, actions, and/or tasks (activities) for developing object-oriented software.

An important feature of a process pattern is that it describes what you should do but not the exact details of how you should do something. Don't worry: I intend to provide a wealth of advice about how to work the process patterns presented in this book, but I will not get into excruciating details.

A process pattern describes a collection of tasks/ techniques/actions for successfully developing software.

Related to process patterns are something called organizational patterns, patterns that describe common management techniques or organizational structures. The fact is that process patterns and organizational patterns go hand-in-hand, so I intend to share with you some of the good work that has been done in this field. The focus of this book, however, is not organizational patterns; instead the focus is to describe a pattern language of process patterns that your organization can use to tailor a mature software process from.

Just as there exists common approaches for successfully solving recurring problems, there also exist common approaches to solving recurring problems that prove to be ineffective. These approaches are called antipatterns. Throughout this book I will describe several process antipatterns to share with you my experiences with techniques that have proven to not work very well in practice.

A process anti- pattern describes a collection of tasks/techniques/ actions that have proven ineffective for developing software.

TIP

Visit The Process Patterns Resource Page

I have developed, and will continue to maintain, a resource web page for process patterns: *http://www.ambysoft.com/processPatternsPage.html.* This page contains references to published material about, and links to key web sites pertaining to, process patterns, organizational patterns, antipatterns, process improvement, and general topics about the software process. I believe you will find this page to be a key resource for your process improvement efforts.

> ### DEFINITIONS
>
> **antipattern** The description of an approach to solving a common problem, an approach that in time proves to be wrong or highly ineffective.
>
> **Object-Oriented Software Process (OOSP)** A collection of process patterns that together describe a complete process for developing, maintaining, and supporting software.
>
> **organizational pattern** A pattern that describes a common management technique or a potential organization structure.
>
> **pattern** The description of a general solution to a common problem or issue from which a detailed solution to a specific problem may be determined. Software development patterns come in many flavors, including but not limited to analysis patterns, design patterns, and process patterns.
>
> **process** A series of actions in which one or more inputs are used to produce one or more outputs.
>
> **process antipattern** An antipattern that describes an approach and/or series of actions for developing software that is proven to be ineffective and often detrimental to your organization.
>
> **process pattern** A pattern that describes a proven, successful approach and/or series of actions for developing software.

1.3 Types of Process Patterns

One feature that I believe is important for process patterns is that it be possible to develop them for all scales of development. For example, process patterns for specific project phases, such as construction or delivery, will be presented as a collection of iterative project stages, and process patterns for each project stage, such as programming or testing, are also presented. The point to be made is that the scope of a single process pattern ranges from a high-level view of how a specific project phase works to a more-detailed view of a specific task/activity. The Object-Oriented Software Process (OOSP), as presented in this book, is described as a collection of process patterns, the OOSP process pattern language.

Patterns can exist at all scales.
—Christopher Alexander

I believe that there are at least three types of process patterns. In order of increasing scale they are:

1. **Task process patterns** This type of process pattern depicts the detailed steps to perform a specific task, such as the Technical Review pattern presented in Chapter 3.

> **DEFINITIONS**
>
> **project phase** The large components of the OOSP that are performed in a serial manner. The four project phases are Initiate, Construct, Deliver, and Maintain and Support. A project phase is depicted by a process pattern.
>
> **project stage** The components of a project phase, performed in an iterative manner, that make up a project phase. For example, the project stages that make up the Construct phase are Model, Test in the Small, Program, and Generalize. A project stage is also depicted by a process pattern.

2. **Stage process patterns** This type of process pattern depicts the steps, that are often performed iteratively, of a single project stage. A stage process pattern is presented for each project stage such as the Model stage (Ambler, 1998b) and the Rework stage (Chapter 4).
3. **Phase process patterns** This type of process pattern depicts the interactions between the stage process patterns for a single project phase. There are four phase process patterns presented in this book, one for each of the four project phases.

1.4 The Object-Oriented Software Process

Let's follow good development practice and begin the discussion of the Object-Oriented Software Process (OOSP) by describing the requirements for it. Once we understand our needs we can put together a process to meet them.

To understand the requirements for an OOSP, we must look at the environment for which we are developing these applications. The business environment of today is constantly changing. The needs of tomorrow are often different than those of today, implying that users and developers must work closely together in order to correctly define, design, and build OO applications. Organizations want to develop mission-critical applications using OO technology, applications that like their structured predecessors will be in production for many years, possibly even decades. Unlike their structured predecessors, however, these applications must be easy to maintain and to enhance because organizations have been badly burned in the past by poorly crafted software—and they will not tolerate it again. To compete effectively, organizations need to have this software in production as soon as possible, with the most critical features being available as soon as possible. Furthermore, the applications that are being demanded by our users are growing larger in both scope and complexity; therefore, we must be able to develop these large, complex applications. In addition to all of this, users[1] want all this to happen as inexpensively as possible.

In Table 1.1 we match the requirements with the development approaches described in the previous section that best meets that requirement. Notice that there is not a single technique that meets all of our needs—not even iterative development, which many people claim to be the only way to develop OO applications. Without considering the requirements for an OOSP first, how would we be able to determine whether or not a development approach actually meets our needs? We wouldn't.

Now that we understand the requirements for an OOSP and the proposed approaches to fulfill each requirement, we can now consider how to implement the OOSP. In Figure 1.1 we see a depiction of the OOSP process pattern, indicating that it is comprised of four serial phases: Initiate, Construct, Deliver, and Maintain and Support. Within each phase are iteratively performed stages. For example, the Construct phase is made up of the Model, Test In The Small, Generalize, and Program stages. Each project phase and stage are described in the following section. The "big arrow" at the bottom of the diagram indicates important tasks critical to the success of a project that are applicable to all stages of development—tasks whose issues will be discussed as we cover each project stage in turn.

For now I want to concentrate on the fact that OO development, at least for non-trivial projects, should proceed in a serial manner in the large, but in an iterative manner in the small.

What is not shown in Figure 1.1, although it will be discussed in greater detail later in this chapter, is the fact that the OOSP easily supports the delivery of incremental releases of an application as well as parallel development activities. OO development is fundamentally serial in the large, iterative in the small, and should deliver incremental releases whenever possible. In the following sections we will discuss in detail the features of the OOSP.

---

[1]Throughout this book I will use the term user to represent the person(s) for which you are ultimately building the application. Your organization may refer to these people as clients, customers, and/or end users.

TABLE 1.1. Trying to Meet the Requirements for an OOSP

Requirement	Development Approach
OO applications must be easy to maintain.	Maintainability is the direct result of good design and good implementation; therefore, both serial and iterative development approaches are applicable.
OO applications must be easy to enhance.	Enhanceability is the direct result of good analysis, design, and implementation; therefore, both serial and iterative development approaches are applicable.
The application must meet the needs of its users.	Both iterative and incremental development best support this requirement, as they both provide many opportunities for users to be involved with system development —which in turn leads to a greater understanding of their real needs.
The application is large and mission-critical.	Serial development best supports this requirement, as it provides better opportunities for managing a project.
Critical features must be put into production as soon as possible.	Incremental development best supports this need, because you can release your application in several, smaller portions instead of one big bang. This means you can get functionality into the hands of your users faster. Parallel development is also important because it reduces the calendar time needed to develop an application.

(continued)

TABLE 1.1. (Continued)

Requirement	Development Approach
The project requires development and operation of complex applications.	The combination of iterative and incremental development approaches best support this need. Iterative development allows you to model and build sections of an application all at once, while releasing in increments puts the application in the hands of users faster, thus providing opportunities for feedback and improvement earlier in the life of the application.
Users want applications built inexpensively.	Iterative development allows you to develop applications in the order that makes the most sense, presumably reducing your costs. Incremental development allows you to build large applications in several releases, making them easier and less expensive to build in the long run.

1.5 Serial in the Large

From a 50,000 foot level, the OOSP is fundamentally serial in nature. You must first get the project started by identifying the initial requirements, justifying that the project is viable, and determining the tools and techniques that you will use to deliver your application. Once these tasks are more or less complete, you actually begin to build the application by developing models, writing code, generalizing your work, and testing it in units. Once construction is complete, you will freeze your code so you can test the entire application and release it to your users. Once the application is released, you maintain and support the application.

The OOSP is serial in the large, and is comprised of four serial project phases:

- Initiate
- Construct
- Deliver
- Maintain and Support

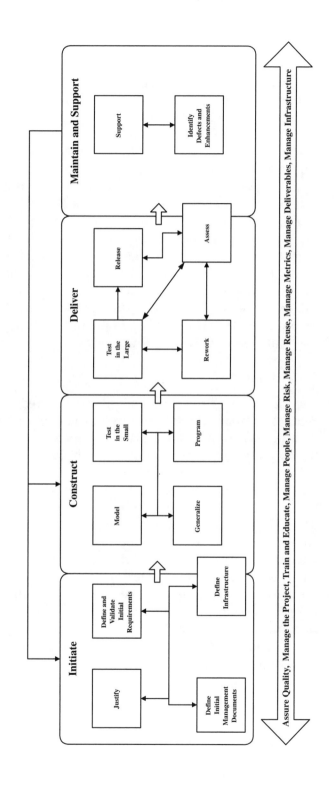

Figure 1.1.
The Object-Oriented Software Process (OOSP)

1.5.1 Initiate

The main goal of the Initiate phase, covered in detail in *Process Patterns* (Ambler, 1998b), is to lay the foundation for a successful project. It is made up of the definition and validation of the initial requirements and management documents, the project justification, and the definition of the project infrastructure. The initial requirements give the project team somewhere to start when construction begins, and the initial management documents provide a basis for managing the project throughout the entire development process. The project justification effort produces a feasibility study that shows whether the project is expected to be successful. (If it shows that the project does not make sense then you shouldn't continue.) The project infrastructure effort puts in place a collection of documents that describe the tools that the project team will use, how they will use them, the standards that the team will follow, how their work will be evaluated, and the deliverables that they must produce during the project.

1.5.2 Construct

The main goal of the Construct phase, covered in detail in *Process Patterns* (Ambler, 1998b), is to build the application in such a way that it is easy to maintain and to enhance. This includes modeling the application via traditional OO techniques such as CRC modeling, use cases, class diagrams, sequence diagrams, and so on. Programming is performed using leading-edge OO languages like Java, Smalltalk, C++, and ObjectCOBOL that support the OO development paradigm. Your modeling and programming efforts are verified using testing-in-the-small techniques such as use-case scenario testing, design walkthroughs, class testing, and inheritance regression testing. During the Construct phase you also want to take the time to generalize your work so that it can be reused successfully; without a distinct generalization stage, this work rarely gets done. By the way, do not forget that modeling, programming, testing in the small, and generalization are all occurring iteratively.

1.5.3 Deliver

The main goal of the Deliver phase, covered in detail in Chapters 2 through 6, is to put a working, high-quality, well-documented application in the hands of your users. This means that you need to perform testing in the large on the application by using techniques such as system testing, installation testing, stress testing, and user acceptance testing. Because your testing efforts will find some problems with your application, you will need to do some rework, effectively more construction, to fix these problems. Once the application has been tested and fixed, you release the application by making it available to users and by training them. Finally, during this phase take the opportunity to improve your development process and to identify training opportunities for your staff by doing a project review, also called a project postmortem, to learn what you did right and wrong on the project.

1.5.4 Maintain and Support

The main goal of the Maintain and Support phase, covered in detail in Chapters 7 through 9, is to keep the application running and as up-to-date as possible. This means that you need to support the needs of users by providing training, answering their questions, and by fixing any problems that they may encounter. You also need to have a change-control process in place so you can identify any possible defects or enhancements for the application, prioritize those changes, and then address the changes in a future release. Change control is an integral part of the OOSP and is put in place during the Initiate phase.

1.6 Iterative in the Small

We've seen that the OOSP is fundamentally serial in the large, so now let's explore the idea that it is iterative in the small by considering the iterative stages of each project phase.

1.6.1 Initiate

The first serial phase of the OOSP is Initiate, which is comprised of four iterative project stages:

- Define and validate initial requirements
- Define initial management documents
- Justify
- Define infrastructure

1.6.2 Define and Validate Initial Requirements

All projects, even the most technical ones, must have a high-level set of requirements defined for them at the beginning of the project.

During this stage, also known as requirements engineering, you want to determine accurately what you are going to deliver to the end user, at least at a high level. There are several techniques that you can employ to do so, including CRC cards, use cases, use-case scenario testing, traditional interviews, and joint application development (JAD) sessions (also known as Joint Requirements Planning (JRP) sessions). There are several ways to gather and validate the initial requirements for your application. Furthermore, it is also possible to get your users actively involved in the project during this stage; they will potentially do the majority of the work of gathering the initial requirements. After all, who knows the user requirements better than the users? The key deliverable of this stage is a definition of the project scope based on validated, high-level requirements.

1.6.3 Define Initial Management Documents

Key project management documents are started during the Initiate phase.

This stage explores the fact that during a project, many critical management documents are started early in a project. Documents like the risk assessment, the project schedule, the project estimate, and the team definition are all started at this time. These documents are not only crucial to the management of the entire project itself, but are also valuable input into the process of justifying the project. Key deliverables of this phase are the management documents themselves, which often have titles such as "Initial Risk Assessment" and "Initial Project Plan."

1.6.4 Justify the Project

The Justify stage is probably the most important part of the Initiate phase, yet it is usually the most poorly done. Because upwards of 85 percent of all large projects fail[2] (Jones, 1996), for various reasons, if you do a good job in this stage then most projects should end here before a large investment has been made in

---

[2]This figure has two components: 65 percent of large projects are absolute failures (canceled) and 21.33 percent are relative failures (delayed). In *The Object Primer* (Ambler, 1995) I take a much harder stance on project failure: any project that is late, over budget, or does not meet the needs of its users should be considered a failure. With this definition, few projects succeed.

them. The key deliverable of this stage is a feasibility study that addresses the project's economic feasibility (does the project make financial sense?), technical feasibility (can it actually be built?), and operational feasibility (can you support and maintain the application?).

You should justify your project on technical, economic, and operational factors.

1.6.5 Define the Project Infrastructure

For a project to be successful, you need to define the team, the tools that you will use, the quality standards to which you will adhere, and the deliverables that you will produce. This naturally needs to be done as soon as possible in the project so that construction can get underway, although sometimes you will start construction before getting the infrastructure completely in place. (That's why this stage overlaps into the Construct phase.) In many ways this stage helps to define how the members of the development team will interact internally with each other and externally with their users. The key deliverables include an indication of the team members and their roles and responsibilities on the project, a description of the development toolset, and a collection of standards and guidelines for construction and testing. This project stage will require a lot of effort the first couple of times that you do it, but will proceed quite quickly on subsequent projects because you can reuse your infrastructure efforts from previous projects.

You need to define the tools that you will use, the environment that you will develop for, and the standards and guidelines that you will follow as early in the project as possible.

1.7 Construct

The second serial phase of the OOSP is the Construct phase, which is comprised of four iterative project stages:

- Model
- Program
- Test in the Small
- Generalize

1.7.1 Model

The Model stage is composed of analysis, which defines what the application does and does not do; and design, which defines how the application will be built. In the structured world, analysis and design were considered two separate stages of the software process, but with the OOSP we really need to consider them as one stage. With OO development the line between analysis and design is blurred, so blurred in fact that both of them share many techniques in common. The bottom line is that the real difference between analysis and design is what you are modeling and who is doing the modeling—not how you are modeling. One way to think about it is that modeling is mostly analysis when users dominate the modeling effort, and mostly design when developers dominate the modeling effort. A better way to think about it, I believe, is that it is just modeling. The key deliverable is a collection of interrelated models/diagrams, which potentially include: class diagrams (object model), interface-flow diagrams, prototypes, CRC models, use cases, use-case diagrams, state diagrams, activity models, collaboration diagrams, deployment diagrams, data diagrams, activity diagrams, and sequence diagrams.

Modeling is a highly iterative process involving different mixes of people for different types of models.

Figure 1.2 shows a task process pattern called Detailed Modeling; the figure depicts many of the common OO modeling techniques and diagrams and indicates the relationships between them. The arrows show the relationships between each technique, with the arrow heads indicating an "input into" relationship; for example, we see that an activity model is an input into a class diagram. In the bottom right-hand corner of each box is a series of one or more letters that indicate who is involved in working on that technique/diagram. The underlined letter indicates which group of people performs the majority of the work for that diagram; for example, we see that users form the majority of the people involved in developing a CRC model, but designers form the majority of those creating state diagrams.

1.7.2 Program

Object-oriented coding is different than procedural/structured coding. First, you are working with classes, methods, and attributes, rather than functions, procedures, and data. Second, your program code should flow right out of your models because they too are based on the same concepts as OO coding. The key deliverable in this project stage is the source code itself and the accompanying documentation, both having undergone testing in the small.

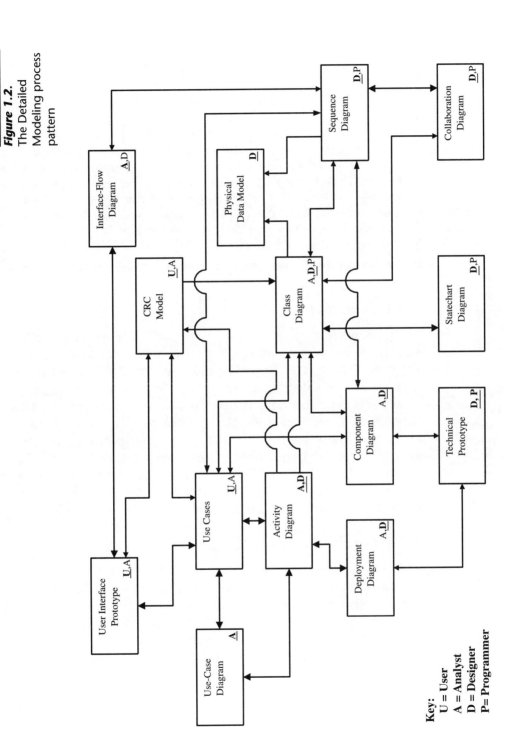

Figure 1.2.
The Detailed
Modeling process
pattern

Interface-Flow Diagram **A**,D

Physical Data Model **D**

Sequence Diagram **D**,P

Collaboration Diagram **D**,P

CRC Model **U**,A

Class Diagram A,**D**,P

Statechart Diagram **D**,P

User Interface Prototype **U**,A

Use Cases **U**,A

Activity Diagram A,**D**

Component Diagram **A**,D

Technical Prototype **D, P**

Use-Case Diagram **A**

Deployment Diagram **A**,D

Key:
U = User
A = Analyst
D = Designer
P = Programmer

SCOTT'S SOAPBOX

OO Modeling is Iterative in Nature

You can see from Figure 1.2 that OO modeling by its very nature is an iterative process. I suspect that because many of the leading methodologies have concentrated on OO analysis and design, instead of the entire OOSP, and that because OO modeling is iterative in nature, many people have concluded that OO development is also iterative in nature. When we step back and think about it, however, we know that this statement is not completely true: OO development is actually serial in the large and iterative in the small.

1.7.3 Generalize

Take the time to actually make your development efforts reusable.

The Generalize stage is critical to your organization's reuse efforts (Meyer, 1995) because it forces project managers to account for the time that it takes to make your work reusable. If you do not invest the time during a project to look for opportunities for reuse, and take the time then to make what you find reusable, then chances are very good that you never will. When a project ends, people always want to go on to the next project; they generally do not want to go through their old work trying to make it reusable. The key deliverable of the Generalize stage is a reusable component, be it model or code, that can be used either on the current project or on future projects.

1.7.4 Test in the Small

This project stage was traditionally referred to as unit testing in the structured world but has been extended to include the testing of your modeling efforts as well. Because OO modeling and coding are iterative efforts, testing in the small is iterative as well because the best time to test your work is immediately after you finish it. If you have developed a new model, walk through it. If you have programmed a new class, or even a new method, test it. You do not want to wait until the end of your project to find out that something does not work; it is far better to find out right away while it is still easy to fix. Object-ori-

---

Jennifer Barzso's Soapbox

Include Technical Writers

To ensure that your application code is properly documented, you should have technical writers working side by side with developers. For some reason information technology (IT) departments think that it is easy to write good documentation and that anyone can do it. Nothing could be further from the truth, so hire an expert who knows how to do it properly.

Note from Scott: Jennifer is a long-time friend and coworker who has provided valuable input into all three of my books, so I felt it was about time that she had an opportunity to directly share some of her thoughts with you. Also, I'm proud to point out that Jennifer has stumbled onto Coplien's (1995) Mercenary Analyst organizational pattern.

---

ented testing is both similar to, yet at the same time significantly different from, structured testing. This can prove frustrating and confusing to experienced developers who are new to OO. Testing in the small techniques combined with testing in the large techniques make up the Full Life Cycle Object-Oriented Testing (FLOOT) methodology (Ambler, 1998a; Ambler, 1998b) which we will discuss later in this chapter. The key deliverable from testing in the small is a working, verified, high-quality portion of the work required to complete an application.

Testing in the small addresses the testing of your construction efforts as they proceed, in order to find and fix any problems as early in the life cycle as possible.

1.8 Deliver

The third serial phase of the OOSP is Deliver, which is comprised of four iterative project stages:

- Test in the Large
- Rework
- Implement
- Review

1.8.1 Test in the Large

You need to freeze the code and test your application before putting it into production.

The Test in the Large stage is the traditional testing phase from structured development, with the caveat that we are now testing an OO application instead of a structured one. Testing in the large, covered in Chapter 3, consists of testing techniques such as function testing, system testing, user acceptance testing (UAT), stress testing, operations testing, and alpha/beta/pilot testing. The key deliverables of this stage are a tested application and test results indicating whether or not the application can be released to the user community. Note that if the test results show that the application should not be released, then that release of the application must be reworked and then retested.

1.8.2 Rework

Very often testing in the large shows that portions of an application need to be improved, or reworked, before it can be released to its users. Although you hope that something like this will not happen, it is unfortunately one of the realities of life—we aren't perfect and we cannot always do a perfect job. Another reality is that we are typically blind to the fact that we aren't perfect and

---

Scott's Soapbox

Release No Application Before Its Time

In the 1970s an American wine company promised to "sell no wine before its time," words of wisdom that should be applied to the release of applications. If you do not have enough time to test, or if testing tells you that you need to rework portions of your application, then it is foolish to release your application. Experience tells us that software does not work the first time that you try to run it, so if you have not tested adequately, then you can safely assume that your application does not work. If your application has failed testing, then you know for certain that it does not work. Releasing an application that does not work is a recipe for disaster, so don't do it. If your users are putting pressure on you to release your application, you have to have the fortitude to not release it until it is ready. Yes, this is often difficult to do, but it is far more difficult and far more expensive to clean up the mess that your defective application will create.

that we make mistakes, the end result being that we forget that we often need to invest time reworking our applications before they can be released to our users. The OOSP includes an explicit Rework stage, described in Chapter 4, so that we do not forget to include the need to rework our applications in our schedules and estimates.

We almost always need to rework an application before it can be released.

1.8.3 Release

Chapter 5 covers the Release stage, the point at which you put the application and its corresponding documentation into the hands of your users. It is also at this point that you train the users, operations staff, and support staff in the application. The key deliverable of this stage is the provision of an application that successfully supports users doing their work.

1.8.4 Assess

Part of the Deliver phase is to review the project to determine what went right as well as what went wrong. The main goal of the Assess stage, described in Chapter 6, is to learn from your experiences so that you may improve the development practices of your organization. The key deliverable here is a report indicating both best and worst practices that occurred on the project, as well as an action plan to improve your development efforts next time. In addition to assessing the project, you should also assess the people who worked on the project, rewarding them appropriately and defining a training plan for them to help them address any skills gap that they may have.

By assessing the project you can improve your development efforts the next time.

1.9 Maintain and Support

The fourth serial phase of the OOSP is Maintain and Support, which is composed of two iterative project stages:

- Support
- Identify Defects and Enhancements

1.9.1 Support the Application

Because the OOSP is concerned with the entire life of an application, including efforts beyond development, the Support stage is included in the OOSP, described in Chapter 8. We are concerned with different levels of support: direct support for users of the application by the support desk (who may in fact be one of the application's developers), as well as technical support for the support people by the developers to help answer difficult questions. The key deliverable of this stage is the summary of collected metrics, such as the number of support calls taken and the average length of time to respond to a support call.

1.9.2 Identify Defects and Enhancements

This stage defines and prioritizes new requirements for future releases of your application.

Because no application works perfectly, or meets 100 percent of the needs of its users, we need a project stage (described in Chapter 9) that handles the identification of defects within the application, as well as desired enhancements for it. A change control process is needed to track and verify these requests. This process should distinguish the differences between something that does not work, something that could work better, and something that simply is not there. If you do not have a process in place to actively manage the identification of defects and enhancements, then the quality of the application will degrade over time because you are making changes to it on an ad hoc basis. The key deliverable of this stage is a series of verified and prioritized requirements for subsequent releases of the application.

I have briefly discussed the serial phases, as well as their iterative stages, of the OOSP. Now it is time to discuss how to deliver incremental releases of an application with the OOSP.

1.10 Delivering Incremental Releases Over Time

There are two keys to incremental development: first, you need to be able to organize the functionality of your application into several distinct packages that you can release one at a time. It is typical that each "functionality package" will build on the previous ones, although this is not always the case. Second, you want to organize your development efforts so that the project teams for each release do not step on the toes of the project teams for the other releases.

Let's consider three approaches to incremental development using the OOSP. In Figure 1.3 you see the aggressive approach for

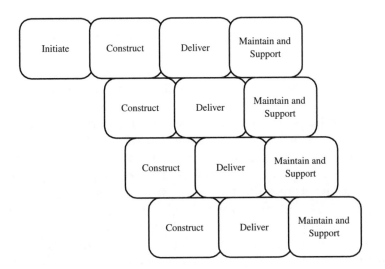

Figure 1.3.
The aggressive
approach to
incremental
development

using the incremental development approach with our OOSP, indicating that the work on the second release starts while development of the first release is still underway, that development of the third release starts while development of the second release occurs, and so on. Although this approach may appear to speed up the development process, chances are very good that it will actually slow it down. The problem is one of version control: having two teams work on the same code simultaneously is very difficult to manage. Note that it is reasonably easy to manage parallel development, however, assuming of course that the parallel components are reasonably uncoupled. With incremental releases, however, release *n* usually builds on release *n-1,* hence they are highly coupled. Another issue is that of staffing: To develop releases in parallel, you need to have enough people to staff each project team.

A less risky approach to incremental development is shown in Figure 1.4 , and a safer one yet, the conservative approach to incremental development in Figure 1.5. At a minimum, you really shouldn't start your next release until the code is frozen from the previous release, as shown in Figure 1.4; but ideally, you want to wait until the previous release has been fully tested and put into production. This ensures that you have a solid, versioned base of code to work from, and it also provides an opportunity for developers to catch their breath between releases. Furthermore, if you wait until the previous release is in the Maintenance and Support phase,

Don't start your next release until after the code is frozen on your current one, and preferably after the code has been tested and fixed.

you have an opportunity to act on the input of the people who are using the previous release, as well as to put into place any recommendations made in the previous release's Assess stage.

Notice how in Figures 1.3, 1.4, and 1.5 that only the first release has a project initiation phase. This probably is not completely true, due to the fact that at the start of a new release you really should revisit your project infrastructure based on the results of the project review of the previous release. Furthermore, you also need to justify, or perhaps rejustify, the requirements for the new release as many of them may be the result of change requests from the user community. The reason why we do not show the project initiation phase for subsequent releases is because of the fact that the change in infrastructure is usually made as part of the recommendations of the review stage, and that justification of any new requirements are made as part of the change control process during the maintenance and support phase.

1.11 Incremental vs. Parallel Development

Incremental development is based on the concept that an application can be delivered in multiple releases: releases that often build on the functionality of previous releases. Parallel development is based on the concept that you can work on portions of an application simultaneously. For parallel development to work smoothly, these portions should have as little overlap as possible; otherwise version control quickly overwhelms you. The basic issue is that it is easier to have two programmers working on different pieces of code simultaneously than it is to have them work on the same piece of code. The good news is that incremental development and parallel development are complementary approaches, not competing ones. In other words, you can have multiple, parallel efforts going on during a single release of an application.

Incremental and parallel development are complementary approaches, not competing ones.

1.12 With a Little Bit of Glue to Hold It All Together

It is not enough to identify the discrete phases and stages of the OOSP, because frankly they aren't enough. There are tasks, or perhaps overriding concerns, that are applicable throughout your project and across projects. Without these tasks being performed, your

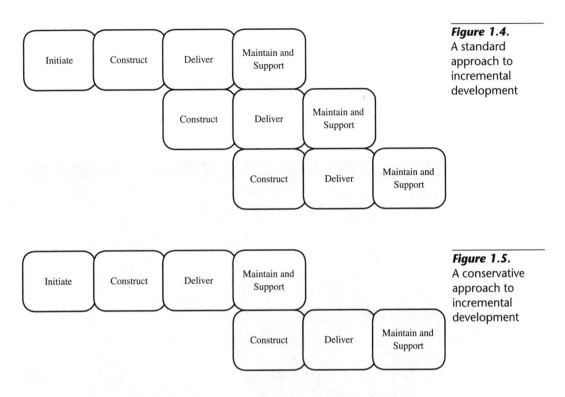

Figure 1.4.
A standard approach to incremental development

Figure 1.5.
A conservative approach to incremental development

project will fail, regardless of how good your developers are. The following project and cross-project tasks make up the glue that hold projects together, helping to increase your chance of success:

- Quality assurance
- Project management
- People management
- Risk management
- Reuse management
- Training and education
- Metrics management
- Deliverable management
- Infrastructure management

Throughout this book I will explore these project/cross-project tasks where appropriate and will even present several task process patterns that are applicable to them. In Chapter 10 I will summarize in detail the issues involved with each task; for now I present a brief overview of each.

1.13 Quality Assurance

Quality assurance is the process of ensuring that the efforts of a project meet or exceed the standards expected of them by the organization. Fundamentally, quality assurance attempts to answer the following questions: *Are you building the right thing?* and *Are you building it the right way?* Quality assurance is critical to

---

DEFINITIONS

deliverable Any document or system component that is produced during the development of a system. Some deliverables are used internally on a project whereas others are produced specifically for users of the application. Examples of deliverables include user requirements, models, plans, assessments, or other documents.

deliverable management The process of organizing, monitoring, and directing the deliverables of a project.

education The process by which people gain knowledge and understanding.

infrastructure management A cross-project effort that includes your organization's architectural and enterprise modeling efforts, as well as the definition and support of your organization's processes, standards, guidelines, and chosen toolsets.

metric A measurement.

metrics management The process of collecting, summarizing, and acting on measurements (metrics) to potentially improve both quality of the software that your organization develops and the actual software process of your organization.

project management The process of organizing, monitoring, and directing a project.

quality assurance (QA) The process of ensuring that the efforts of a project meet or exceed the standards expected of them.

reuse management The process of organizing, monitoring, and directing the efforts of a project team that lead to reuse on a project, either reuse of existing or purchased items.

risk management The process of identifying, monitoring, and mitigating the risks faced by a project team. These risks may typically be strategic, technical, and/or political.

training The process by which people gain tangible skills.

the success of a project, and should be an integral part of all project stages. At all points in the OOSP you should be reviewing your work to ensure its quality.

1.14 Project Management

Project management is the process of organizing, monitoring, and directing a project. Project management is planning. Project management is scheduling. Project management is estimating. Project management is people. As you will see throughout this book, projects must be skillfully managed if they are to be successful.

1.15 People Management

People management is the process of organizing, monitoring, coaching, and motivating people in such a manner to ensure that they work together effectively and contribute to a project/organization positively. People develop software; therefore, managing people must be part of the software development process.

1.16 Risk Management

Risk management is the process of identifying, monitoring, and mitigating the risks faced by a project team. These risks may come from a range of sources and may be strategic, technical, and/or political. The key concept of risk management is that you want to identify and deal with risks as soon as possible, and if you are unable to deal with them, or at least unwilling to deal with them, then you should at least keep an eye on them to ensure that they do not harm your project (at least not too badly). Risk management is one of the keys of success for system development projects, a task that must be performed throughout the project.

Risk management is a key factor in the success of an OO project.

1.17 Reuse Management

Reuse management is the process of organizing, monitoring, and directing the efforts of a project team that lead to reuse on project (or on subsequent projects); either reuse of existing or of purchased items. It is possible to achieve reuse throughout the entire OOSP, but it is not free and it is not automatic. You have to work at it. Furthermore, although we have a project stage called Generalize (Ambler, 1998b) that is dedicated specifically to building reusable components during the Construct phase, this is only a start. You can reuse your project plans, your estimates, your risk analysis, your test strategies, your construction standards, and your documentation templates—but only if you put in the effort. Reuse management is key to reducing the overall cost of application development. Table 1.2 describes several approaches to reuse (Ambler, 1998b).

Reuse is not free and it is not automatic. You need to manage the process.

1.18 Training and Education

Training and education (T&E) are both important to the success of a project. Training gives people the skills that they need to do their jobs, whereas education provides them with the knowledge that they need to understand their jobs. For example, people may take a course that teaches them the fundamentals of application development. This is education because it provides them with knowledge. The same people may attend a five-day course to learn how to program in Java. This is training because it teaches them a specific skill. Education generally deals with knowledge that is useful for a long period of time, whereas training often has a much shorter shelf life, often on the order of months or years. You want to distinguish between training and education because in many ways training is an investment that needs to pay for itself in the short term, perhaps over one or two projects, whereas education pays for itself over the long term, typically the employment of an individual. At some point most projects require the training and/or education of both developers and users; therefore T&E is an important part of the OOSP.

1.19 Metrics Management

Metrics management is the process of collecting, summarizing, and acting on measurements (metrics) to potentially improve both the quality of the software that your organization develops

TABLE 1.2. The Various Approaches to Reuse

Reuse Strategy	Description
Artifact reuse	The reuse of previously created development artifacts: use cases, standards documents, domain-specific models, procedures and guidelines, and other applications to give you a kick start on a new project.
Code reuse	The reuse of source code within sections of an application and potentially across multiple applications.
Component reuse	The reuse of pre-built, fully encapsulated components in the development of your application.
Domain-component reuse	The reuse of pre-built, large-scale domain components that encapsulate cohesive portions of your business domain.
Framework reuse	The reuse of collections of classes that together implement the basic functionality of a common technical or business domain.
Inheritance reuse	The use of inheritance in your application to take advantage of behavior implemented in existing classes.
Pattern reuse	The reuse of publicly documented approaches, called patterns, to solving common problems.
Template reuse	The reuse of a common set of layouts for key development artifacts—documents, models, and source code—within your organization.

and the actual software process of your organization. As the old saying goes, "You cannot improve it if you cannot measure it." Metrics management provides the information that is critical to understanding the quality of the work that your project team has performed and how effectively that work was performed. Metrics range from simple measurements of work effort such as the number of hours invested to develop a model to code quality measurements such as the percentage of comments within your code.

1.20 Deliverable Management

Deliverable management is key to the management of a project, to the successful operation of an application, and to the successful maintenance and support of an application. A deliverable is any information, either printed or electronic, that describes all or part of an application or system such as models, documents, and plans. Deliverables may be internal, used only by members of the project team; or external, delivered as part of the application. Deliverables may be for developers, for users, for support staff, or for operations staff. The review and update of deliverables is a fundamental part of quality assurance, and the existence of accurate and complete documentation is a fundamental part of risk management. Deliverables are created and updated by all members of a project team throughout the entire project.

1.21 Infrastructure Management

Infrastructure management is a cross-project effort that includes the architectural and enterprise modeling efforts of the Model stage (Ambler, 1998b), and the definition and support of your organization's processes, standards, guidelines, and chosen toolsets. The Define Infrastructure stage (Ambler, 1998b) is a key function of infrastructure management because it defines and/or selects the infrastructure for a single project. However, from the point of view of your organization, the Define Infrastructure stage is not sufficient to promote a common infrastructure between projects; hence the need for infrastructure management.

DEFINITIONS

guideline A description, ideally with an example provided, of how something should be done. It is recommended, but not required, that you follow guidelines (unlike standards that are mandatory).

standard A description, ideally with an example provided, of how something must be done. It is required that you follow standards (unlike guidelines that are optional).

1.22 The Advantages and Disadvantages of the OOSP

The OOSP, and the OOSP pattern language, presented in this book have many advantages:

- The emphasis on quality assurance, testing, and working closely with users leads to greater quality in your applications and helps to promote the traceability of requirements throughout an application.
- The OOSP defines how applications are built and shows the interrelationships between development processes, promoting understanding and teamwork within and between project teams.
- The emphasis on project management and risk management reduces the risks associated with development, increasing your chances of success.
- The OOSP provides a consistent, proven approach to OO development, based on real-world experience and not the musings of ivory-tower academics.
- The OOSP provides insight into how developers, users, managers, and external vendors interact with one another to build an OO application.
- The OOSP helps to define staffing requirements for projects, as well as the deliverables.
- The emphasis on reuse management and generalization increases the chance that you actually will achieve reuse within your organization.
- By explicitly defining how you do things you have the opportunity to measure and reflect on the development process, allowing you to improve it over time.
- The OOSP promotes a mature approach to development and creates an environment that is inhospitable to hacking.

The OOSP is mapped to the Software Engineering Institute's Capability Maturity Model, an industry-standard framework for improving the software maturity of an organization.

The OOSP pattern language shows how to apply process patterns in a consistent and comprehensive manner, providing a framework within which other process patterns may be added later.

There are also a few disadvantages:

- You still need to fill in the details: for example, Chapter 3 covers the testing in the large process in general, reviewing the various testing techniques and how they fit together, as well as providing a testing strategy for large projects but what it does not do is teach you how to test.
- It becomes difficult to underestimate the effort required for developing OO applications, making it harder to justify pet projects and to ram through emergency projects that have little chance for success.

1.23 Toward a Mature Object-Oriented Software Process: The SEI CMM

The Software Engineering Institute (SEI) at Carnegie Mellon University has proposed the Capability Maturity Model (CMM), which provides a framework from which a process for large, complex software efforts can be defined (Software Engineering Institute, 1995). Sponsored by the United State's Department of Defense (DoD), the CMM has been adopted by hundreds of organizations worldwide who want to improve the way that they develop software.

The CMM distinguishes between immature and mature software organizations. Immature software organizations are typically

---

TIP

Spread the Costs Over Several Projects

Implementing an OOSP such as this within your organization is only possible if you spread the costs of it over several projects. A process is an investment made by your organization, not just by a single project.

reactionary and have little understanding as to how to success-fully develop software. Mature software organizations, on the other hand, understand the development process that enables them to judge the quality of the software products and the process that produces them. Mature software organizations have a

---

DEFINITIONS

Baseline A tested and certified version of a deliverable representing a conceptual milestone which thereafter serves as the basis for further develop-ment and that can be modified only through formal change control procedures. A particular version becomes a baseline when a responsible group decides to designate it as such.

Capability Maturity Model (CMM) A strategy, defined by the Software Engineering Institute (SEI), that describes the key elements of an effective software process.

Immature software organization A software organization that is reactionary, its managers are usually focused on solving immediate crises. There is no objective basis for judging product quality or for solving product or process problems. There is little understanding of how the steps of the soft-ware process affect quality, and product quality is difficult to predict.

Key process area (KPA) An issue that must be addressed to achieve a spe-cific Capability Maturity Model (CMM) maturity level.

Mature software organization A software organization where the managers monitor the quality of the software products and the process that produces them. There is an objective, quantitative basis for judging product quality and analyzing problems with the product and process.

Maturity level A well-defined evolutionary plateau toward achieving a mature software process. According to the Capability Maturity Model (CMM), for an organization to achieve a specific maturity level it must satisfy and insti-tutionalize all of the key process areas (KPAs) for that level and the levels below.

Software Engineering Institute (SEI) An organization within Carnegie Mel-lon University whose goal is to provide leadership in advancing the state of the practice of software engineering to improve the quality of systems that depend on software.

Software process A set of project phases, stages, methods, techniques, and practices that people employ to develop and maintain software and its associ-ated products (plans, documents, models, code, test cases, and manuals).

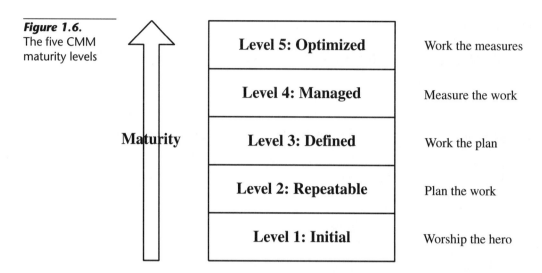

Figure 1.6.
The five CMM
maturity levels

Maturity

Level 5: Optimized	Work the measures
Level 4: Managed	Measure the work
Level 3: Defined	Work the plan
Level 2: Repeatable	Plan the work
Level 1: Initial	Worship the hero

higher success rate and a lower overall cost of software, across the entire life of a software product, than do immature software organizations. The goal of this book is to describe a mature OOSP.

1.24 The Five CMM Maturity Levels

The CMM defines five maturity levels, evolutionary plateaus toward achieving a mature software process, that an organization can attain with respect to the software process. The five maturity levels of the CMM are shown in Figure 1.6 and described in Table 1.3. All organizations are at least at the Initial Level, the lowest level of software process maturity, by definition.

As you can see, each maturity level builds upon aspects and features of the previous levels. This implies that for your organization to achieve CMM Level 4 is must satisfy the requirements for CMM Levels 2 and 3 as well as those for CMM Level 4. The goal of this book is to define an OOSP that meets the needs of a mature software organization, one that aims for CMM Level 5. For our purposes the important thing is to identify the issues, called key process areas, for each maturity level so that you can determine which aspects of the software process you should concentrate on.

The true value of the SEI CMM is the fact that it defines the issues that must be addressed by a software process to achieve each maturity level. These issues are called key process areas (KPAs) and are shown by maturity level in Figure 1.7 (Ambler, 1998b).

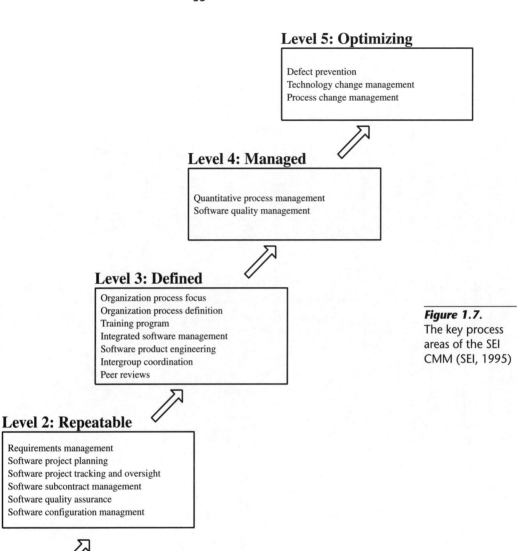

Level 5: Optimizing

Defect prevention
Technology change management
Process change management

Level 4: Managed

Quantitative process management
Software quality management

Level 3: Defined

Organization process focus
Organization process definition
Training program
Integrated software management
Software product engineering
Intergroup coordination
Peer reviews

Level 2: Repeatable

Requirements management
Software project planning
Software project tracking and oversight
Software subcontract management
Software quality assurance
Software configuration managment

Level 1: Initial

Figure 1.7.
The key process areas of the SEI CMM (SEI, 1995)

1.25 How the Rest of This Book Is Organized

Chapters 2 through 9 describe the phase and stage process patterns for the Deliver phase and the Maintain and Support phase. These chapters are organized into four parts, one for each project phase and its associated stages. Chapter 10 describes the project and cross project tasks of the OOSP, summarizing and expanding

TABLE 1.5 The Five CMM Maturity Levels

Level	Description	Characteristics
1. Initial	The software process is ad hoc, and occasionally even chaotic. Few processes are defined, and success depends on individual effort and heroics.	• Overcommitment is common. • During a crisis, planned procedures are abandoned and project teams revert to coding and testing. • Success depends on having an exceptional manager and a seasoned and effective software team. • The software process is effectively a black box to the user community. Resources go in and software potentially comes out.
2. Repeatable	Basic project management processes are established to track cost, schedule, and functionality. The necessary process discipline is in place to repeat earlier successes on projects with similar applications.	• The planning and management of new projects is based on experience with similar projects. • Process capability is enhanced at the project level by establishing basic process management techniques. • Software requirements and deliverables are baselined. • Processes often differ between projects, reducing opportunities for teamwork and reuse. • The user community is provided visibility into the project at defined occasions, typically via the review and acceptance of major project deliverables, allowing limited management control.

3. Defined

The software process for both management and development activities is documented, standardized, and integrated into a standard software process for the entire organization. All projects use an approved, tailored version of the organization's standard software process for developing and maintaining software.

- A standard process is used, with possible tailoring, on all projects.
- Management has good insight into technical progress on the project.
- Defined processes allow the user community greater visibility into the project and enable accurate and rapid status updates.

4. Managed

Detailed measures, called metrics, of the software process and product quality are collected. Both the software process and products are quantitatively understood and controlled.

- Productivity and quality are measured for important software process activities across all projects.
- The user community can establish an accurate, quantitative understanding of the software process capability of your organization/team and the project risk before the project begins.

5. Optimized

Continuous process improvement is enabled by quantitative feedback from the software process and from piloting innovative ideas and technologies.

- Innovations that exploit the best software engineering practices are identified and shared throughout the organization.
- The software process is improved by changing common causes of inefficiency.
- Disciplined change is the norm, not the exception.
- The user community and the software organization work together to establish a strong and successful relationship.

on the material presented in the previous chapters. Chapter 11 describes strategies for successfully introducing the OOSP and process patterns into your organization, and Chapter 12 presents some parting words to you.

Each *phase overview* chapter, describing a single phase process pattern, is organized into the following sections:

- Overview
- Initial context: Entry conditions to begin the phase
- Solution: How work proceeds during the phase
- Solution: Project task issues
- Resulting context: Exit conditions to end the phase
- Secrets of success
- Phase process checklist
- What you have learned in this chapter
- References and suggested reading

Each *stage* chapter, describing a single stage process pattern, is organized into the following sections:

- Overview
- Initial Context: Entry conditions to enter the stage
- Solution: How work proceeds during the stage
- Solution: Project tasks (quality assurance, risk management, reuse, metrics)
- Resulting context: Exit conditions to leave the stage
- Secrets of success
- Stage process checklist
- What you have learned in this chapter
- References and suggested reading

The approach that I will take throughout this book is to present the phase and stage process patterns as templated patterns, patterns that follow a consistent documentation format. I've stuck as close as possible to the generally accepted format, albeit reworking it a bit to move away from its reference-oriented nature to what I consider to be a more readable format. I suspect that this decision will cause heartburn for some of the theoreticians in the patterns community—sorry about that. Task process patterns, on the other hand, are presented as degenerate patterns, patterns that are described without using a template (personally, I feel the term

> **DEFINITIONS**
>
> **degenerate pattern** A pattern that has been described without the use of a pattern template.
>
> **process checklist** An indication of the tasks that should be completed while working a defined process.
>
> **templated pattern** A pattern that has been documented using a pattern template.

untemplated pattern would have been a little more forgiving than degenerate pattern). Yes, at some point I should document each of these patterns using a common, "standard" template, but for the sake of readability I have chosen to simply present task process patterns as simple prose, not as structured reference material.

The overview section for each project phase and stage describes the pertinent issues and forces applicable to the process pattern being described by the chapter. The next section describes the initial context, the situation before the process pattern is worked, focusing on the entry conditions that should be met for the process to begin. The solution to resolving the issues of the process pattern is described in two parts, one describing the mechanical tasks/activities to be performed and one describing project task-related issues (the *big arrow* of the OOSP). The resulting context, the situation after the process pattern is worked, is described in the following section via a focus on the exit conditions for the process. The chapters end with a summary of the secrets of success for the process, many of which hint at possible task process patterns for those of you interested in extending the OOSP pattern language, and a process checklist that you can tailor to meet the unique needs of your organization. Process checklists should be used as part of your software process improvement efforts as they provide a feedback mechanism about your internal processes. I highly suggest adding standard questions at the end of each checklist that investigate needed improvements to the process.

1.26 What You Have Learned in This Chapter

In this chapter I discussed several common approaches to application development—serial, iterative, incremental, parallel, and

There is no reason why good cannot triumph as often as evil. The triumph of any-thing is a matter of organization.
—Kurt Vonnegut, Jr.

hacking—and discussed their advantages and disadvantages. The OOSP is serial in the large, iterative in the small, delivering incremental releases over time, taking a more realistic approach to OO development than the "traditional"iterative-only approach. I also introduced you to the concept of the OOSP pattern language, a collection of process patterns that describe the OOSP. I ended the chapter with a discussion of the Capability Maturity Model (CMM) and the advantages and disadvantages of the OOSP.

1.27 References and Recommended Reading

Alexander, C. 1979. *The Timeless Way of Building.* New York: Oxford University Press.

Ambler, S. W. 1995. *The Object Primer: The Application Developer's Guide to Object Orientation.* New York: SIGS Books/Cambridge University Press.

Ambler, S. W. 1998a. *Building Object Applications That Work: Your Step-by-Step Handbook for Developing Robust Systems with Object Technology.* New York: SIGS Books/Cambridge University Press.

Ambler, S. W. 1998b. *Process Patterns: Building Large-Scale Systems Using Object Technology.* New York: SIGS Books/Cambridge University Press.

Baudoin, C., and Hollowell, G. 1996. *Realizing the Object-Oriented Life Cycle.* Upper Saddle River, New Jersey: Prentice-Hall, Inc.

Boehm, B.W. 1988. *A Spiral Model of Software Development and Enhancement.* IEEE Computer 21(5), 61–72.

Coplien, J.O. (1995). *A Generative Development-Process Pattern Language. Pattern Languages of Program Design,* eds. Coplien, J.O. and Schmidt, D.C., Addison Wesley Longman, Inc., pp. 183–237.

Emam, K. E.; Drouin J.; and Melo, W. 1998. *SPICE: The Theory and Practice of Software Process Improvement and Capability Determination.* Los Alamitos, California: IEEE Computer Society Press.

Fowler, M. 1997. *Analysis Patterns: Reusable Object Models.* Menlo Park, California: Addison Wesley Longman, Inc..

Gamma, E.; Helm, R.; Johnson, R.; and Vlissides, J. 1995. *Design Patterns: Elements of Reusable Object-Oriented Software.* Reading, Massachusetts: Addison-Wesley Publishing Company.

Jones, C. 1996. *Patterns of Software Systems Failure and Success.* Boston, Massachusetts: International Thomson Computer Press.

Meyer, B. 1995. *Object Success: A Manager's Guide to Object Orientation, Its Impact on the Corporation and Its Use for Engineering the Software Process.* Englewood Cliffs, New Jersey: Prentice Hall, Inc.

Software Engineering Institute. 1995. *The Capability Maturity Model: Guidelines for Improving the Software Process.* Reading Massachusetts: Addison-Wesley Publishing Company, Inc.

Part 1

Deliver

THE THIRD SERIAL PHASE of the OOSP is the Deliver phase, commonly referred to as delivery or implementation in the structured world. This is where you verify and deliver the application to its users by:

- Testing in the large, an object-oriented version of integration and function testing, to verify that your application works as a whole and that it meets the needs of your users.
- Implementing the application, to put it in the hands of its users.
- Reviewing the project so that you can learn from both your successes and from your mistakes.

Chapter 2

The Deliver Phase

THE main goal of the Deliver phase, the third serial phase of the object-oriented software process (OOSP), is to deploy your application, including the appropriate documentation, to your user community. A major theme/force throughout the Deliver phase is that although your user community is the primary customer of your efforts, you must never forget your secondary customers, which are your organization's operations and support departments. An important force applicable to the Deliver phase is the need to meet your schedule yet still test and rework your software appropriately.

The Deliver phase puts your application and supporting documentation into the hands of your user community, operations department, and support department.

As shown in Figure 2.1, the Deliver phase is made up of four iterative stages: Test in the Large, Rework, Release, and Assess. The inputs to the Deliver phase are the development deliverables of the Construct phase, comprised of the packaged application; the models and source code; the initial versions of the test, training, and release plans; and the user, operations, and support documentation which accompany the packaged application.

The Test in the Large stage (Chapter 3) takes as its main inputs the packaged application and the supporting documentation to verify that the application works as a whole and meets the needs of the user, operations, and support communities. The purpose of the Rework stage (Chapter 4) is to make the necessary corrections to the application and its documentation as identified by the Test in the Large stage. Although the Rework stage is effectively a sub-

Figure 2.1.
The Deliver
process pattern

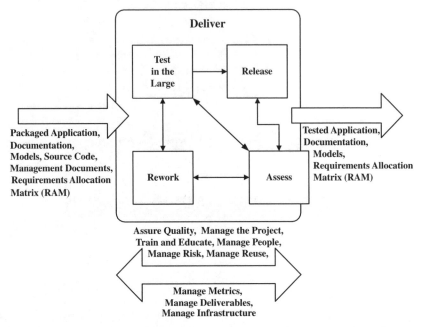

set of the Construct phase, my experience is that it needs to be its own stage for two reasons: (a) you always have some rework to do, and (b) by explicitly including the Rework stage, you will remember to include it in your project planning efforts. The Release stage (Chapter 5) is where the actual work of deploying your application to your user, operations, and support communities takes place. It is also during this stage that people are trained to use, operate, or support the application. Finally, the Assess stage (Chapter 6) is where you invest the time to review what happened on the project, to learn from your experiences so that you may improve your software process. As with the Rework stage, my experience is that the Assess stage needs to be explicitly called out in the object-oriented software process (OOSP): otherwise, it will not be planned for.

As you can see in Figure 2.1, the Assess stage may overlap into the Maintain and Support phase (Chapter 7) for one of several reasons. The most common reason is one of prioritization: the number one priority of the Deliver phase is to deploy your application to the user community, and as a result the Assess stage may be left to the end of the Deliver phase. A second reason is that you may choose to wait until the application is in production to include users in the assessment process who have had on-the-job experience with the application. Yes, you should at least start the Assess stage during the Deliver phase because your experiences on the project are still fresh in the minds of the project team, but you might decide to continue your assessment after the application has been deployed.

The Assess stage may, for valid reasons, run past the end of the Deliver phase.

The Deliver phase is interesting because it exhibits iterative, serial, and parallel properties. The iterative nature is shown by the relationship between the Test in the Large and Rework stages: you perform some testing, you do some rework, then you perform more testing, and so on. The serial nature comes about from the fact that the Test in the Large and Rework stages must both finish before the application may be released. Finally, the Assess stage can effectively be run in parallel to the three other stages, because many of the resources that it requires, the developers who worked on the Construct phase, are often available at least on a part-time basis during the Deliver phase.

The Deliver phase includes iterative, serial, and parallel properties.

2.1 Initial Context: Entry Conditions to the Deliver Phase

There are several entry conditions that must be met before the Deliver phase may begin:

1. **A development (code) freeze has taken place.** A baselined version of all models, documents, and source code files must be defined before the Deliver phase may begin. This is important because your test engineers must be assured that they are testing the official, baselined version of your application, and because the Rework stage will require these deliverables so that the application may be updated appropriately to fix the defects found during the Test in the Large stage.
2. **The application has been packaged for delivery.** The packaged application, including the installation utility, support documentation, operations documentation, and user documentation must be available for testing, rework, and release.
3. **The initial training plans have been developed.** The initial plans for training your user, operations, and support communities must be at least started, if not completed, so that the appropriate training may take place during the Release stage.

DEFINITION

baseline A tested and certified version of a deliverable, representing a conceptual milestone that thereafter serves as the basis for further development and that can be modified only through formal change control procedures. A particular version becomes a baseline when a responsible group decides to designate it as such.

The management of your training efforts is often a complex and difficult task, a task for which you need to start planning very early if you want it to succeed.

4. **The initial operations and support documentation have been developed.** Never forget that your operations and support departments are your customers, not just your users. The operations and support personnel have specific documentation needs, described in the Release stage, needs that must be met for you to successfully deliver your application.

2.2 Solution: How Work Generally Proceeds During the Deliver Phase

The Deliver phase will often begin with the Test in the Large stage, which as Figure 2.2 shows, should comprise fifty to seventy percent of your efforts during this phase. If your application fails testing (you can count on this happening), then you may choose to fix some or all of the defects in the Rework stage. The Rework stage typically requires between zero and forty percent depending on the quality of the application being tested and the willingness of senior management to invest the necessary resources to make the needed fixes. The Release stage comprises between five and twenty percent of the effort of the Deliver phase and, as mentioned previously, occurs after your application has been tested and reworked as necessary. The Assess stage, where you take the opportunity to learn from your experiences on the project, often takes between five and ten percent of your efforts.

Figure 2.3 presents a more detailed look than Figure 2.2 at the work to be performed during the Deliver phase. Notice how the Test in the Large, Rework, and Release stages all decompose into relatively serial processes. The Test in the Large stage comprises two distinct components: system testing, wherein test engineers

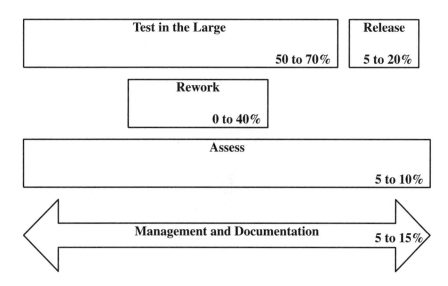

Figure 2.2.
Organizing the
Deliver phase

verify that the application and supporting documentation performs as defined, and user testing, wherein members of the user
community perform the testing to verify that the application
truly meets their needs. The Rework stage also comprised two distinct components:, the first, wherein the defects identified during
the Test in the Large stage are prioritized (you may choose to fix
many, if not all, defects in a later release of the application), and
the second, wherein the defects are fixed if necessary. As you can
see, the Release stage also comprises three sequential tasks: preparing to release the application, releasing the application to operations and support, and releasing the application to your user
community. It is important to note that the application must first
be released to the operations and support community to prepare
them to operate and support the application appropriately.

DEFINITIONS

system testing A testing process in which you find and fix any known
problems to prepare your application for user testing.

user testing Testing processes in which the user community, as opposed to
developers, performs the tests. User testing techniques include user-
acceptance testing, alpha testing, beta testing, and pilot testing.

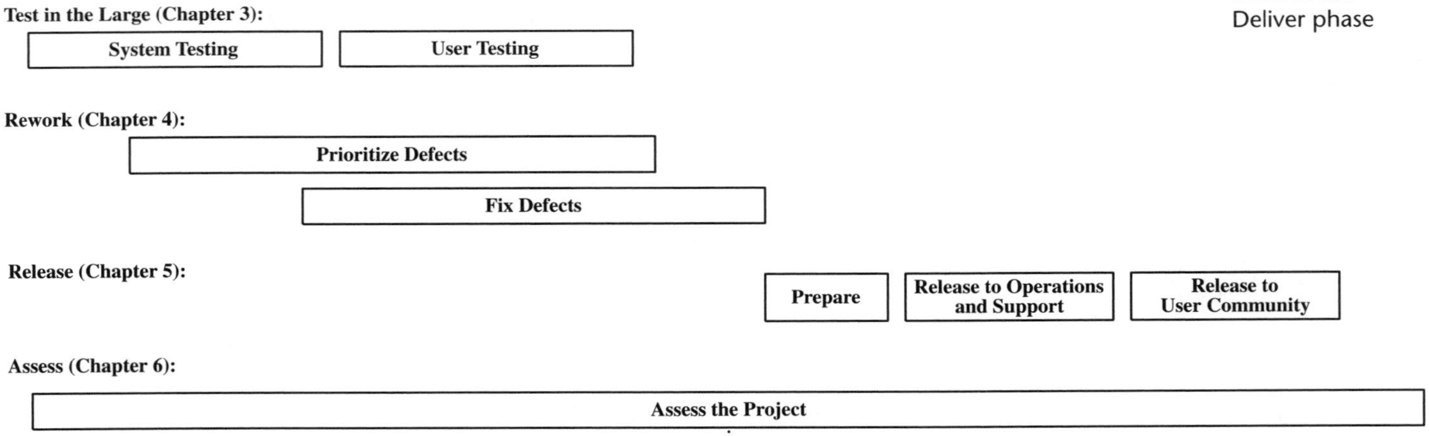

Test in the Large (Chapter 3):

System Testing

User Testing

Rework (Chapter 4):

Prioritize Defects

Fix Defects

Release (Chapter 5):

Prepare

Release to Operations and Support

Release to User Community

Assess (Chapter 6):

Assess the Project

Figure 2.3.
Organizing the work of the Deliver phase

2.3 Solution: Project Tasks

In this section I will discuss the issues associated with the various project tasks during the Deliver phase.

2.3.1 *Managing the Deliver Phase*

The Deliver phase is often the most frustrating one for project managers, because they spend a significant portion of their time fighting with senior management to do the right thing. Very often, by the time a project enters the Deliver phase it is late and overbudget, two things that shouldn't happen if you follow the advise presented in this book, typically because of ill-advised shortcuts taken during the Initiate and Construct phases. Regardless of the cause, the fact still remains that at this point in the software process, there is significant pressure placed on the project manager to find ways to reduce the remaining time to delivery for the project. The temptation to reduce the time invested in the Test in the Large stage will be great, as will be the temptation to leave identified defects to a subsequent release instead of fixing them immediately in the Rework stage. You will also be pressured to forgo training of users, operations, and support people in favor of learning on the job to reduce the time for the Release stage.

You will be pressured to reduce testing and rework time to get the application deployed to the user community as soon as possible.

A second management issue that you will face during the deliver phase is that of obtaining support for the Assess stage. At this point in the software process, your project team is likely exhausted from overtime during the Construct phase; and the last thing that they want to do is talk about what happened on the project, unless, of course, your project has become a miserable failure and everyone is eager to point the finger at someone else. You also have the issue that senior management is likely to be completely focused on getting the application in the hands of its users and is unwilling to allow you to take the time to assess the project to learn from your experiences, at least not until after the application has been deployed. The result is that there is usually significant pressure to skip the Assess stage, pressure to which you do not want to buckle under. My experience is that it is a sign of process maturity that an organization is willing to invest the resources to learn from their experiences, which undoubtedly is why this is a key process area for Level 5 of the Capability Maturity Model (Software Engineering Institute, 1995).

You have to choose to learn from your mistakes as well as your successes; it doesn't happen automatically.

DEFINITIONS

user testing Testing processes in which the user community, as opposed to developers, performs the tests. User testing techniques include user-acceptance testing, alpha testing, beta testing, and pilot testing.

key process area (KPA) An issue that must be addressed to achieve a specific Capability Maturity Model (CMM) maturity level.

Software Engineering Institute (SEI) An organization within Carnegie Mellon University whose goal is to provide leadership in advancing the state of the practice of software engineering to improve the quality of systems that depend on software.

2.3.2 People Management

A wide range of roles are taken during the Deliver phase, many of which are not adequately appreciated in many organizations.

In this section I would like to describe the various roles fulfilled by people during the Deliver phase. These roles are shown in Figure 2.4 and described in Table 2.1. An interesting thing about the roles during the Deliver phase is that the majority of them are often considered "secondary" within many organizations: that of your testing, support, and operations departments. My experience is that these roles are just as important as those taken during the Construct phase—roles such as domain programmer and architectural modeler. The people who test, support, and operate an application are just as important as the people who build the application and should be recognized as such.

DEFINITIONS

function testing A part of systems testing in which development staff confirm that their application meets the user requirements specified during analysis.

operations testing The act of ensuring that the needs of operations personnel who have to support and/or operate the application are met.

As you would expect, you need a project manager throughout the Deliver phase to manage it. During the Test in the Large stage a test manager and test engineers are needed to test the application, and are supported by its developers to help track down and identify defects. Support engineers are often needed during the Test in the Large stage to aid in function testing, and the operations manager and operations engineers are required to aid in operations testing. Developers and technical writers, supported by test engineers, are needed during the Rework stage to fix identified defects in the application and its documentation that were discovered during the Test in the Large stage. During the Release stage, support and operations managers/engineers are trained, a process which is worked by the training manager and trainers. Finally, everyone involved with the project, and potentially an auditor, participate during the Assess stage to learn from their experiences.

Project Manager	Support Manager	Operations Manager	Training Manager
Developer	Support Engineer	Operations Engineer	Trainer
Project Auditor	Testing Manager	Test Engineer	Technical Writer

Figure 2.4.
Potential roles during the Deliver phase

2.3.3 Potential Risks During the Deliver Phase

There are several risks specific to the Deliver phase:

1. **Testing is cut short.** There is always pressure to reduce the time invested in the Test in the Large stage so as to deploy the application to your user community that much quicker. The reality is that you have to test your application to find and fix defects before you release your application. Remember, defects that get into production are significantly more expensive to fix (Ambler, 1998a) than those fixed before your application is released.
2. **Rework has not been planned for.** You know that the Test in the Large stage will find defects, some of which you will want to fix before the application is deployed. Knowing that you will need to rework your application, doesn't it make sense to plan to do so? Many projects run into trouble during the Deliver stage because sufficient resources to fix defects weren't planned for ahead of time. When it comes time to fix the application, project managers find that key developers have moved on to other projects or have taken several weeks' vacation. Include resources to rework your application in your project plan and avoid these problems.
3. **Your developers quit.** It is quite common for developers to quit immediately following the end of the Construct phase. Developers who are unhappy with their current position (perhaps the project has been less-than-ideal and they are

TABLE 2.1. Common Roles Held During the Deliver Phase

Role	Description
project auditor	A professional who specializes in the review and assessment of projects.
developer	Any person directly responsible for the creation of software, including, but not limited to, modelers, programmers, and reuse engineers.
operations engineer	A person responsible for operating one or more applications once they are placed in production.
operations manager	The person responsible for managing your organization's operations department and operations engineers.
project manager	The person responsible for obtaining funding and authorization for the project from senior management.
support engineer	A person whose job is to collaborate with users needing help to use your software.
support manager	The person responsible for managing your organization's support center and support engineers.
technical writer	The person responsible for writing, updating, and/or improving the technical documentation produced on the project, potentially including the requirements, models, standards, guidelines, and project plans.

(continued)

frustrated with your organization, or perhaps they simply want to work somewhere else) will often look for another job once they believe that they have met their obligation to the project team. For many developers, once the Construct phase ends the "real work" is complete; therefore, they are free to look for employment elsewhere.

TABLE 2.1. (continued)

Role	Description
test engineer	The person responsible for verifying that the application works as defined by the requirements for the application.
test manager	The person responsible for managing the testing engineers and testing process within your organization. This person works closely with your organization's project managers to ensure that the testing of applications is being performed in an effective manner.
trainer	A person responsible for the delivery, and possibly development, of training courses.
training manager	The person responsible for managing your organization's training department. The person oversees your organization's internal trainers, if any, and is responsible for hiring outside training firms to deliver courses to your organization's employees.

4. **Resources to assess your project have not been allocated.** Project deadlines often do not allow you the luxury of learning from your experiences, at least not until the application has been delivered. My advice is to take the time to assess your project as this is a primary source of information for improving your object-oriented software process (OOSP).

5. **The needs of operations and support are not adequately considered.** A common mistake made by many projects is to focus solely on the needs of the user community while ignoring the needs of the operations and support communities. Don't leave the issues associated with operations and support to the last minute, otherwise you may find that you cannot put your application into production when you need to due to difficulties with operations or support.

6. **The data conversion task has been underestimated.** Your data conversion effort, in which you take your legacy data schema and modify it to meet the needs of your object-oriented (OO) application, is always a complex and onerous task. Your data conversion plan, a subsection of your release plan, should have been started during the Construct phase.

7. **Training has been poorly planned.** Managing the training of your user, operations, and support communities is a complex task. You need to determine what courses are needed, determine who should take each course, have course materials developed, schedule training facilities to hold the courses, schedule trainers to teach the courses, and schedule students into the courses. You must plan your training efforts ahead of time for them to be effective.

2.3.4 Training and Education Issues

In this section I will discuss the training and education needs of the people who will be working the Deliver phase. I will not discuss the training and education efforts that are performed during the Deliver phase, specifically the training of the user, operations, and support communities regarding application-specific information—training that is performed as part of the Release stage (Chapter 5).

Technical issues, such as the hardware and software environment that the application will operate within, are critical skills for everyone involved with the Deliver phase. Test engineers must understand the technical environment that they are testing in, and operations and support personnel must also understand the technical environment. Training and education on technical issues will need to be performed only for new employees or when the application requires a change in the technical environment, a change such as an upgrade of the operating system or the installation of middleware for object-oriented application environments.

Test, operations, and support engineers will need training in the technical environment.

Support engineers and trainers will need training in people-oriented skills. For example, support engineers should be given training in dealing with difficult people, basic phone skills (you cannot assume that people know how to answer the phone politely), and basic domain skills (in other words, support engineers at an insurance company need to understand the basics of the insurance industry). Trainers will also need to be given training in dealing

DEFINITION

middleware The technology that allows computer applications to communicate with one another. This includes the network itself, its operating system, and anything needed to connect computers to the network.

with difficult people as well as in how to deliver a training course. More importantly, the trainers will need to be trained on the application that they will be training others on: trainers need to understand the material, in this case the application, that they are teaching. Inexperienced trainers will often assume that because they know how to train people, they can teach anything; anyone who has attended a presentation given by someone who didn't know what they were talking about can attest to the validity of this claim. Similar to support engineers, trainers will also need a basic understanding of the business domain so they can effectively explain the context in which the application is used.

Support engineers need training in people, phone, and domain skills. Trainers need training in people, training, application, and domain skills.

Test engineers will naturally need training in system testing techniques. Because test engineers who are involved in function testing will test the user interface of your application, they will need training in the basics of user interface design and the chosen user interface design standards of your organization. The same can be said of any support engineers who are involved in function testing.

2.4 Resulting Context: Exit Conditions from the Deliver Phase

For the Deliver phase to end, the following deliverables must be in place:

1. **The application has been deployed to the user community.** The primary goal of the Deliver phase is to deploy the application, including the corresponding user documentation, to the user community.
2. **The support and operations documentation has been accepted.** Because your application needs to be operated and supported once it is in production, your operations and support departments need the appropriate documentation to do so. Part of deploying an application is ensuring that the operations and support departments have reviewed, understood, and accepted the documentation about your application that they need to perform their jobs.
3. **The users, operations staff, and support staff have been trained.** With the exception of the most trivial of applications,

> **DEFINITION**
>
> **Requirements allocation matrix (RAM)** A mapping of requirements, defined in your requirements document, to the portions of your model(s) that implement them.

you will always need to train your user, operations, and support communities so that they understand how to work with your application effectively. The money that you invest training your users will pay for itself in reduced support costs and reduced mistakes using the application.

4. **The models and requirements allocation matrix (RAM) are up-to-date.** Your models and RAM should have been updated during the Rework stage (Chapter 4) to reflect any changes made to your application to fix defects found during the Test in the Large stage (Chapter 3). These deliverables are needed by the Identify Defects and Enhancements stage (Chapter 9) to allocate maintenance changes appropriately.

2.5 Secrets of Success

I would like to share with you some of my secrets of success for the Deliver phase:

1. **Recognize the importance of testing and rework.** I cannot say this too many times: you need to invest the time to detect and fix defects within your application before it is deployed to your user community. It is significantly easier and less expensive to fix defects before an application is in production than after. The Deliver phase is your last opportunity for getting your application running correctly.

2. **Assess your efforts.** Don't let senior management pressure you into not taking the time to work the Assess stage and learn from your experiences. Invest in the future by improving your software process.

3. **Work closely with support and operations staff.** Your operations and support communities are your customers, as is your user community. In fact, not only are the operations and support departments your customers they are also your partners, partners who will help you to make your application successful. Train operations and support staff as early as you can, and actively involve them in the Test in the Large stage. By working closely with the operations and support communities you increase the chance of success for your application.

2.6 Process Checklist

The following process checklist can be used to verify that you have completed the Deliver phase.

DELIVER PHASE PROCESS CHECKLIST

Fulfillment of Entrance Conditions:
✔ A development freeze has taken place.
✔ The application has been packaged for delivery.
✔ The training plans are in place.
✔ Development of the support documentation has started.
✔ Development of the operations documentation has started.

Processes Performed:
✔ Testing in the large has been successfully completed.
✔ High-priority defects have been addressed and retested.
✔ Your support staff has received training and documentation to support the application effectively.
✔ Your operations staff has received training and documentation to operate the application effectively.
✔ The project and project staff have been assessed.
✔ Risk management has been performed regularly.
✔ Decisions made, and forgone, have been documented in your project's group memory.

Fulfillment of Exit Conditions:
✔ The application has been deployed successfully to your user community.
✔ The user, support, and operations documentation has been accepted.
✔ The user, support, and operations communities have received adequate training.
✔ The models and documentation are up-to-date.

2.7 What You Have Learned in This Chapter

The main goal of the Deliver phase is to deploy your application to your user community. During the Deliver phase you must test your application to verify that it both works in its entirety and that it meets the needs of your users. Because testing will reveal defects with your application you will need to rework it to fix those defects. Once the application has been tested and fixed, you are ready to release it to your user, operations, and support communities. To release an application, you need to train people in its use and operation, and deploy both the application and its documentation. At some point during the Deliver phase you should take the opportunity to assess your project so that you learn from your experiences, enabling your to improve your software process.

2.8 References and Recommended Reading

Ambler, S. W. 1998a. *Building Object Applications That Work—Your Step-by-Step Handbook for Developing Robust Systems with Object Technology.* New York: SIGS Books/Cambridge University Press.

Ambler, S. W. 1998b. *Process Patterns—Building Large-Scale Systems Using Object Technology.* New York: SIGS Books/Cambridge University Press.

Software Engineering Institute 1995. *The Capability Maturity Model: Guidelines for Improving the Software Process.* Reading Massachusetts: Addison-Wesley Publishing Company, Inc.

Chapter 3

The Test in the Large Stage

THE goal of the Test in the Large stage is to ensure that your application works in its entirety. Testing in the large is the object-oriented equivalent of the traditional Test stage of structured development, and you will see in this chapter that the techniques of testing in the large are the same as those of traditional testing. Although testing was performed during the Test in the Small stage (Ambler, 1998b) it was not sufficient to ensure that the application works together as a whole: testing in the small only tests portions of your application. Furthermore, the Test in the Large stage includes user testing in which the application is specifically tested by members of your user community.

The Test in the Large stage ensures that your application works as a whole.

As you see in Figure 3.1, the main inputs into the Test in the Large stage are the packaged application that is to be tested, the master test/QA plan, and in the case of applications being retested the previous test results. Applications will be retested after being fixed by the Rework stage (Chapter 4) or when a new version is being released. The main outputs of the Test in the Large stage are the tested application and the results of testing which indicate whether the application can be released to the user community or needs to be reworked and then retested.

The techniques of the Test in the Large stage are a subset of those of Full Life Cycle Object-Oriented Testing (FLOOT) (Ambler,

Figure 3.1.
The Test in the
Large stage

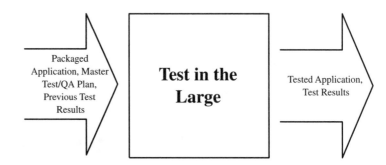

Packaged
Application, Master
Test/QA Plan,
Previous Test
Results

**Test in the
Large**

Tested Application,
Test Results

1998a), depicted in Figure 3.2, composed of the techniques for system testing and user testing.

The Test in the Large stage is critical to the success of your application because it is during this stage that you determine if your application is suitable for release to your user community. I am a firm believer that regardless of your project's schedule, if your application has not been thoroughly tested (and passed those tests), you should not release it to your users. I have seen several applications rushed through testing and put into production, only to fail miserably once people start using it. In fact, the key force/issue that you must address is senior management's insistence that your software be put into production, regardless of whether it was tested sufficiently. Giving people software that doesn't work is usually of little value, but it is what many organizations choose to do instead of taking the time to fix the software first. Fixing defects in software in production is significantly more difficult and costly than fixing them before software is released. The goal of the Test in the Large stage is to identify defects in your software so that you can fix them before you release your application.

The Test in the Large stage strives to identify software defects so they can be fixed before your application is released to your user community.

3.1 Initial Context: Entry Conditions for Testing in the Large

Several entry conditions must be met before the Test in the Large stage may begin:

1. **The application has been packaged for delivery.** Testing in the large tests the application in its entirety, including the installation utility, the documentation, the application support strategy, and the application itself. The implication is

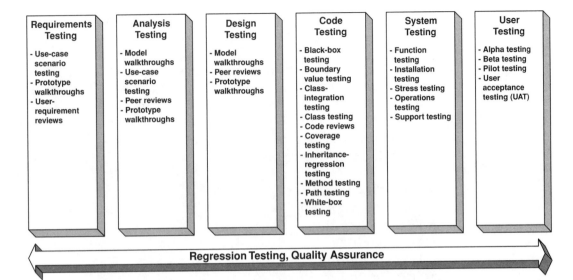

Requirements Testing	Analysis Testing	Design Testing	Code Testing	System Testing	User Testing
- Use-case scenario testing - Prototype walkthroughs - User-requirement reviews	- Model walkthroughs - Use-case scenario testing - Peer reviews - Prototype walkthroughs	- Model walkthroughs - Peer reviews - Prototype walkthroughs	- Black-box testing - Boundary value testing - Class-integration testing - Class testing - Code reviews - Coverage testing - Inheritance-regression testing - Method testing - Path testing - White-box testing	- Function testing - Installation testing - Stress testing - Operations testing - Support testing	- Alpha testing - Beta testing - Pilot testing - User acceptance testing (UAT)

Regression Testing, Quality Assurance

that you need the packaged application, a deliverable of the Construct phase, so you may test it.

2. **The master test/QA plan is available.** You need it to manage and track your testing efforts, which is the purpose of the master test/QA plan that was developed/updated during the Construct phase.

3. **Previous test results.** It is important to have the previous results from your testing-in-the-large efforts if you are testing the new version of an existing application, or if the application has been reworked and is going into testing again. The previous test results help to provide insight for your regression testing efforts and for your entire testing efforts in general.

Figure 3.2.
The techniques of Full Life cycle Object-Oriented Testing (FLOOT)

3.2 Solution: Testing in the Large

Figure 3.3 depicts the process pattern for the Test in the Large stage. The first step is to accept the master test/QA plan, which

---

DEFINITION

master test/quality assurance (QA) plan A document that describes your testing and quality assurance policies and procedures, as well as the detailed test plans for each portion of your application.

often includes updating it so that it reflects all testing to be performed. Testing begins once the test plan is accepted. Testing is composed of two general tasks: system testing, in which the development community tests the application; and user testing, in which the user community tests the application. Throughout both types of testing you must regression-test the application and you must record defects discovered in the application.

As you can see in Figure 3.3, the Test in the Large stage is composed of the following tasks:

- Accept the test plan
- Record defects
- Regression testing
- System testing
- Function testing
- Stress testing
- Installation testing
- Operations testing
- Support testing
- User testing
- User acceptance testing (UAT)
- Alpha/beta/pilot testing

3.2.1 Accepting the Master Test/QA Plan

The first task of the Test in the Large stage is to accept the master test/QA plan. Although this plan should have been appropriately

---

DEFINITIONS

regression testing The act of ensuring that previously tested behaviors still work as expected after changes have been made to an application.

software problem report (SPR) A description of a potential software defect identified by someone who is not directly responsible for a given software deliverable.

system testing A testing process in which you find and fix any known problems to prepare your application for user testing.

user testing Testing processes in which the user community, as opposed to developers, performs the tests. User testing techniques include user acceptance testing, alpha testing, beta testing, and pilot testing.

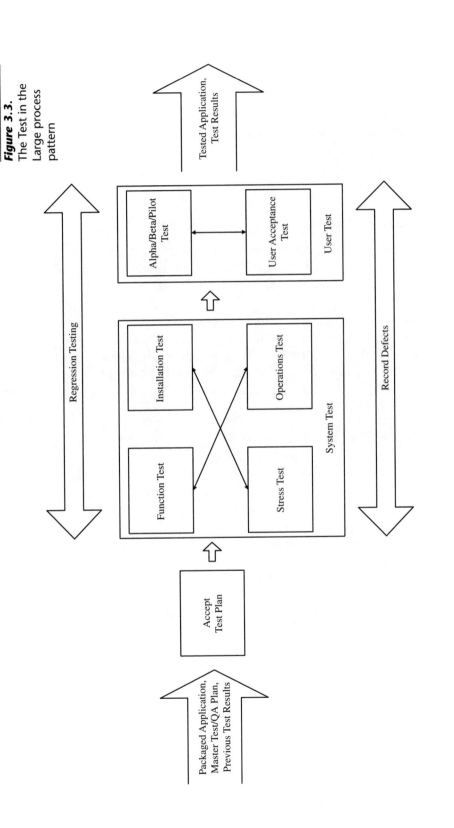

Figure 3.3.
The Test in the Large process pattern

You need an accurate, up-to-date plan before you may begin testing.

updated during the Construct phase, you still need to review it at this point to ensure that it is adequate for your needs. Your test plan should indicate what will be tested, how it will be tested, who will do the testing, and when the testing will be performed. If the existing plan is not complete, then you will need to update it at this point before testing may begin. The point to be made is that before testing can begin you must understand what you are going to test and how you will test it.

3.2.2 Recording Defects

As we saw in *Process Patterns* (Ambler 1998b), software configuration management (SCM) is an important part of the Construct phase. Part of SCM is to manage change requests for an application. With respect to the Test in the Large stage you want to record a specialized form of a change request, called a software problem report (SPR), that describes a defect found in software. The need to document SPRs is identified in DeLano and Rising's (1998) Document the Problem task process pattern.

Humphrey (1997) suggests that the following information be recorded about a defect:

- Description of the defect
- Date the defect was found
- Name of the person who found it
- Defect type (user interface bug, application crash, and so on)
- Stage the defect was found in
- Stage that the defect was introduced in
- Stage the defect was removed in
- Date the work was started
- Date the defect was fixed
- Steps to recreate the defect
- Effort, in work hours or work days, to fix the defect
- Description of the solution

Collecting this information is important for several reasons. First, it provides an accurate description so that the defect may be fixed. Second, in provides the metrics (measurements) that you need to analyze and then improve your work practices. This data should be used to avoid defects in the first place—an important key process area — or at least to find defects sooner in the development process to reduce the cost of fixing them.

DEFINITIONS

change request (CR) A formal document describing a potential modification to an application or system. Software problem reports (SPRs) and enhancement descriptions are specializations of change requests.

enhancement description A type of change request that specifies a new feature for an application or system.

key process area (KPA) An issue that must be addressed to achieve a specific Capability Maturity Model (CMM) maturity level.

software configuration management (SCM) A set of engineering procedures for tracking and documenting software and its related deliverables throughout their life cycles to ensure that all changes are recorded and the current state of the software is known and reproducible.

work day A standard amount of time, measured in hours, that your organization considers a day. Most organizations define a standard work day as being seven, seven-and-a-half, or eight hours.

3.2.3 Regression Testing

Regression testing is the act of ensuring that changes to an application have not adversely affected existing functionality. We have all had experiences where we made a small change to a program and then put the program into production, only to see it fail because our small change affected another part of the program that we had completely forgotten about. Regression testing is all about avoiding problems like this.

The goal of regression testing is to ensure that existing functionality still works after changes have been made.

Regression testing is the very first thing that you should be thinking about when you begin the actual testing in the large of your application. How angry would you get if you took your car into a garage to have a new stereo system installed just to discover afterward that the new stereo works but that the headlights do not? Pretty angry. How angry do you think your users would get when a new release of an application no longer allows them to fax information to other people because the new e-mail feature that you just added has affected it somehow? Pretty angry.

Users expect that all of the functionality they had in a previous version of a system will either still exist or will be enhanced by new releases.

How do you do regression testing? The quick answer is to run all of your previous test cases against the new version of your application. Although this sounds like a good idea, it often proves not to be realistic. First, you may have changed part of, or even all of, the design of your application. This will mean that you need to modify some of the previous test cases. Second, if the changes

Changes in the design may result in changes to your old testing procedures.

you have made truly affect only a component of the system, then potentially you only need to run the test cases that affect this single component. Although this approach is a little risky because your changes may have had a greater impact than you suspect, it does help to reduce both the time and cost of regression testing.

It is important to recognize that incremental development (remember, OO development is incremental in the small) makes regression testing critical. Whenever you release an application, you have to ensure that its previous functionality still works, and because you release applications more often when taking the incremental approach, it means that regression testing becomes that much more important.

Incremental development dramatically increases the importance of regression testing.

3.2.4 System Testing

System testing is a testing process in which you aim to determine the system's capabilities so you may then fix known problems before your application is sent for user testing (section 3.2.5). System testing is comprised of the following techniques:

System testing is performed by developers to verify that your application is ready for user testing.

- Function testing
- Stress testing
- Installation testing
- Operations testing
- Support testing

3.2.4.1 Function Testing

Function testing is a systems-testing technique in which development staff verify that their application meets the defined needs of their users. The idea is that developers, typically test engineers, work through the main functionality that the system should exhibit to assure themselves that their application is ready for user acceptance testing (UAT). It is during user testing that the users will confirm for themselves that the system meets their needs. In many ways the only difference between function testing and user acceptance testing is who does it: testers and users respectively. The End User Viewpoint task process pattern (DeLano and Rising, 1998) describes a major goal of function testing: having test engineers work with the application as if they were users to detect and fix flaws before the software is deployed to your user community.

Why function-test an application when it will just be retested

Function testing is performed by developers to verify that your application is ready for user acceptance testing.

DEFINITIONS

function testing A part of systems testing in which development staff confirm that their application meets the user requirements specified during analysis.

support engineer A person whose job is to collaborate with users needing help to use your software. This is a key role during the Support stage and Test in the Large stage.

test engineer This person is responsible for verifying that the application works as defined by the requirements for the application. This is a key role during all stages of the Construct phase and the Test in the Large stage.

test script The steps to be performed to run a test case. Test scripts will be implemented using a variety of techniques, from source code for code tests to written steps for function testing.

user acceptance testing (UAT) A testing technique in which users verify that an application meets their needs.

---

again by your users? The answer is simple: you do not want to go into UAT unless you are sure that your application will pass. Because you want to build your users' confidence in your application, you do not want to ask them to test something that doesn't work. I want people to work with the best-quality application that I can deliver, even when they are testing it, and that means that I will test it as thoroughly as possible before making it available to them.

Use cases, a technique of the Define and Validate Initial Requirements stage (Ambler, 1998b), are typically used to develop

---

TIP

Involve Support Engineers in Function Testing

Support engineers are responsible for providing support and assistance to the users of your application. Tourniaire and Farrell (1997) suggest that these people are perfect candidates to help you function-test your application for several reasons. First, they know your users often better than you do, and they know the existing environment that your users work in. Second, since support engineers have to live with your application once it is in production, they are highly motivated to test thoroughly. Third, function-testing an application is a great way to get familiar with it, aiding in the training process of your support engineers, an important part of the Release stage (Chapter 5).

test scripts for function testing because they describe the exact behavior of how your users work with your application. You may find that changes in the design of your application will force you to revisit your use cases to verify that they are still applicable, although these problems should have been identified and fixed during construction.

3.2.4.2 Installation Testing

The installation utility/process for your application is part of your overall application package and therefore must be tested. Installation testing is a form of system testing in which the focus is whether your application can be installed successfully. There are several important issues to be considered:

- Can you successfully install the application into an environment that it hasn't been installed into before?
- Can you successfully install the application into an environment where it, or a previous version, already exists?
- Is configuration information defined correctly?
- Is previous configuration information taken into account?
- Is online documentation installed correctly?
- Is there a distribution plan for the application?
- Are other applications affected by the installation of this one?
- Are there adequate computer resources for the application and does the installation utility detect this?

3.2.4.3 Stress Testing

The goal of stress testing is to determine the load/volume levels under which your application no longer works properly.

Stress testing is the process of ensuring that your application works with high numbers of users, high numbers of transactions (testing of high numbers of transactions is also called volume testing), high numbers of data transmissions, high numbers of printed reports, and so on. The goal is to find the stress points of your application under which it no longer operates, so that you can gain insights into how it will perform in unusual and/or stressful situations.

Although stress testing must be performed during the system testing process, it is also commonly performed at the start of a project to verify whether or not a technical alternative works or simply to test the validity of your software. For example, many database administrators will set up a sample database and "pound it" with high numbers of transactions, access requests, and concurrent users to determine its strengths and weaknesses. At the end of a project the real database will be stress-tested again to verify that it will meet the needs of peak demand periods.

Stress testing, for the most part, is a technical process that should be executed by developers who are experienced in both the application and the aspect of it that they intend to stress. Stress testing will often take anywhere from several days to several months, depending on the complexity of what is being stressed and the number of environments that it must be stressed in. For example, one form of stress testing involves using the application on what is considered to be the minimal computer/network hardware/software configuration(s) to verify that it will run in less-than-ideal environments. Stress testing is often performed as part of technical prototyping, a technique of the Model stage, to determine whether a proposed technical solution is viable.

Related to stress testing is DeLano and Rising's (1998) Busy System task process pattern which states that you need to test in an environment that simulates the type of load when the system is considered busy, a load that might not necessarily stress the system. The purpose is to ensure that the system will still operate under a load that it is likely to experience on a regular basis.

A stress test plan, a component of your master test/QA plan, should be created that defines exactly how you intend to go about "pounding" your application. How do you intend to stress the

---

DEFINITIONS

proof-of-concept prototype Software written to prove/test the viability a technology, language, or environment. Also called a technical prototype.

stress testing The act of ensuring that the system performs as expected under high volumes of transactions, high numbers of users, and so on.

stress test plan The test plan that describes how you intend to go about stress-testing your application.

volume testing A subset of stress testing that deals specifically with determining how many transactions or database accesses that an application can handle during a defined period of time.

DEFINITIONS

operations testing
The act of ensuring that the needs of operations personnel who have to support/operate the application are met.

support testing The act of ensuring that the needs of support personnel who have to support the application are met.

database? The network connection? The printer from which you will be printing reports? How many users logons do you wish to test your application under? All of these questions and more should be addressed in your stress test plan.

3.2.4.4 Operations and Support Testing

Operations testing is a type of system testing that verifies that the requirements of operations personnel are met. The main goal of operations testing is to ensure that your operations staff will be able to run your application successfully once it is installed. The issues that must be addressed by operations testing include:

- Are the operations documents current?
- Do the operations documents meet the documentation standards required by your operations department?
- Are there technical manuals available for every component (database, operating system, language, and so on) of your application?
- Is an error-handling facility in place?
- Is someone available on call to answer questions if something goes wrong?

Tourniaire and Farrell (1997) suggest that the needs of your support organization, in addition to those of your operations organization, be tested for before your application is allowed to go into production. Support testing addresses similar issues as does operations testing, obviously with a support focus.

3.2.5 User Testing

User testing is comprised of testing processes in which members of your user community perform the tests. The goal of user testing is to have the users verify that an application meets their needs. User testing is comprised of the following techniques:

- Alpha testing
- Beta testing
- Pilot testing
- User acceptance testing (UAT)

3.2.5.1 Alpha, Beta, and Pilot Testing

One of the major problems with testing is that you can only test for the things that you know about. Unless you do the job of your users day in and day out you can never know the needs of the problem domain as well as they do. The implication is that you'll never be able to define as many real-life testing scenarios as your users can, therefore it makes sense to get your users to test for you.

Your users can devise more and better real-life test scenarios than you can.

Two common approaches to this are alpha testing and beta testing (alpha/beta testing is referred to as pilot testing for applications being developed for use by internal users). Alpha testing is a process in which you send out software that is not quite ready for prime time to a small group of your users to let them work with it and report back to you the problems that they encounter. Although the software is typically buggy and may not meet all of their needs, they get a heads-up on what you are doing a lot earlier than if they waited for you to formally release the software. Beta testing is basically the same process, except the software has many of the bugs fixed that were identified during alpha testing (beta testing follows alpha testing) and the software is distributed to a larger group. The main goal of both alpha and beta testing is to test-run the product to identify and then fix any bugs before your release your application.

Before you alpha/beta/pilot test your application, you need to define your goals so that the users working with the application understand what they are to do with the product. Furthermore,

---

DEFINITIONS

alpha testing A testing period in which pre-release versions of software products, products that are often buggy, are released to users who need access to the product before it is to be officially deployed. In return these users are willing to report back to the software developers any defects that they uncover. Alpha testing is typically followed by a period of beta testing.

beta testing Similar to alpha testing except that the software product should be less buggy. This approach is typically used by software development companies who want to ensure that they meet as many of their client needs as possible.

pilot testing A testing process equivalent to beta testing that is used by organizations to test applications that they have developed for their own internal use.

TIP

You Can Beta Test Your Application While It is Reworked

Although your application may have failed system testing, and therefore is sent to the Rework stage (Chapter 5) to fix the identified defects, you may still decide to release the application to your users for alpha/beta/pilot testing. Although your users are working with a product with known bugs, there is still value in making it available to them so that they work with the application to find additional problems that you have missed. The advantage to this approach is that you perform two tasks in parallel, rework and user testing; but the disadvantage is that the reworked application is out of synch with what is being tested in the field which increases the difficulty of updating the application based on defects found by users. Yes, this tip contradicts my previous advice of only providing the best-quality software that you can to your users, but sometimes you will choose to make this trade-off.

---

you want to release your application to users that you believe will provide you with valuable feedback—often users that have done so in the past—as well as key users who need to see that you have made progress in the development of your application.

3.2.5.2 User Acceptance Testing (UAT)

After your system testing proves successful, your users must perform user acceptance testing, a process in which they determine whether your application truly meets their needs. This means that you have to let your users work with the software that you produced. Because the only person who truly knows your own needs is you, the people involved in the user acceptance test should be the actual users of the system. Not their managers and not the vice presidents of the division that they work for, but the people who will work day in and day out with the application. Although you may have to give them some training to gain the testing skills that they will need, actual *users* are the only people who are qualified to do *user* acceptance testing. The good news is that if you have function-tested your application thoroughly, then the UAT process will take only a few days to a week at most.

Your users are the only ones who can determine if an application truly meets their needs.

The first step of UAT is get a group of users working with the application to learn its basics. You should pay careful attention to their initial reactions—reactions that will reveal either deficiencies in your system or areas in which your user community may need training. For example, when presented with a graphical user interface (GUI) for the first time, many users will have difficulties working with it—often an indication that they need basic training in GUIs and not an indication of problems with your application.

UAT begins with users gaining a basic understanding of the application.

The second step is to get your users working through some of your simpler use cases in addition to their own efforts to use the application to perform everyday tasks. Then have them slowly build up to more complex or esoteric functions in the application, giving them time to learn how to use the application on their job.

The next step is for the users to use the application to do their jobs.

The third step of UAT is test the additional supporting deliverables that are released with your application, such as the user documentation, the support process, and the training materials. In the minds of your users, these are all important parts of the user interface for your application; therefore, they need to be tested to ensure that they meet the needs of your users. To test the user documentation, you want to have users try to work through a series of problems with the user documentation as their only source of information. To test your application support process, you should have users contact support with common problems. Note that you may have to simulate a support desk worked by support engineers familiar with your new application. To test the training materials, run a training course for a group of users who have not worked with the application yet.

DEFINITION

graphical user interface (GUI) A style of user interface in which graphical components, as opposed to text-based components, are used.

The third step of UAT is to test the documentation, support process, and training materials.

To manage your UAT efforts, you must develop a user acceptance test plan, a subsection of your master test/QA plan, that defines exactly how your users intend to go about testing the application. Without such a plan you'll find that the user acceptance test process quickly becomes chaotic and will not produce the results that you want: verification of whether or not your application meets the needs of your users. Both users and test engineers should be involved with the definition of the user acceptance test plan, users providing the business knowledge and test engineers providing the testing expertise. Although your function test plan can be used as input in the development of your user acceptance test plan, the important thing is to let your users drive the process of creating it so that you can be assured that the test plan accurately reflects their needs. As with your function test plan, use cases should be used as input into the development of your user acceptance test plan.

3.3 Solution: Project Tasks

In this section I will discuss project task issues pertinent to the Test in the Large stage.

3.3.1 Managing the Test in the Large Stage

When planned properly, the Test in the Large stage is easy to manage because it is a very mechanical process: you run a series of tests and you record and report on the results. The key to managing this stage is to work to your master test/QA plan, which is why this stage begins with the acceptance of the plan. With the master test/QA plan in place, it is significantly easier to justify and obtain the resources necessary to the Test in the Large stage. This is important because test engineers are constantly being pressured to take shortcuts during testing: the project is often late at this point in the software process and the project manager is trying to make up time. With a reasonable test plan defined and presented to senior management, they understand the implications of reducing the testing effort, making it harder for them to do so.

Work your master test/QA plan.

3.3.2 Training and Education

To provide for appropriate training and education of staff involved with testing in the large, you should consider the following issues:

1. **Test engineers need training in system testing.** Test engineers need to be given training in function testing, installation testing, stress testing, and operations testing to give them the skills needed to perform these tasks properly.
2. **Test engineers need training to submit software problem reports (SPRs).** Anyone involved in reporting defects, including both test engineers and users involved with user testing, needs the necessary training to fill out and submit SPRs properly. This should not be a significant amount of training, perhaps less than an hour; but it still needs to be done.
3. **Management needs to understand that testing is an investment, not a cost.** It is critical that you release software to your user community that works, and the only way to ensure

that it works is to test it thoroughly. We saw in Chapter 11 of *Process Patterns* that the later a defect is detected, the more expensive it is to fix; and that defects that make it into production are always the most harmful to your organization. The implication is that senior management needs to view testing as an investment in quality.

4. **Developers need to understand that testing is a learning opportunity, not an onerous burden.** Testing is one of the few opportunities, with the exception of peer reviews, that developers have to get feedback on their work. This is the perfect opportunity for developers to discover what they are doing wrong so that they may improve their development methods in the future.

> **DEFINITION**
>
> **software problem report (SPR)** A description of a potential software defect identified by someone who is not directly responsible for a given software deliverable.

3.3.3 People Management

The main issue regarding people management during the Test in the Large stage is one of attitude. Everyone must understand that testing is an important and critical part of developing software, one that should not be reduced simply because it comes towards the end of development. Testing is just as important as modeling and programming.

3.3.4 Quality Assurance

Quality assurance is an issue during all project stages, including the Test in the Large stage. The deliverables of your test engineers—test plans, test scripts, and test cases—can be peer reviewed. Remember the golden rule of quality assurance: if you can create it you can review it.

You can, and should, review the deliverables of your test engineers.

TIP

Treat Your Test Engineers with Respect

I have never understood it, but within the vast majority of organizations developers are typically held in higher regard than test engineers. When you stop and think about it, the situation should be reversed: who is more valuable, the person who created a defect or the person who found it? My experience is that test engineers deserve far more respect than they get.

3.3.5 Potential Risks While Testing in the Large

There are several risks specific to the Test in the Large stage:

1. **There are no testing standards or guidelines.** Your organization must come to a consensus on the standards and guidelines that it will follow during testing. These standards and guidelines should have been defined and selected during the Define Infrastructure stage (Ambler, 1998b).
2. **Lack of resources.** Testing is often shortchanged due to the project slipping its schedule during construction, or to a lack of understanding by management about why testing is important. There is little value in delivering something on time that doesn't work.
3. **Underestimating the importance of regression testing.** Taking either an incremental or iterative approach to development, both fundamental aspects of object-orientation, requires that you regression test your work effectively.

3.3.6 Opportunities for Reuse

Here are the opportunities for reuse within and between projects during the Test in the Large stage:
1. **Templates for software problem reports (SPRs).** If your organization has not already done so, you should create a common template for recording SPRs—an example of template reuse. This might be as simple as a common word processing document, or as complex as a common data entry screen that saves the SPRs into a shared persistence mechanism.
2. **Standards, guidelines, and procedures.** Your organization should define and support a common set of standards, guidelines, and procedures for testing that should be used across all projects. There should be procedures for review and testing activities, and standards and guidelines against which deliverables will be reviewed against. This is an example of artifact reuse.

3.3.7 Metrics

You should consider collecting several common metrics during the Test in the Large stage:

> ### DEFINITIONS
>
> **artifact reuse** The reuse of previously created development artifacts: use cases, standards documents, domain-specific models, procedures and guidelines, and other applications.
>
> **guideline** A description, ideally with an example provided, of how something should be done. It is recommended, but not required, that you follow guidelines (unlike standards which are mandatory).
>
> **persistence mechanism** The permanent storage facility used to make objects persistent. Examples include relational databases, object databases, flat files, and object/relational databases.
>
> **procedure** A series of steps to be followed to perform a given task.
>
> **standard** A description, ideally with an example provided, of how something must be done. It is required that you follow standards (unlike guidelines which are optional).
>
> **template reuse** The reuse of a common set of layouts for key development artifacts—documents, models, and source code—within your organization.

1. **Time to fix defects.** The time to fix a defect is the difference between when it is first identified and when it fixed and verified to work by testing. This is an important metric because it indicates how serious defects are—information that you can use to determine whether or not you need to try to find defects earlier (the earlier a defect is found the easier it is to fix).

2. **Defect recurrence.** This is a count of the number of times that the same defect occurs in your work. This metric indicates the true effectiveness of your efforts to fix bugs: if you declare a defect to be fixed, only to find the same bug again a few months later, then you know that it wasn't fixed the first time; instead, it is likely that it was only patched.

3. **Defect-type recurrence.** This is a count of the number of times that a given defect type occurs in your work. For example, if you find that your modelers are constantly indicating key attributes in their class diagrams (keys are indicated on data diagrams, not class diagrams) then it is clear that they need to be trained on class diagramming. This metric is an important means of determining whether your developers are improving their work processes.

4. **Defect severity count.** This is a count of the number of defects of each severity, to provide management with a better understanding of the results of testing. For example, if you know that application A has fifty outstanding defects and application B has fifty outstanding defects, then it is difficult to determine which application needs more work. On the other hand, if application A has twenty-five outstanding level-one defects (severe), twenty level-two defects and five level-three defects, whereas application B has five level-one defects, five level-two defects, and forty level-three defects then you know that application B is likely to be in better shape than application A.

5. **Defect source count.** This is a count of the number of defects caused during each stage of development. This is an important metric because it provides insight into where you need to focus your process improvement efforts—a key process area.

3.4 Resulting Context: Exit Conditions for Testing in the Large

The Test in the Large stage is interesting because there are two valid ways to exit it. Either your application passes testing and is ready to be released to your user community, or it fails testing and needs to be fixed in the Rework stage (Chapter 4). Note that you may iterate several times between the Test in the Large stage and the Rework stage until your application is suitable for release.

3.5 Secrets of Success

I would like to share with you with a few tips and techniques that are helpful when testing object-oriented applications:

1. **Successful tests find errors.** The main goal of testing is to find problems in your application so that you are able to fix them. If your tests do not find any problems, then the chances are infinitely more likely that you need to improve your testing techniques rather than that your application is perfect.

2. **Learn from your mistakes.** We can never find all of the errors in our applications, and some of them will get past us and

into production. Because I believe in making the best of a bad situation, I always try to determine how the error got past me so that I can improve my testing strategy on the next application that I work on. The least you can do is add the problem to your technical review checklists.

3. **Get training in testing.** The material that was covered by this chapter is just the tip of the testing iceberg. The only way to ensure that your developers will have the necessary skills to properly test systems is to invest in object-oriented-testing training courses for them.

4. **Test to the importance of the system.** I would hope that you would put significantly more effort into testing an air-traffic control system than you would a "hello world" program. You need to invest enough time and effort in testing so that you are comfortable that if there is a problem with the application, its consequences would be acceptable to yourself and to your users.

5. **Consider paying for every defect found.** A really successful way to motivate your testers is to consider paying for every defect that they find. I have seen schemes in which a pot of money was allocated to the testing process. For every problem the tester found he or she got so much of the pot, and whatever was left at the end of testing was split among the development team. I have also seen beta tests where every original problem found by a user resulted in them being given a bottle of wine. The major drawback to this approach is that it is easy to abuse and must be managed carefully.

6. **Provide feedback to developers about defects.** A person will never be able to improve their work habits if they do not know that they're doing something wrong. By tracking defects found in the models and source code created by individual developers, and then providing them with feedback about those defects you provide them with the opportunity to learn from their mistakes. Constantine (1995) reports that quality in one organization went up when they started providing such feedback to developers.

7. **Do not ship substandard features.** If user testing shows that a feature is too slow, or doesn't work as expected, or has unintended side effects, then users become disenchanted with your application (Maguire, 1994).

8. **You need a software configuration management (SCM) strategy.** SCM is critical to the testing effort because there

needs to be a planned and coordinated impound of software before testing can begin. Furthermore, SCM makes it easy to identify new features and modified areas of your code so that testing can be focused on those areas. Finally, a configuration item (CI) has a status that cannot be both development and test at the same time, providing a control mechanism with which you can "freeze" your code and declare it to be ready for test (Compton and Conner, 1994).

3.6 Process Checklist

Use the following process checklist to verify that you have completed the Test in the Large stage.

TEST IN THE LARGE STAGE PROCESS CHECKLIST

Fulfillment of Entrance Conditions:
✔ The application has been packaged for delivery.
✔ The master test/QA plan is available.
✔ Previous test results are available.
✔ Team members have been given the appropriate training for their part in this stage.

Processes Performed:
✔ The master test/QA plan was accepted.
✔ Defects have been recorded.
✔ Regression testing has been performed to show that existing behaviors still work.
✔ Function testing has been performed as appropriate.
✔ Stress testing has been performed as appropriate.
✔ Operations testing has been performed as appropriate.
✔ Installation testing has been performed as appropriate.
✔ Support testing has been performed as appropriate.
✔ User acceptance testing (UAT) has been performed as appropriate.
✔ Alpha testing has been performed as appropriate.
✔ Beta testing has been performed as appropriate.
✔ Pilot testing has been performed as appropriate.

✔ Artifacts that are potentially reusable by your project team during this stage have been identified and used where appropriate.

✔ Your risk assessment document has been updated where appropriate.

✔ Decisions made, and decisions forgone, have been documented in your group memory.

✔ Metrics have been collected.

Fulfillment of Exit Conditions:

✔ The application has passed testing.

3.7 What You Have Learned in this Chapter

In this chapter you discovered that you should use several approaches to testing to verify that an application works in its entirety. You saw that system testing—composed of function testing, installation testing, stress testing, and operations testing—is performed by developers to ensure that your application is ready to be user-tested. User testing, comprised of user acceptance testing and alpha/beta/pilot testing, is performed by your user community to ensure that your application truly does meet the needs of its users. Once your application passes testing in the large, it is ready to be released to your users.

3.8 References and Recommended Reading

Ambler, S. W. 1998a. *Building Object Applications That Work—Your Step-by-Step Handbook for Developing Robust Systems with Object Technology.* New York: SIGS Books/Cambridge University Press.

Ambler, S. W. 1998b. *Process Patterns—Building Large-Scale Systems Using Object Technology.* New York: SIGS Books/Cambridge University Press.

Compton, S. B. and Conner, G. R. 1994. *Configuration Management for Software.* New York: Van Nostrand Reinhold.

Constantine, L. L. 1995. *Constantine on Peopleware.* Englewood Cliffs, New Jersey: Yourdon Press.

DeLano, D.E. & Rising, L. (1998). *Patterns for System Testing.* Pattern Languages of Program Design 3, eds. Martin, R.C., Riehle, D., and Buschmann, F., Addison Wesley Longman, Inc., pp. 503–525.

Humphrey, W. S. 1997. *Introduction to the Personal Software Process.* Reading, Massachusetts: Addison-Wesley Longman, Inc.

Maguire, S. 1994. *Debugging the Development Process.* Redmond, Washington: Microsoft Press.

Siegel, S. 1996. *Object Oriented Software Testing: A Hierarchical Approach.* New York: John Wiley and Sons, Inc.

Tourniaire, F. and Farrell, R. 1997. *The Art of Software Support: Design and Operation of Support Centers and Help Desks.* Upper Saddle River, New Jersey: Prentice Hall PTR.

Chapter 4

The Rework Stage

THE focus of the Rework stage is to fix the critical defects discovered by the Test in the Large stage (Chapter 3) to ensure the successful deployment of your application. The implication is that not all defects need to be fixed immediately—many can be addressed by a later release of your application. The Rework stage is effectively a miniature version of the Construct phase, although due to project pressures to deploy your application the generalization of items to make them reusable is left out.

The Rework stage is effectively a mini-Construct phase that focuses on fixing critical defects discovered during the Test in the Large stage.

Figure 4.1 shows that the main inputs into the Rework stage are the tested application and test results from the Test in the Large stage, as well as the current version of the models and requirements allocation matrix (RAM), source code, and documentation for the application which should be under software configuration management (SCM) control. Based on the prioritized defects, the models, source code, and documentation will be reworked appropriately and sent back to the Test in the Large stage so that they may be retested.

The Rework stage is called out explicitly by the object-oriented software process (OOSP) to remind you to plan for it. You know that defects will be found by testing in the large, many of which will need to be addressed before the application is deployed; therefore, you must include the need to rework your application in your project plan. Just as I explicitly include the Generalize stage (Ambler, 1998b) within the Construct phase, I include the

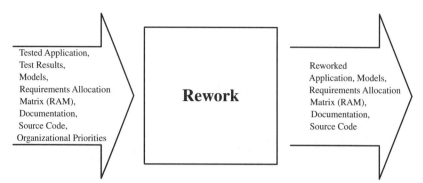

Figure 4.1.
The Rework stage

An explicit Rework stage provides you an opportunity to plan for it early in the software process, and a distinct stage against which you can measure work effort.

Rework stage in the Deliver phase to force you to consider it in your planning efforts. Another advantage of having an explicit Rework stage is that it provides a distinct, measurable stage against which you can track costs. By having a measure of your rework effort you can easily gauge the quality of your construction efforts and you will have something that you can now manage to, for example a goal for your next project may be to reduce the rework effort by fifty percent.

1.1 Initial Context: Entry Conditions for Reworking Your Application

The following conditions must be met before you may begin the Rework stage:

1. **The test results are available.** The application needs to have been tested and the defects documented, typically in the form of software problem reports (SPRs). The SPRs define the issues that potentially need to be addressed by the Rework stage. An

---

DEFINITIONS

requirements allocation matrix (RAM) A mapping of requirements, defined in your requirements document to the portions of your model(s) that implement them.

software configuration management (SCM) A set of engineering procedures for tracking and documenting software and its related deliverables throughout their life cycles to ensure that all changes are recorded and the current state of the software is known and reproducible.

SPR may indicate that a screen needs to be reworked to conform to the user interface standards of your organization, that the information in a report isn't being calculated properly, that the application crashes at a certain point, or that the documentation is out of synch with the application.

DEFINITION

software problem report (SPR) A description of a potential software defect identified by someone who is not directly responsible for a given software deliverable.

2. **Your organization's priorities are known.** To determine which defects will be fixed now and which will be left for a future release, you need to understand the expectations of senior management for your project. Are you under contract to deliver the application on a given date? Do you have the opportunity to push back your delivery date in favor of delivering a better product? What level of defects is your user community willing to accept in your application? What application features are critical to your organization right now, and what can be delivered later? These are all questions that you need to have answered so you may accurately determine how to rework your application.

3. **The current versions of your models, requirements allocation matrix (RAM), documentation, and source code are available.** To rework your application you must modify the models, RAM, documentation, and source code for your application, therefore you must have access to them.

4.2 Solution: Reworking Your Application

The process pattern depicted in Figure 4.2 shows that there are two steps to the Rework stage. The first step is to prioritize the defects found during the Test in the Large stage, to determine which defects will be fixed now and which will be left for a future release. The second step is to fix the selected defects, which is done by updated the models where needed, programming the necessary changes, updated the documentation to reflect the changes, and then to perform testing in the small to verify that the changes have been made properly. In many ways, to fix defects you simply work through the Construct phase again, although now the focus is on fixing specific problems instead of fulfilling specific requirements.

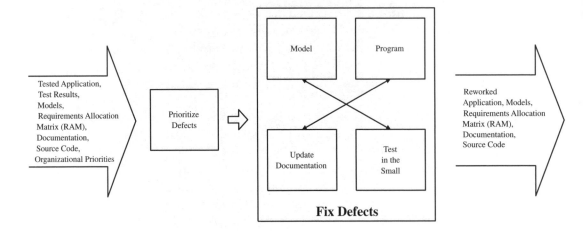

Figure 4.2.
The Rework
process pattern

4.2.1 Prioritizing Defects

The first step of the Rework stage is to prioritize the defects described by the software problem reports (SPRs). You begin prioritizing potential defects by determining whether the SPR documents an actual defect or a new or changed requirement. To do this you need to trace the defect to the requirements for your application, described in your requirements document. If you find that the SPR describes either a new or changed requirement then you need to negotiate with your users whether you need to "fix" the SPR at this time, resulting in scope creep for your project, or if it should be reassigned to a future release of your application.

You begin by determining if each SPR describes a defect, a new requirement, or a changed requirement.

Next you perform an impact analysis for each SPR. An impact analysis determines how your application will be affected by a given change, describing the modifications that need to be made to your models, documentation, and source code. Your requirements allocation matrix (RAM) is used to trace where the impacted

---

TIP

Many New Requirements Indicates Modeling Deficiencies

If you discover that a large percentage of the software problem reports (SPRs) that you receive from testing in the large are actually change requests for new or improved features, it is an indication that you didn't do an effective job during the Define and Validate Initial Requirements stage (Ambler, 1998b) and/or the Model stage (Ambler, 1998b).

requirements are implemented in your application. You will also want to include an estimate of the work effort involved in fixing each defect to aid in your determination of which defects to be addressed (perhaps you will choose not to fix defects that require significant levels of effort). The estimates to fix each defect will be used as input into your overall estimate of how long it will take to rework your application, key information for senior management.

You need to perform an impact analysis for each defect.

Once you have performed an impact analysis for each defect, you are ready to perform requirements triage, in which you select the defects that you must fix immediately, the defects that you would prefer to fix given adequate resources, and defects that can be left until a later date. Depending on the priorities of your organization, you may decide to fix none of the defects, or perhaps all of them, before deploying your application. The priorities of your organization will often boil down to:

- What level of quality must your application exhibit?
- When must the application be deployed?
- How much is your organization willing to spend to fix the defects?
- What features is your organization willing to forgo to deliver the application sooner and/or cheaper?

4.2.2 Fixing Defects

Once you have determined which defects your intend to fix you must do the work to fix them. This work will be driven by the

---

TIP

Document The Implications of Not Fixing a Defect

It is common to have senior management unilaterally decide to ship an application that has known defects—defects that you would have preferred to fix—to meet the delivery date for an application. The issue is that when the defects are found by users once the application is in production, your team will be blamed for them, not the managers who decided to ship the application anyway. To protect yourself from this, my suggestion is to document the potential implications of not fixing each defect. That way management understands the potential risks associated with not fixing the defects and therefore can be held responsible, at least in the eyes of your users, for shipping a buggy application.

DEFINITIONS

feature creep The addition as development proceeds of new features to an application that are above and beyond what the original specification called for. This is also called scope creep.

impact analysis A determination of how your application will be affected by a given change. Your analysis should describe the modifications that need to be made to your models, documentation, and source code and should provide an estimate of the work effort involved to make those changes.

requirements document A document, also called a System Requirements Specification (SRS), that describes the user, technical, and environmental requirements for an application. This document potentially contains the major use cases for the application, detailed use-case scenarios for the application, and traditional requirements for the application as well. Requirements documents are a deliverable of the Initiate phase and are updated regularly during modeling. Requirements documents are also updated during the Maintain and Support phase as bugs and enhancements are identified.

requirements triage The act of prioritizing requirements—for example, "must have," "nice to have," and "nonessential"—to aid in the definition of an application that can be delivered with the limited resources at hand.

work day A standard amount of time, measured in hours, which your organization considers a day. Most organizations define a standard work day as being seven, seven-and-a-half, or eight hours.

---

results of your impact analysis, which describes the modifications that need to be made to your application. To fix the defects in your application you must:

- Rework your models.
- Rework your source code.
- Update the documentation.
- Retest in the small.

4.2.2.1 Reworking the Models and RAM

Your first task is to make the appropriate changes to the detailed models for your application and to update your requirements allocation matrix (RAM) where needed. If you have maintained traceability throughout your models, as suggested in the Model stage (Ambler, 1998b), then this will be a straightforward process. During the prioritization of each SPR, you traced each one back to the

---

DEFINITIONS

capability Maturity Model (CMM) A strategy defined by the Software Engineering Institute (SEI) that describes the key elements of an effective software process.

key process area (KPA) An issue that must be addressed to achieve a specific Capability Maturity Model (CMM) maturity level.

traceability The ease with which the features of one deliverable, a document, model, or source code, can be related/traced to the features of another.

---

original requirements for the application—requirements that are traceable to your models. Because you can trace each defect to the appropriate portions of your models, you merely need to follow the object-oriented modeling techniques (Ambler, 1998a) of the Model stage to update them appropriately.

You need to trace each defect into your models and make the appropriate changes.

The Software Engineering Institute (1995) points out that an important feature of a mature software process is the effective negotiation and management of requirements between your information technology (IT) department and your user community. This is a goal of the Level 2 Requirements Management key process area (KPA) of the Capability Maturity Model (CMM), a goal that is supported by keeping your models and RAM up-to-date as you rework your application.

4.2.2.2 Reworking the Source Code

Once you have reworked your models the effort to reworking your source code is similar to that of the Program stage (Ambler, 1998b), as you would expect. You begin by understanding the changes to the models, then document in the code the changes that you need to make; you then update the code to reflect those changes, and then inspect and improve your code based on the results of the inspection. Once the application has been tested in the small (see below), you will need to repackage the application just as you did in the Program stage so that the application may be sent back to the Test in the Large stage (Chapter 3).

DEFINITION

application package The software and supporting documentation that is deployed to your user community.

4.2.2.3 Updating the Documentation

Because defects may be found in the documentation for your application—very often portions of the documentation will be

Technical writers may be needed to fix defects in the documentation for the application.

DEFINITION

technical writer
The person responsible for writing, updating, and/or improving the technical documentation produced on the project, potentially including the requirements, models, standards, guidelines, and project plans. This is a key role throughout all project phases.

missing, out of synch with the application, or difficult to understand—you will be required to update the documentation. The most effective way to fix your application's documentation is to assign the work to technical writers—ideally, the same technical writers who wrote the documentation to begin with, as they have the necessary skills. Also, remember that defects may be found in the user documentation, the operations documentation, and/or the support documentation.

4.2.2.4 Retesting in the Small

As you make changes to your models, source code, and documentation you need to apply the techniques of the Test in the Small stage (Ambler, 1998b) to verify that they work. You need to review the changes you have made to ensure that the quality of your application is being maintained. You also want to test your source code to ensure that the new changes work, and regression-test to ensure that previous working behaviors still do so. Yes, it is tempting to not perform testing in the small, because you know that your application will return to the Test in the Large stage once it is reworked. However, the fact is that testing in the small and testing in the large focus on different issues; therefore, you need to perform both on your reworked application.

You need to perform testing in the small, in particular regression testing, on your reworked application.

4.3 Solution: Project Tasks

In this section I will discuss project task issues that are pertinent to the Rework stage.

4.3.1 Managing the Rework Stage

Avoid the temptation to rush the Rework stage. Do it once and do it right.

In addition to the management issues associated with construction, the key management issue during the Rework stage is to avoid the temptation to rush this stage to get your application ready to be retested. By rushing you will do a sloppy job, virtually ensuring that your application will fail testing again and still need to be reworked. A motto that I live by is "do it right and do it once," a philosophy that is definitely pertinent to the Rework stage.

4.3.2 People Management

People management can become a serious problem during the Rework stage. First, because of overtime put in by your team toward the end of the Construct phase, developers are likely to be burnt out and tired of working on your application. The last thing that they want to do is fix the mistakes in their work. Second, at this point some developers may have already left the project, either for another project within your organization or for a completely different organization, and are no longer available to fix defects in your application. Third, developers are tempted to rush their work, often because they are eager to get the work over with so they can move onto another project, or simply because they have vacations and/or training courses scheduled that they wish to attend.

Developers are often unwilling to rework your application, are unavailable to do so, or want to rush through the Rework stage to get it over with.

To avoid these problems, or at least to minimize their impact, you need to include rework in your project plan, providing developers with an indication that they'll still be needed once your project is in the Deliver phase.

4.3.3 Quality Assurance

As you would expect the quality assurance issues of the Construct phase are completely relevant for the Rework stage. Developers should follow the same standards and guidelines that they used during construction, and you need to hold peer reviews of all updated models, documents, and source code.

The quality assurance issues of the Construct phase are applicable to the Rework stage.

4.3.4 Potential Risks While Reworking Your Application

Several risks are inherent to the Rework stage:

1. **The temptation to rush.** Take the time to perform your rework properly, following the same standards, guidelines, and procedures employed during the Construct phase.
2. **The temptation to reduce testing.** Because your application will return to the Test in the Large stage for retesting there is a temptation to reduce or even eliminate testing in the small efforts during the Rework stage. You cannot afford to do this because testing in the small focuses on a different set of testing issues than does testing in the large. You need to do both.
3. **The temptation to only update the source code.** One way to reduce the amount of time taken for the Rework stage is to only update the source code for your application, with the intention to update the models and potentially the documentation at a later date. The problem is that the later date never arrives, other pressing matters get in the way, and your source code is out of synch with your models and documen-

---

DEFINITIONS

guideline A description, ideally with an example provided, of how something should be done. It is recommended, but not required, that you follow guidelines (unlike standards which are mandatory).

procedure A series of steps to be followed to perform a given task.

standard A description, ideally with an example provided, of how something must be done. It is required that you follow standards (unlike guidelines which are optional).

---

tation, increasing the difficulty and cost of maintaining and supporting your application.

4. **The temptation to not fix known defects.** You are often between a rock and a hard place during the Rework stage. You want to ship a high-quality working product that is free of defects but at the same time need to meet delivery dates. If you choose to not fix a defect, and you often will, at a minimum you want to invest the time to understand and document the expected consequence of not doing so. Not fixing known defects is a risk to your application, and a fundamental task of risk management is that you document known risks.

4.3.5 Opportunities for Reuse

Template reuse for software problem reports (SPRs) is achievable during the Rework stage.

The main opportunity for reuse during the Rework stage is that of template reuse—the document template that you use for software problem reports (SPRs) should include a section for the impact analysis of the SPR, and potentially a section for describing the implications of not addressing the SPR. The forms of reuse that are common to the Construct phase, such as code and pattern reuse, are typically not taken advantage of during the Rework stage because you are fixing existing work that should have already taken advantage of these forms of reuse.

4.3.6 Metrics

There are several metrics applicable to the Rework stage that you may choose to collect:

1. **Work effort to fix a defect.** This is an important measure because it indicates the loss to your organization due to a defect.

DEFINITIONS

code reuse The reuse of source code within sections of an application and potentially across multiple applications.

pattern reuse The reuse of publicly documented approaches, called patterns, to solving common problems.

template reuse The reuse of a common set of layouts for key development artifacts—documents, models, and source code—within your organization.

---

2. **Percentage of SPRs reworked.** This is calculated by dividing the number of software problem reports (SPRs) that were reworked by the total number of SPRs considered to be reworked. For example, if testing submits ten SPRs to be reworked, and three of them actually are reworked, then the percentage of SPRs reworked is thirty percent. This is an important metric because it indicates your project team's ability to fix identified defects in the time provided.

4.4 Resulting Context: Exit Conditions for Reworking Your Application

The following conditions must be met before the Rework stage is considered complete:

1. **The selected defects have been fixed.** All defects that were chosen to be fixed must be.
2. **The documentation, models, and requirements allocation matrix (RAM) are current.** As your development team fixed the identified errors they should have also updated the corresponding documentation, models, and portions of your application's RAM to keep them in synch.
3. **The application has been packaged.** The final step of the Rework stage is to repackage the application so that it may be retested by the Test in the Large stage (Chapter 3).

4.5 Secrets of Success

I would like to share with you a few tips and techniques for making your rework efforts successful:

1. **Plan for rework.** The Test in the Large stage is guaranteed to find defects in your application, some of which will need to be fixed before your application is ready to be deployed. By planning to rework your application, something that you know that you will need to do, you are better able to manage your resources to ensure that you are able to do the rework that needs to be performed.

2. **Maintain rigor within the Rework stage.** The Rework stage is just as important as the Construct phase, even more so because you know that what you are fixing must work before you are able to deploy your application to your user community. Your development team must follow the same standards, guidelines, and procedures that they did during construction to ensure similar quality in their work.

3. **Follow your object-oriented software process (OOSP).** The Software Engineering Institute (1995) points out that a key to success during construction is to perform the engineering tasks to build and maintain your application in accordance with the project's defined software process and appropriate methods and tools. This is an important part of the Level 2 Software Product Engineering key process area (KPA) of the Capability Maturity Model (CMM).

4.6 Process Checklist

The following process checklist can be used to verify that you have completed the Rework stage.

REWORK STAGE PROCESS CHECKLIST

Fulfillment of Entrance Conditions:
✔ The testing results are available.
✔ Your organization's priorities are known.
✔ The current versions of Construct phase deliverables are available to be reworked.
✔ Team members have been given the appropriate training for their part in this stage.

Processes Performed:
- ✔ Defects have been prioritized.
- ✔ The models have been reworked.
- ✔ The requirements allocation matrix (RAM) has been reworked.
- ✔ The support documentation has been reworked.
- ✔ The user documentation has been reworked.
- ✔ The operations documentation has been reworked.
- ✔ The source code has been reworked.
- ✔ The application has been tested in the small.
- ✔ Artifacts that are potentially reusable by your project team during this stage have been identified and used where appropriate.
- ✔ Your risk assessment document has been updated where appropriate.
- ✔ Decisions made, and decisions forgone, have been documented in your group memory.
- ✔ Metrics have been collected.

Fulfillment of Exit Conditions:
- ✔ The selected defects have been reworked and are ready to be retested.
- ✔ The Construct phase deliverables have been reworked and are consistent.
- ✔ The application has been repackaged for testing.

4.7 What You Have Learned in this Chapter

The goal of the Rework stage is the fix the defects found during the Test in the Large stage so that your application may be released. The Rework stage is explicitly called out within the Deliver phase because of the surety of needing to fix the defects identified during testing. In this chapter you saw that software problem reports (SPRs) which describe potential defects must be analyzed and prioritized to determine the defects to be fixed immediately, and which can be left for a future release of the application. The chosen defects must be fixed following the same standards, guidelines, and procedures that were applied during the Construct phase to ensure consistency within your application. Your application is then tested in the small and then packaged so that it may be sent back to the Test in the Large stage for further retesting.

4.8 References and Recommended Reading

Ambler, S. W. 1998a. *Building Object Applications That Work—Your Step-by-Step Handbook for Developing Robust Systems with Object Technology.* New York: SIGS Books/Cambridge University Press.

Ambler, S. W. 1998b. *Process Patterns—Building Large-Scale Systems Using Object Technology.* New York: SIGS Books/Cambridge University Press.

Software Engineering Institute 1995. *The Capability Maturity Model: Guidelines for Improving the Software Process.* Reading Massachusetts: Addison-Wesley Publishing Company, Inc.

Chapter 5

The Release Stage

THE goal of the Release stage is to deploy your application and its corresponding documentation successfully to your user community. To do that you must ensure that the needs of your operations department are met—after all, these are the people that will keep your application running once it is in production—and that the needs of your support department are met, as these are the people that will help your users work with your application effectively. The Release stage includes training your customers—your user community, your operations department, and your support department.

During the Release stage you train your customers and deploy your application and associated documentation to them.

Figure 5.1 shows that there are several inputs into the Release stage. First, the release procedures, if any, that were selected during the Define Infrastructure stage (Ambler, 1998) are needed to drive the management of this stage, as are the training plans developed during the Construct phase. The items that will be deployed to your customers, the application package (also known as your product baseline) and the corresponding operations and support documentation are also required. The outputs of the Release stage are the released application package itself and its corresponding procedures and documentation for your operations and support departments.

It is important to understand that there are different types of software releases. Although this book has concentrated on the development, and therefore the release, of a new application, there are in fact four types of software release: an application release in which your entire application is deployed; a mainte-

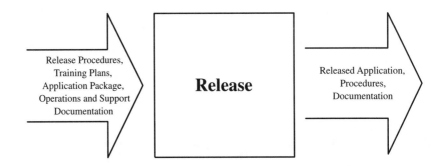

Figure 5.1.
The Release stage

nance release where your application is released but only contains fixes to previous functionality; a patch release where a portion of your application is released to fix specific bugs; and a testing release in which your application is released for alpha/beta/pilot testing to support the Test in the Large stage (Chapter 3). In this chapter I will concentrate on application releases, the most complex of the three types, and will leave it to you to select the tasks appropriate for any maintenance or patch releases that you perform.

There are four different kinds of formal software release: application, maintenance, patch, and testing.

5.1 Initial Context: Entry Conditions for Releasing Your Application

The following conditions must be met before you may begin the Release stage:

1. **The application has been packaged for release.** The implication is that your application has passed the Test in the Large stage (Chapter 3) as well as the Rework stage (Chapter 4) if necessary. The application package includes the installation procedures, the appropriate documentation, and the application itself.

2. **The release procedures have been defined and selected.** The release procedures that were defined and selected during the Define Infrastructure stage (Ambler, 1998) are used to help plan and manage your efforts during the Release stage.

3. **Training plans have been developed.** The plans to train your customers to use, operate, and support your application should have been developed during the Construct phase in parallel with the application itself. You need these plans to help you manage the training portion of the Release stage.

DEFINITIONS

alpha testing A testing period in which pre-release versions of software products, products that are often buggy, are released to users who need access to the product before it is to be officially deployed. In return these users are willing to report back to the software developers any defects that they uncover. Alpha testing is typically followed by a period of beta testing.

application package The software and supporting documentation that is deployed to your user community.

application release A software release that delivers an application containing new, improved, and/or fixed functionality.

beta testing Similar to alpha testing, except that the software product should be less buggy. This approach is typically used by software development companies who want to ensure that they meet as many of their client needs as possible.

maintenance release An application release that contains only bug fixes and does not contain new functionality.

patch release A software release that contains one or more bug fixes, replacing only a portion of the total application.

pilot testing A testing process equivalent to beta testing that is used by organizations to test applications they have developed for their own internal use.

product baseline The exact version of the software that is released to the user community.

testing release A software release in which your application is released for alpha/beta/pilot testing.

---

4. **Operations and support documentation have been developed.** The operations and support documentation for your application should have been developed during the Construct phase.

5.2 Solution: Releasing Your Application

The process pattern shown in Figure 5.2 indicates that the Release stage is comprised of three sequential tasks: preparing for release, releasing the application to operations and support, and releasing the application to your user community. The effort to prepare for the release of your application will range from very simple to very complex depending on what your project team accomplished previous to the Release stage—all of this work should have already been accomplished and will merely need to be given one last check to verify that it is complete. The next step is to release your application to your operations and support communities, which involves delivering the appropriate documentation and training the appropriate staff. The third step is to release your application to your user community, a step that you will likely choose to run in parallel to the second one, a step which includes deploying your application and training your users to work with your application effectively.

The Release stage is comprised of three sequential tasks, the second two of which may potentially run in parallel.

5.2.1 Preparing for Release

The purpose of preparing to release your application is twofold. First, you want to ensure that everything is in place for your release to go smoothly. Second, you want to obtain authorization to release your application from your operations department, support department, and from senior management. Depending on your organization, this authorization will range from a simple verbal agreement to a formal document that your application is ready to go into production. There are four tasks, typically performed in parallel, to prepare for the release of your application:

- Accept the training and release plans.
- Accept the user, support, and operations documentation.
- Package the application.
- Finalize conversion of legacy data.

5.2.1.1 Accepting the Training Plan and Release Plan/Procedures

Your training manager must accept your training plan, and your operations and support managers must accept your release plan and procedures. Senior management must accept both.

Ideally, your training plans should have been started, and potentially completed, during the Construct phase (Ambler, 1998) and your release procedures during the Define Infrastructure stage (Ambler, 1998). To accept your training plan, you need to review it with your organization's training manager, the person whom you likely worked with to define it in the first place. To accept your release plan and procedures you need to review them with your support and operations managers to verify that their needs are being met. Senior management must also accept both your

Figure 5.2.
The Release
process pattern

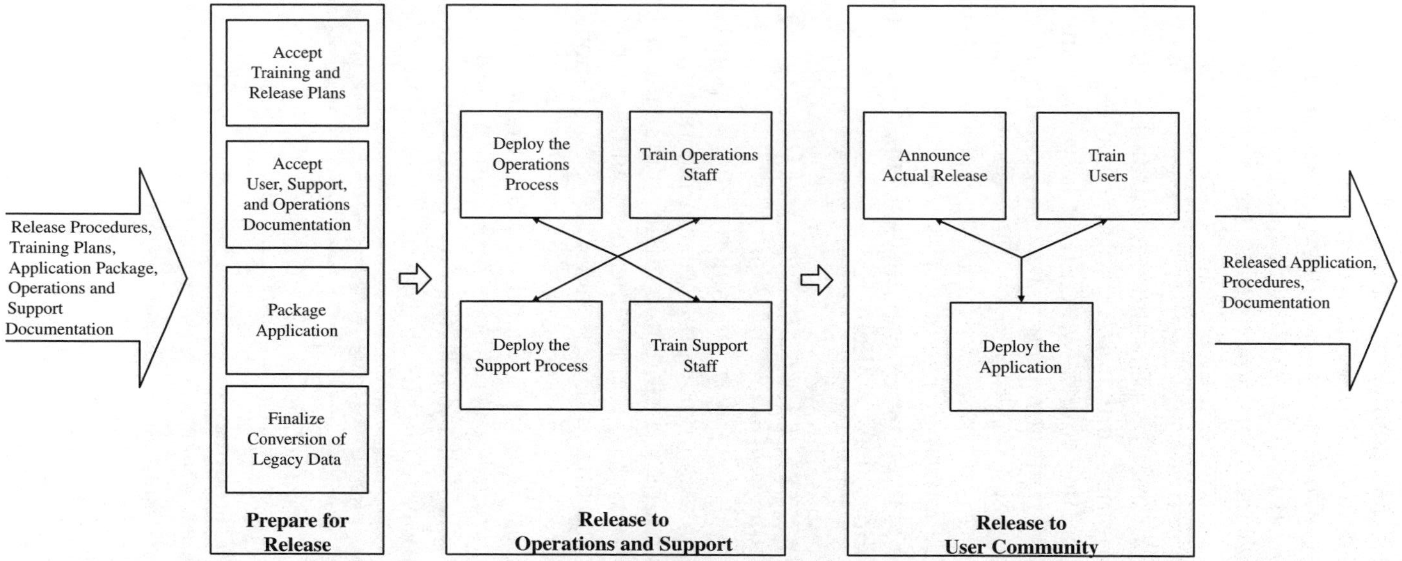

training plan and your release plan to ensure that your application will be deployed appropriately.

A training plan is crucial to the success of the Release stage, because there is potentially a significant amount of training to be given to your users, operations staff, and support staff. The issues surrounding training and education are discussed in detail in Chapter 10, where you will see that the management of training and education is a complex and difficult task which you need to start planning very early if you want it to succeed.

Your release procedures, which refer to your training plan and to your data conversion plan (data conversion is covered later in this chapter), describe the tasks that you will follow to release your application to your customers. This chapter provides a basis from which your organization may define release procedures. Your release plan shows when you will apply your release procedures and who will apply them.

5.2.1.2 Accepting the User, Support, and Operations Documentation

Your customers, your user, operations, and support communities, must be assured that your project team has met their documentation requirements. These requirements, summarized in Table 5.1, are quite extensive. These documents should have been developed during the Construct phase (Ambler, 1998) and should have been validated during the Test in the Large stage (Chapter 3). The purpose of this task is to verify that the documentation is complete and that your customers accept them. Although this task is essentially a formality, I would like to take the time to explain what each of your customer groups require in the way of documentation.

DEFINITIONS

release plan A plan which describes when your release procedures will be applied, and by whom, to release your application.

release procedures A description of the tasks, and the order in which to take them, to release an application. Release procedures will refer to your data conversion plan and your training plan for your release.

training plan A plan that describes the training to be delivered, to whom it will be delivered, how it will be delivered, when it will be delivered, and where it will be delivered.

TABLE 5.1. The Documentation Needs for Each Customer Group

Customer	Documentation Needs
Operations	• Backup procedures • Batch job and printing requirements • Data extraction/sharing requirements • Installation procedures • Resource requirements • Version description document (VDD)
Support	• Contact points within development and operations • Escalation procedures • Support call recording process • User documentation (all versions)
Users	• Reference manual • Support user's guide • Tutorial manual • User manual

Mayhew (1992) states that the user documentation is part of the user interface for an application, and that well-written user documentation is no excuse for a poorly designed user interface. The user documentation to be deployed to your users has several components, including a tutorial manual for novice users, a user manual for intermediate users, and a reference manual for expert users. Weiss (1991) points out the need for different kinds of manuals to support the needs of different types of users; the lesson to be learned is that one manual does not fit all. Tourniaire and Farrell (1997) suggest that a support user's guide describing the support services provided to your user community should be included with the user documentation for your application.

The user documentation for your application includes a tutorial manual, a reference manual, a user manual, and a support user's guide.

Your user documentation should include a description of the skills needed to use the application. For example, your users may require training in your business domain or in basic computer skills such as using a mouse. This information is needed to develop training plans for users and by support engineers when they are attempting to determine the source of a problem. Very often support engineers will receive support calls for which the solution is to send the user for additional training.

Your support department requires a document describing the support call recording process for filling out and submitting software change requests (SCRs) and software problem reports (SPRs) resulting from contacts with your user community. Your call escalation procedures—in which your support department passes difficult support calls to people with specific expertise, both within your support organization and your development community—need to be documented. This document will include the contact information for the relevant positions within your development and operations departments. Finally, to help users work through problems, the support staff needs access to all documents that are deployed to the user community.

Your operations department needs to have documentation that describe all processes and procedures that they must follow to operate your application. This includes:

- Backup procedures for your persistence mechanism(s)
- The installation procedures for your application in case it needs to be reinstalled
- The version description document (VDD) describing all components of your application
- The printing and batch job requirements for your application (perhaps your application includes a monthly reporting batch job)
- Data extraction/sharing requirements to support your organization's data warehouse and/or reporting database(s)
- A description of the physical computer resources required by your application

5.2.1.3 *Finalizing the Application Package*

This task is the creation of the final version of the application package; essentially the same process that was followed during the Program stage (Ambler, 1998) to prepare the application for the Test in the Large stage (Chapter 3) is followed again. The main difference is that this application package contains the official product baseline—the version of your application to be released to your user community—and its associated documentation.

To package the application, you need to:

- Gather the software files to be deployed.
- Create a master set of the files to be versioned within your software configuration management (SCM) tool.

DEFINITIONS

escalation procedures The process by which difficult support calls are forwarded to people with greater expertise, both within your support organization and your development community.

operations documentation The documentation deployed to your operations department, including backup procedures, batch job and printing requirements, data extraction/sharing requirements, installation procedures for your application, resource requirements for your application, and the version description document (VDD) describing the product baseline for your application.

persistence mechanism The permanent storage facility used to make objects persistent. Examples include relational databases, object databases, flat files, and object/relational databases.

reference manual A document, either paper or electronic, aimed at experts who need quick access to information.

software change request (SCR) A description of a potential improvement to a software deliverable, often identified by users of that deliverable.

software problem report (SPR) A description of a potential software defect identified by someone who is not directly responsible for a given software deliverable.

support documentation The documentation deployed to your support department, including your support call recording process, applicable call escalation procedures, relevant points of contact within your development and operations departments, and all user documentation for your application.

support user's guide A brief document, usually a single page, which describes the support services for your application that are available to your user community. This guide will include support phone numbers, fax numbers, and Web site locations as well as hours of operations and tips for obtaining the best services.

tutorial manual A document, either paper or electronic, aimed at novice users who need to learn the fundamentals of an application.

user documentation The documentation deployed to the user community, potentially including a user manual, tutorial manual, reference manual, and support user's guide.

user manual A document, either paper or electronic, aimed at intermediate users who understand the basics of an application but may not know how to perform all applicable work tasks with the application.

version description document (VDD) A complete list of all items included in a product baseline release of software, including all configuration items and supporting deliverables. The VDD includes an indication of all changes made to the software from the previous version and a list of all applicable SPRs and SCRs implemented in the current version.

- Finalize the version description document (VDD) describing this product baseline.
- Create/update release notes, to be deployed with the application, summarizing the VDD.
- Prepare/finalize installation procedures.
- Prepare/finalize the external documentation (see previous section).

You should only have to verify that the application package is complete and that is has been defined as your product baseline.

There should be very little work to do to complete this task, because your application should have been packaged in the exact same manner for testing. The only thing that you need to do is verify that the application package is complete and that the appropriate software configuration management (SCM) procedures have been followed to define your product baseline.

5.2.1.4 Finalizing the Conversion of Legacy Data

The vast majority of object-oriented applications require access to existing, legacy data. We saw in the Program stage (Ambler, 1998) that the task of mapping objects to relational databases is a complex one, one that is made even more complicated when you attempt to map directly to a legacy schema. Due to the object/relational impedance mismatch, the design of your legacy database is rarely sufficient for the needs of your object-oriented application. The result is that you need to convert some or all of your legacy data.

The design of legacy databases rarely meets the needs of modern, object-oriented applications.

The development of the program to convert your legacy database should have been performed in parallel with the Construct phase; in fact, many organizations choose to treat data conversions as a project in their own right due to the complexity of the effort. Your data conversion efforts should include the following:

DEFINITIONS

product baseline The exact version of the software that is released to the user community.

software configuration management (SCM) A set of engineering procedures for tracking and documenting software and its related deliverables throughout their life cycles to ensure that all changes are recorded and the current state of the software is known and reproducible.

1. A data model and corresponding data access maps for the existing database
2. A data model and corresponding data access maps for the new version of the database
3. A strategy for converting the existing data to the new data format, potentially one of:
   - Tested data conversion program code that takes the existing data and converts it into the new format
   - Database views that simulate the existing schema in the new database
   - Database views that simulate the new schema in the legacy database
   - An application server that takes requests from both your new, object-oriented application(s) and your existing legacy applications and performs the appropriate accesses in both your legacy database and new database to keep them both current

You will potentially need to perform a data/object conversion when you release an updated version of an existing object-oriented application. The object schema of your application is likely to have changed to meet new business needs; and as a result, your persistence schema is also likely to have changed. The point to be made is that data conversion is an important issue for both the initial release of an application and for subsequent releases.

You will likely need to perform data conversions when releasing an update to an existing OO application.

SCOTT'S SOAPBOX

Put Object Modelers in Charge of Data Conversion

Data conversion is often a project itself—a project that should be led by OO modelers who understand the full needs of the OO application and supported by data modelers who understand the existing data. A common mistake is to put data modelers in charge of your data conversion efforts, the problem being that data modelers only consider half the picture in their designs, that of data, and typically do not consider the full picture, behavior and data. OO modelers, on the other hand, focus on the full picture and as a result produce more robust models. Think of it like this: if your data modelers had taken the full picture into account, then you wouldn't have a data conversion issue to deal with now.

DEFINITIONS

data access map A depiction of a query into a database, made by an application or report, showing the tables accessed and the order in which they are accessed.

data conversion plan A plan describing how a legacy data schema will be reworked to meet the new needs of your organization. A data conversion plan will likely refer to data models for both the existing and new data schema as well as the data access maps associated with both models.

data diagram A diagram used to communicate the design of a (typically relational) database. Data diagrams are often referred to as entity-relationship (ER) diagrams.

data model A data diagram and its corresponding documentation.

object/relational impedance mismatch The difference resulting from the fact that relational theory is based on relationships between tuples that are queried, whereas the object paradigm is based on relationships between objects that are traversed.

5.2.2 Releasing the Application to Operations and Support

Once your application has been prepared for release you are ready to release it to your customers. Ideally, your application should be released to your operations and support staffs before it is released to your user community, enabling them to detect and resolve any remaining problems before your users begin working with it. Unfortunately, because many applications now operate in a seven-days-a-week, twenty-four-hours-a-day (7/24) environment, they must be released to your operations, support, and user communities simultaneously. Regardless, to release the application to your operations and support departments, you must:

- Train the operations staff
- Deploy the operations process
- Train the support staff
- Deploy the support process

5.2.2.1 Training The Operations Staff
The operations staff will need to be trained in your new and/or updated operations processes for your application, and will need to be trained in any new or updated technologies used by your

---

WAR STORY

Operations Needs to Understand the Technology

A friend of mine once worked on an application that used a multi-user, server version of Smalltalk for a business application. The application passed testing and was put into production, but once in production crashed on an almost weekly basis. The operations people would restart the server, recover from the most recent backup, and continue running the application. As more users started working with the application, it began to crash more frequently, so operations upgraded their server, resulting in less-frequent crashes. The organization went through several cycles until operations finally gave up and demanded that the development team to fix the problem.

The developer assigned to the problem determined the cause almost instantly—because users were always logged on to the Smalltalk application, the operations department kept a status window open 24 hours a day to monitor the application. The version of Smalltalk did not have the opportunity to manage its memory, which resulted in the application eventually running out of memory and crashing. Had someone in operations understood the development language, they would have avoided the unnecessary upgrades to the server by simply logging everyone off the application during off-peak hours, allowing the application to recover unused memory.

---

application. It is important that your operations staff have an understanding of the technology used to develop an application because they are the ones who will need to determine the source and potential cause of operational problems with your application. The better they understand the technology employed by your application the more effective operations engineers will be.

5.2.2.2 Deploying the Operations Process

The operations process, documented by the operations documentation described previously and implemented by the batch jobs and programs needed to operate the application, must be deployed to the operations department. The documentation must be distributed to the applicable operations staff, often it is printed and placed in a common accessible area, and the batch jobs and programs must be installed.

W_{AR} S_{TORY}

Don't Forget the Needs of Operations

Several years ago I worked on the redevelopment, using object technology, of a legacy billing system. The existing system had been in place for years, and although it functioned properly, it wasn't very flexible. The team that I was on developed a new design for the billing statement, changing everything from the layout of the statement to the paper that it was printed on. A graphics design company design new letterhead for the statement with a new envelope design to match it. The new billing application was designed and coding began. Then we talked to the operations manager.

One of the things that we did not find out during modeling, because we did not bother to talk to operations staff, was that this company ordered envelopes in batches large enough to last them an entire year. By ordering them in such large quantities, they were able to obtain a very good price for them; plus, it meant that they only had to worry about envelopes once a year. The problem was twofold: nobody had told them that we were redesigning the envelopes and we had assumed that we could switch to a new set of envelopes at any time. The point to be made is that the requirements of your operations department need to be taken into account and that you need to have a firm understanding of the operations procedures associated with your application.

5.2.2.3 Training the Support Staff

Your support staff will need to be trained on any new and/or updated features in your application before it goes into production (Tourniaire and Farrell, 1997). This training should include the same training given to your users, described in a forthcoming section, so that the support engineer understands what training their users have received. My experience is that the training for support engineers should be enhanced by a role-playing session in which they are required to field simulated support calls for the new application. This sort of hands-on training is easy to do, is fun, and verifies that the support engineers have understood the training that they received. Note that the effort to train support staff can be greatly reduced for the support engineers involved in function testing during the Test in the Large stage (Chapter 3).

TIP

Summarize New Features for Support Staff

When you are releasing a new version of an existing application your support staff will only need to be trained on the new features, and many experienced staff may only need a brief document summarizing the new features.

Support engineers will also need training in your organization's call escalation and support call recording processes and be made aware of the key contact points within your operations and support departments, if applicable.

5.2.2.4 *Deploying the Support Process*

Your support process, described by your support documentation, must be deployed to your support department. Copies of the user documentation for your application must be distributed to each support engineer supporting your application so that they have their own personal copies that they can mark up as necessary. The other documentation, reference material such as the escalation process and the support call recording process, should be printed and stored in a common area accessible by all support engineers.

A problem reproduction environment, described in detail in Chapter 8, is a critical tool used by your support engineers to simulate problems reported by your user community. This environment is simply a copy of your application running in isolation that is used by support engineers to help them to understand what your users are telling them over the phone. The problem reproduction environment typically has its own version of your persistence mechanism loaded with a known set of

DEFINITIONS

function testing A part of systems testing in which development staff confirm that the application meets the user requirements specified during analysis.

support engineer A person whose job is to collaborate with users needing help to use your software. This is a key role during the Support stage and Test in the Large stage.

DEFINITIONS

persistence mechanism The permanent storage facility used to make objects persistent. Examples include relational databases, object databases, flat files, and object/relational databases.

problem reproduction environment An environment in which a copy of your application runs in isolation. This environment is used by support engineers to simulate problems reported by your user community.

You need to deploy an updated version of your problem reproduction environment.

objects (the persistence mechanism is regularly reloaded to its original state, allowing support engineers to update the objects as they need to). Whenever your application is released to your user community, the problem reproduction environment must be updated to reflect the new release. The training of your support engineers and your users is typically performed using this environment to avoid the risk of updating real objects during training.

5.2.3 Releasing the Application to the User Community

You must perform three tasks to release your application to your user community:

- Announce the actual release
- Train your users
- Deploy the application

5.2.3.1 Announcing The Actual Release

You need to announce to your user community when your application will be released and how to gain access to it.

You need to announce the actual release date for your application to all affected users along with a general description of what people need to do, if anything, to gain access to your application. I use the term "actual release date" in recognition that release dates for software are often preannounced months in advance, dates that are then missed due to delays during construction and testing. The implication is that not only do you need to announce the release of your application, you might also be required to do some damage control by explaining why your application is late.

Update your application release schedule to reflect your current status.

Now is the time to update your application release schedule, initially developed during the Define Initial Management Documents stage (Ambler, 1998), to reflect the actual release date for the current release your application. Furthermore, you should rework the release dates for all future releases to reflect the actual release date for your current version. For example, if your current release is two months late, then you need to consider pushing back the release dates for future releases by two months to reflect the time that you have lost.

DEFINITION

application release schedule A schedule indicating the dates of the incremental releases of your application.

5.2.3.2 Training Users

The users of your application will need to be trained in its new and updated features. Depending on the level of com-

---

DEFINITIONS

computer-based training (CBT) A program designed for the purpose of training users in a specific topic. CBT programs often use multimedia features such as animated graphics and sound.

mentor An experienced developer who transfers their skills to less experienced developers to aid in their education experience. This is a key role during all phases, but specifically during the Construct phase.

puter literacy within your user community, some users may also require basic computer training such as how to use the computer, the operating system, and even the mouse. There are various training methods that you may employ, including computer-based training (CBT), mentoring, and formal classroom training. The advantages and disadvantages of these methods are described in detail in Chapter 10.

Users should be given the appropriate training on your application before they are required to work with it. As mentioned previously, this training is typically performed using the support department's problem reproduction environment to avoid the risk of updating real objects during the training process. Ideally, once the user has received training on your application, the next time they log in to their system they will discover that the application has been deployed to them. The implication of this approach is that because you may choose to train your users in groups, the users who are trained first will have access to the application before the users who have not yet received training.

Train your users first, and then deploy your application to them.

5.2.3.3 Deploying the Application

Once your users have been trained to use your application, you must deploy it to them. To deploy an application, you must deliver the entire application package, which includes both the software and the accompanying documentation. Table 5.2 compares and contrasts common techniques for deploying an application package.

Part of the task of deploying an application is ensuring that the hardware/software environment of your user is sufficient for the needs of your application. Very often you will discover that some or all of your user community will require upgrades to their computer systems. Some will need memory added to their computers,

TABLE 5.2. Common Techniques for Deploying an Application

Strategy	Strengths	Weaknesses
A person visits every user and installs the application by hand.	• It works well for a small user base. • Contact with the user community is made. • Installation can be customized by an expert installer. • Hardware/software configuration of the user's computing environment can be evaluated for potential upgrade. • You are assured that the application has been installed. • Physical documentation can be easily distributed.	• It is time-consuming.
The application package is physically distributed to each user to install.	• Each user can customize his or her installation. • Each user has a copy of the application. • Physical documentation can be easily distributed.	• It is error-prone. • It is expensive when the total time for inexperienced users to install the software is considered. • The application may not be installed by everyone.
Users log on to a specific server and download the application.	• Users control when and if they install the application. • The release procedure is simple, as you only need to install the application to the common server and inform your users.	• It requires reasonably sophisticated users. • The application may not be installed by everyone. • It doesn't support distribution of physical documentation.

(continued)

TABLE 5.2. (continued)

Strategy	Strengths	Weaknesses
Automatic installation of entire (updated) application when the user logs on.	• Users are guaranteed to have the latest software. • Users do not need to install the application themselves. • Requires a sophisticated computing environment.	• Doesn't support distribution of physical documentation.
Automatic installation of updated portions of an application.	• Users are guaranteed to have the latest software. • Users do not need to install the application themselves. • This is a common approach for Java-based software involving the use of Java applets. • Requires a very sophisticated computing environment.	• Doesn't support distribution of physical documentation.

some will need more disk space, while others will need a better monitor or the latest version of the operating system installed. Your installation procedure should define the minimum hardware/software configuration for your application, and ideally, it should automatically detect whether your user's system needs to be upgraded, and if so how.

When deploying your application, you will find that some users will need hardware and/or software upgrades.

5.3 Solution: Project Tasks

In this section I will discuss project task issues pertinent to the Release stage.

TIP

Evaluate and Perform Necessary Upgrades Before Deploying Your Application

In parallel with the Construct phase (Ambler, 1998), you should consider evaluating the current system configurations of your users and making the necessary upgrades before you deploy your application. This will help to streamline the deployment process.

DEFINITIONS

client A single-user PC or workstation that provides presentation services and appropriate computing, connectivity, and interfaces relevant to the business need. A client is also commonly referred to as a "front end."

Java applet A program written in Java that is commonly operated in a Web browser.

proof-of-concept prototype Software written to prove or test the viability a technology, language, or environment. Also called a technical prototype.

server One or more multi-user processors with shared memory that provide computing connectivity, database services, and interfaces relevant to the business need. A server is also commonly referred to as a "back end."

5.3.1 Managing the Release Stage

The management of the Release stage is reasonably straightforward, requiring the management of a number of small but simple tasks. The most difficult task will be the scheduling of training classes for your customers, due to the variables involved: training room availability, trainer availability, and the schedules of the people being trained. My approach to scheduling is to first identify the groups of people with unusual scheduling needs (it is likely that I will need to hold training sessions for some operations and support people during off-hours because they need to maintain at least skeleton staffs while their coworkers are being trained), and schedule them first. I then schedule several training sessions and allow everyone to pick their own training times, making it clear that I will arbitrarily put people into classes after a given cut-off date. This approach is reasonably straightforward and provides sufficient scheduling flexibility.

WAR STORY

Sometimes You Need to Deploy to Hundreds of Sites

I was once involved in the development of an application that needed to be installed to hundreds of sites around the world, the majority of them in North America. These sites were the equivalent of retail stores, and from a information technology point of view were completely isolated from the head office. Each site had its own computer system, comprising a server and several client machines, and our application required either system upgrades or complete replacement of the existing systems (there was a range of configurations among the sites).

We determined that it would take between six and eight hours to install the system at each site; this included the time to run the data conversion batch job and to replace the hardware. Even worse, the users were virtually computer illiterate and couldn't perform the installation themselves; we were going to have to have someone do the installation for them. Furthermore, because the business was being run by this computer system, the installation would have to be done at night while the site was closed.

Although I left the project before this problem was solved (my role was to prototype the hardware/software environment), the team was considering the following deployment options:

1. Have an installation team go to each site, one per night, over a two-year period (that's how many sites there were) to install the new system.

2. Have several installation teams go to the various sites to reduce the calendar time.

3. Fly in representatives from each site to train them to install the application and then provide a support team to answer questions over the phone.

4. Stop the project and continue using the existing application as is.

5.3.2 People Management

People management for the Release stage focuses on basic change management issues. Within your user community, and potentially within your support and operations communities too, you will find a wide range of support for the release of your application, from

Some people will be reluctant to work with your application, whereas others will clamor for it.

refusal to use it to complete elation. Users who invested a significant amount of time learning their existing work processes, and those who are afraid of new technology, will be reluctant to be trained on your application or to have it installed. At the other end of the spectrum you will have users who are clamoring to use your application—users who are often frustrated with their current ways of doing business. It is likely, however, that the majority of your users are indifferent to your application and will be content to use it, provided that it works. The point to be made is that you will start out with some friends, some foes, and a large group of people who will become friends or foes based on the quality of your application.

A second issue is the need to convince people to take time away from their daily jobs to be trained on your application. For some people this will be no problem at all; for other people you will find it incredibly difficult to schedule them for training.

5.3.3 Training and Education

In addition to the training and education needs described in previous sections, support engineers and trainers will need training in people-oriented skills. Support engineers should be given training in dealing with difficult people, basic phone skills (you cannot assume that people know how to answer the phone politely), and basic domain skills (i.e. support engineers at an insurance company need to understand the basics of the insurance industry). Trainers will also need to be given training in dealing with difficult people, as well as in how to deliver a training course. More importantly, the trainers will need to be trained on the application that they will be training others on—trainers need to understand the material (in this case the application) that they are teaching. Inexperienced trainers will often assume that because they know how to train people, they can teach anything. Anyone who has attended a presentation given by someone who did not know what they were talking about can attest to the validity of this claim. Similar to support engineers, trainers will also need a basic understanding of the business domain so they can effectively explain the context in which the application is used.

5.3.4 Quality Assurance

There are two quality assurance issues that you need to address during the Release stage. First, you want to ensure that your training efforts were effective, and the easiest way to do this is to test people after the training and retrain them if necessary. It is critical that your operations and support staff understand how to work with your application, and depending on the business domain of your application this is also true for your users (for example, it's important for users of an air traffic control system to be competent with its use). Second, you want to ensure that your application deployment goes smoothly, and the best way to do this is to deploy your application to a few users, analyze what went right and wrong, and then update your deployment strategy to reflect the knowledge gained.

5.3.5 Potential Risks While Releasing Your Application

Several risks are specific to the Release stage:

1. **Pressure to forgo training.** If your project is late, and at this point in the software process it often is, you will often be pressured to reduce or even forgo training of your users, operations, and support people to make up lost time. Your customers need to understand how to use, operate, and support your application properly for it to be effective.
2. **Pressure to accept poor documentation.** Documentation is often left to the end of a project when there is insufficient time to develop it properly. It is common to see people forced into accepting poor documentation in the name of keeping the project on schedule. The solution is to write documentation as early as possible, at least during the Construct phase, to give you the time needed to do a good job.
3. **Late and/or failed data conversion efforts.** Data conversion is often a difficult and complex task, one that may take longer than originally anticipated or that may even fail. You can avoid this problem by starting your data conversion efforts early (during the Model stage (Ambler, 1998) you can begin by modeling both the existing and new schemas), and by managing them closely throughout your project so that you are not surprised when you are trying to release your application.

5.3.6 Opportunities for Reuse

There are two opportunities for reuse during the Release stage. The first is artifact reuse of your installation procedures, which

> **DEFINITIONS**
>
> **artifact reuse** The reuse of previously created development artifacts: use cases, standards documents, domain-specific models, procedures and guidelines, and other applications.
>
> **template reuse** The reuse of a common set of layouts for key development artifacts—documents, models, and source code—within your organization.

You can reuse your installation procedures on other projects and achieve template reuse for your user, support, and operations documents.

can be modified by other project teams for their applications. The second opportunity is for template reuse of your user, support, and operations documentation. By using consistent formats for your common documentation within your organization, you make them easier to develop and easier to use.

5.3.7 Metrics

Several metrics are commonly collected during the Release stage:

1. **Enhancements implemented per application release.** This is a count of the number of software change requests (SCRs) implemented in the release of an application. This is an easy metric to collect, because the SCRs implemented in a product baseline are referred to by your application's version description document (VDD). This metric provides an indication of the functionality delivered by a release.

2. **Problems closed per release.** This is a count of the number of software problem reports (SPRs) implemented in the release of an application. This is an easy metric to collect, because the SPRs implemented in a product baseline are referred to by your application's VDD. This metric provides an indication of the functionality fixed by a release and, when analyzed over a period of time, provides an measurement of the effectiveness of your defect prevention and repair efforts.

3. **Percentage of customers trained.** This metric is calculated by dividing the total number of people trained during the Release stage by the number of people who should have been trained. It is common to collect this metric for each customer type: users, support staff, and operations staff. This metric provides an indication of the coverage of your training efforts. Low training percentages among your user community will be reflected in higher support costs for your application.

DEFINITIONS

product baseline The exact version of the software that is released to the user community.

software change request (SCR) A description of a potential improvement to a software deliverable, often identified by users of that deliverable.

software problem report (SPR) A description of a potential software defect identified by someone who is not directly responsible for a given software deliverable.

version description document (VDD) A complete list of all items included in a product baseline release of software, including all configuration items and supporting deliverables. The VDD includes an indication of all changes made to the software from the previous version and a list of all applicable SPRs and SCRs implemented in the current version.

---

4. **Average training time per person.** This metric measures the average training investment per person—a metric that, once again, should be collected by customer type. When this metric is compared with your support costs over time, it provides an indication of the effectiveness of your training program; a greater investment in training should result in reduced support costs.

5.4 Resulting Context: Exit Conditions for Releasing Your Application

The following conditions must be met before the Release stage is considered complete:

1. **Your customers are trained.** For your application to be successfully released, your user, support, and operations communities must be properly trained.
2. **The application has been deployed.** Your application must be successfully deployed to your user community.
3. **The documentation has been accepted and deployed.** The user, support, and operations documentation must be reviewed, accepted, and deployed to your appropriate customer groups.
4. **The support production environment is installed.** The support production environment that is used by your support engineers to simulate problems experienced by users must be successfully deployed to your support department.

5.5 Secrets of Success

I would like to share with you a few tips and techniques to make the Release stage successful:

1. **Work closely with your operations and support departments.** Never forget that your operations and support departments are both your customers (you produce deliverables for them) and your partners; they help make your application successful once it is in production. Work closely with these two communities to ensure that your application is the best that it can be.

2. **Develop your training program early.** Putting together the training program for the release of an application can be a difficult and time consuming task. My advice is to start developing the training program for your application during the Construct phase to ensure that it is ready when you want to release your application.

3. **Develop your documentation early.** The user, support, and operations documentation should also be developed during the Construct phase to ensure that it is ready for when you need to release your application.

4. **Update your release schedule.** Incremental releases, discussed in *Process Patterns* (Ambler, 1998), are a common way to implement a large application. During the Define Initial Management Documents stage (Ambler, 1998) you will have put together a release schedule for your application, a schedule that you should now update to reflect the actual date that your application was released on. For example, if your current release is two months late, then you should either push back all future release dates by two months or reduce the functionality to be delivered by your next release to make up time in your schedule.

5.6 Process Checklist

The following process checklist can be used to verify that you have completed the Release stage.

RELEASE STAGE PROCESS CHECKLIST

Fulfillment of Entrance Conditions:
✔ The application has been packaged for release.
✔ Your organization's release procedures are available.
✔ The training plans for your user, operations, and support communities are available.
✔ The documentation is available to be deployed.
✔ Team members have been given the appropriate training for their part in this stage.

Processes Performed:
✔ The training and release plans have been accepted.
✔ The user documentation has been accepted.
✔ The support documentation has been accepted.
✔ The operations documentation has been accepted.
✔ The legacy data has been converted (if applicable).
✔ The product baseline has been finalized.
✔ The version description document (VDD) has been finalized.
✔ The release notes have been finalized.
✔ The installation procedures have been finalized.
✔ The operations staff has been trained.
✔ The operations process has been deployed.
✔ The support staff has been trained.
✔ The support process has been deployed.
✔ The release was announced.
✔ The user community was trained.
✔ The application was deployed to the user community.
✔ Artifacts that are potentially reusable by your project team during this stage have been identified and used where appropriate.
✔ Your risk assessment document has been updated where appropriate.
✔ Decisions made, and decisions forgone, have been documented in your group memory.
✔ Metrics have been collected.

Fulfillment of Exit Conditions:
- ✔ The user, support, and operations communities have been trained.
- ✔ The application has been deployed.
- ✔ The application and documentation has been accepted.
- ✔ The support reproduction environment has been installed.

5.7 What You Have Learned in This Chapter

In this chapter you saw that there is a significant amount of work to be performed during the Release stage. You begin by accepting the training and release plans, as well as the external documentation for your application. In parallel you will finalize the application package and any data conversion needed to support your application. The next step is to release your application to your operations and support communities, which involves training them and deploying the appropriate processes for your application. The third step, often performed in parallel with the second, is to release your application to your user community. This is done by announcing the actual release, training your users to work with your application, and to deploy your application to them.

5.8 References and Recommended Reading

Ambler, S. W. 1998. *Process Patterns—Building Large-Scale Systems Using Object Technology.* New York: SIGS Books/Cambridge University Press.

Mayhew, D. J. 1992. *Principles and Guidelines in Software User Interface Design.* Englewood Cliffs, New Jersey: Prentice Hall, Inc.

Tourniaire, F. and Farrell, R. 1997. *The Art of Software Support: Design & Operation of Support Centers and Help Desks.* Upper Saddle River, New Jersey: Prentice Hall PTR.

Weiss, E. H. 1991. *How To Write Usable User Documentation.* Phoenix, Arizona: The Oryx Press.

Chapter 6

The Assess Stage

THE Assess stage has two goals: (a) for your project team to learn from its experiences developing your application, and (b) to provide an opportunity to evaluate the members of your project team to support their personal growth. Similar to the Generalize stage (Ambler, 1998) and the Rework stage (Chapter 4), the Assess stage is explicitly included in our object-oriented software process (OOSP) to ensure that it will be included in your project plan. This assessment, also called a project postmortem (Maguire, 1994), should occur at some point during the Deliver phase while your memory of your project is still fresh. Although project assessments provide an excellent opportunity for learning from your experiences, it is common to find that this project stage is not sufficiently supported by senior management who mistakenly see assessments as an overhead, not an investment. How unfortunate.

The Assess stage is an explicit attempt to learn from your experiences and to support the personal growth of your staff.

As you can see in Figure 6.1 the inputs to the Assess stage are the deliverables produced by the project team, metrics collected during the project, and your group memory that records the decisions made and the lessons learned on your project. During the Assess stage the work performed by your project team is reviewed and analyzed to determine the strengths and weaknesses of both your software process and of your project team members. Assessments of your project and project team are made, a learning history is developed, and a plan to improve your software process based on what you have learned is developed.

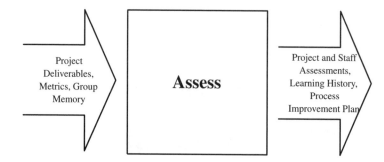

Figure 6.1.
The Assess stage

Project Deliverables, Metrics, Group Memory

Assess

Project and Staff Assessments, Learning History, Process Improvement Plan

You should always assess your project.

It is as important to perform a project assessment for successful projects as it is for not-so-successful projects. Yourdon (1997) asks of successful projects: "What made it possible for you to succeed in the first place?" and "What makes you think that you could pull that stunt off again?" The point to be made is that you should always work through the Assess stage.

The act of learning from your experiences to improve your software process supports the Process Change Management Level 5 key process area (KPA) of the Capability Maturity Model (Software Engineering Institute, 1995). This KPA focuses on the effort required to improve your software process, and the Assess stage as described in this chapter goes a long way toward implementing this KPA within your organization.

6.1 Initial Context: Entry Conditions for Assessing Your Efforts

The following conditions must be met before you may begin the Assess stage:

TIP

An Assessment Is Crucial for Your First Projects

Following the object-oriented paradigm to develop large-scale, mission-critical systems is new to many organizations. You first few projects will be where you make the most mistakes, mistakes that you want to learn from. As a result it is imperative that you take the time to do a full assessment of your initial projects to learn from your initial experiences.

1. **Management support for the Assess stage exists.** Senior management must be willing to invest the resources necessary to perform a proper assessment of your project and project staff. Furthermore, management must also be willing to consider and act on your assessment's recommendations to improve the software process.
2. **Project team members and key customer representatives** are **available.** The people who worked on the project, both developers and members of the user, operations, and support communities, are needed during the Assess stage for interviews

---

DEFINITIONS

Capability Maturity Model (CMM) A strategy, defined by the Software Engineering Institute (SEI), that describes the key elements of an effective software process.

group memory A record of what your project team accomplished, decisions made by your team and the reasoning behind them, deferred decisions, and the lessons learned on your project. A group memory provides a mechanism to record this information when it is first recognized so that it isn't lost.

key process area (KPA) An issue that must be addressed to achieve a specific Capability Maturity Model (CMM) maturity level.

learning history A written narrative of an organization's recent critical experience, often the experiences of a software development project team.

process improvement plan A plan identifying potential improvements to your existing object-oriented software process (OOSP), including an estimate, schedule, and staff assignments for making the improvements.

project assessment A two- or three-page document that summarizes what occurred on a project. This document is often used as introductory material to your learning history for the given project, and for the process improvement plan that results from the lessons learned on the given project.

Software Engineering Institute (SEI) An organization within Carnegie Mellon University whose goal is to provide leadership in advancing the state of the practice of software engineering to improve the quality of systems that depend on software.

staff assessment A summary of the performance of a single staff member with your organization. An assessment of the staff member's skills is included, as is a training plan for maintaining and improving those skills.

and/or focus group sessions. These are the people who were actively involved in the project, therefore these are the people who best know what happened.

3. **Project deliverables, group memory, and project metrics are available.** During the Assess stage you will review your project deliverables, including the metrics gathered and the group memory that you maintained throughout the project, to remind you of what occurred on the project.

6.2 Solution: Assessing Your Efforts

The process pattern depicted in Figure 6.2 shows that the Assess stage is comprised of two main tasks: (a) assessing the project and the team, and (b) documenting the results of the assessment. To assess your project and project team you will review the project deliverables, including your group memory; assess team member performance; analyze the metrics collected during the project; and assess the involvement, or lack of involvement, of your customers throughout the project. To document the results of your assessment you need to produce the following deliverables: a project assessment which summarizes what occurred on the project; staff assessments documenting the performance of individual project team members, their skills, and a training plan to improve those skills; a learning history describing in narrative form what occurred on the project; and a software process improvement plan indicating how to improve the object-oriented software process (OOSP) within your organization.

TIP

Bring in a Project Auditor to Aid in the Assessment

A project auditor is a professional who specializes in the review and assessment of projects. Your organization may choose to have a project auditor to either fully manage or to aid you in managing the Assess stage. Project auditors have the experience needed to analyze a project, experience that you likely do not have. Furthermore, project auditors are unbiased and will see things in a different light than you do, seeing strengths and weaknesses in your staff and software process that you may miss.

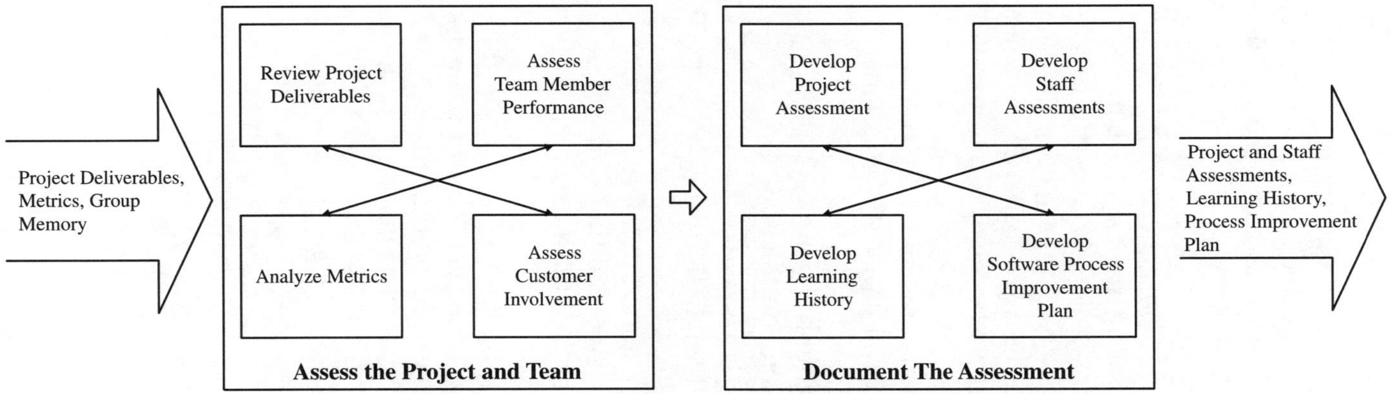

Figure 6.2.
The Assess
process pattern

Project Deliverables,
Metrics, Group
Memory

Assess the Project and Team

Review Project
Deliverables

Assess
Team Member
Performance

Analyze Metrics

Assess
Customer
Involvement

Document The Assessment

Develop
Project
Assessment

Develop
Staff
Assessments

Develop
Learning
History

Develop
Software Process
Improvement
Plan

Project and Staff
Assessments,
Learning History,
Process Improvement
Plan

6.2.1 Assessing The Project and Project Team

You need to review the project deliverables and determine the views of both project team members and the customers of your application.

To properly assess your project and project team, you need to review the deliverables that the team produced, determine what each team member believes happened on the project, and determine what your customers believe happened on the project. You will find that everyone has a similar yet different story—everyone one will likely agree on general facts, but will have their own views about what went right and what went wrong. This is the information that is critical to unearth, because very often some things that you felt were quite successful weren't in the minds of others, and things that you believed were not as successful may have been just perfect in the eyes of others. Different people, different opinions.

Some of the general issues that you need to consider when assessing a project and project team include:

- What went right on the project?
- What went wrong on the project?
- Why did it go right/wrong?
- What information do new team members need to know when joining the project?
- Was that information available?
- What political issues did the team face during the project?
- How could the political issues have been avoided and/or resolved earlier and/or better?
- How well did people work together on the team?
- Did everyone do their fair share of the work?
- What have we learned on this project?
- What did the project team need to do its job? What did it actually have?
- What did the team expect to happen on the project? What actually happened? Why is there a difference?

To assess the project and the project team you need to perform the following tasks iteratively:

- Review project deliverables.
- Analyze metrics.
- Assess the performance of project team members.
- Assess your customer's involvement on the project.

6.2.1.1 Reviewing Project Deliverables

An important part of determining how to improve your software process is to review the results of that process, your project deliverables. During the Assess stage you want to quickly review each project deliverable, specifically the results of the peer reviews for each deliverable, to identify portions of your software process that weren't necessary, that were overly complex, or that were not sufficient for producing the project deliverables.

Your group memory, the repository of decisions made during the project, will prove to be an excellent source for identifying needed improvements to your software process. First, the group memory contains descriptions of lessons learned that were identified during the development of your application. These lessons learned should be reviewed, improved where necessary, and incorporated into your project assessment. Second, decisions that you deferred for later potentially indicate the need to rework your modeling practices and/or your information gathering techniques.

Your group memory describes lessons learned during the project as well as deferred decisions which can be analyzed to reveal the need for process improvement.

Another source of information is the weekly status reports, common project management deliverables (Chapter 10) that should be reviewed to glean lessons learned from them. The weekly status reports should act as reminders of what happened, or perhaps what didn't happen, throughout your project. The status reports will provide insight into how the development of the other project deliverables progressed, as well as provide input into the assessments of individual team members discussed below.

Your weekly status reports provide reminders for what did or did not happen on your project.

6.2.1.2 Analyzing Project Metrics

The reason why you collect metrics during a project is so you may later analyze them to reveal areas of your software process that need to be improved. The Assess stage is a key time to analyze the metrics collected about a specific project. Furthermore, you want to compare the metrics for a given project against those collected from previous projects to compare against. Metrics management is discussed in detail in Chapter 10.

At this point in your project you will likely have only the raw data of the measurements that were collected, it is unlikely that anyone has taken the time to perform a statistical analysis of the metrics. For example, although time reporting information may have been input by team members throughout the project it may

You will need to summarize and compare the raw measurements taken during the project to extract meaningful information.

not have been summarized in a meaningful manner yet. Meaningful metrics that could be calculated from this information include the total work effort expended on a given deliverable or a given project stage; the amount of overtime worked on the project, and the amount of time invested in training. These figures in turn could be compared against those of other projects to determine the project factors that result in overtime—perhaps you'll find that projects that spend little time in requirements definition or modeling require significant amounts of overtime during the Program stage.

The metrics that you collected during your project can also be used to confirm, and sometimes even deny, some of the lessons learned on your project. For example, you may believe that a change in the way that your organization performs peer reviews has made you more productive, whereas the metrics that you collected about the results of those reviews do not show an increase in your productivity. The reality is that not all process improvements turn out to be actual improvements once put into practice, and the metrics that you collect often show this.

DEFINITION

metric A measurement.

Metrics can be used to verify the effectiveness of previous process improvements.

6.2.1.3 Assessing the Performance of Project Team Members

As we saw in the Define Infrastructure stage (Ambler, 1998), a skills assessment should be performed for each team member at the end of a project so that a training plan may be developed for them, and that they may be moved into an appropriate role on a new project. Now is the time to perform skill assessments because everyone's accomplishments, strengths, and weaknesses are still fresh in your memory.

Document the skills and experiences gained by each team member on your project.

Each team member should be rated on the roles that they took on the project; for example, programmer, designer, or project manager, to determine both their strengths and weaknesses. Maguire (1994) suggests that you should document the skills and experiences the person has gained during your project, because this is the type of information that other managers need to determine how this person will fit into their projects. This information, typically stored in a skills database, is also needed to justify raises, promotions, and bonuses in addition to promoting the personal growth of team members.

The Software Engineering Institute (1995) suggests that each

TIP

Determine the Goals of Each Team Member

Not only do you want to assess each team member's performance on your project, effectively looking at the past; you also want to look to the future and determine what each person wants to do with his or her career. Does Pavel, one of your programmers, want to become a designer, an analyst, a project manager, or does he want to remain a programmer? This is an important piece of information that should be included in your assessment so that he can be given the proper training that he needs to achieve his goals and that he will be assigned to an appropriate project.

TIP

People Do Not Quit Because They Get Training

Many managers incorrectly believe that people quit because they've been given training. The real reason why people quit is because they do not like their job, do not like the people that they are working with, or are not being paid fairly. Yes, giving people training makes them more attractive to other organizations interested in hiring them; but what is the use of having staff that nobody else would want to hire?

---

team member also be rated on their knowledge and understanding of your organization's software process to determine the need for further training and education. This is a goal of the Level 5 Process Change Management key process area (KPA) of the Capability Maturity Model (CMM).

You performed a skills assessment for each team member at the beginning of the project during the Define Infrastructure stage (Ambler, 1998) and have now performed one at the end of the project; the implication is that you should be able to compare the two assessments to determine how each team member grew on your project. With the phenomenal rate of change in the information technology industry, it is important for technical people to be constantly improving their skills—technical people who believe their skills are stagnating in a given position will quickly decide to look elsewhere for employment.

An important side benefit of comparing the skill assessments of

---

TIP

Have an Outsider Interview Project Team Members

It is often effective to have an outsider to your project, ideally a project auditor, to interview each team member privately. The purpose of this interview is to give your team members the opportunity to communicate what they truly think about the project, what everyone's strengths and weaknesses truly are, and what improvements need to be made to your software process. Very often people will not share their true feelings with the people that they work with, for fear of retribution, but will do so with an outsider, provided that their input is considered anonymously.

Comparing skill assessments from the start and end of your project provides insight into the effectiveness of your training and education efforts.

each individual over the project is that it provides insight into the quality of the training and education that they received. For example, if you provided several developers with Java programming training at the beginning of the project, only to find that their Java programming skills show little improvement at the end of the project, you know that your approach to training and education needs to be improved. Perhaps the training course wasn't effective; perhaps you needed to provide mentors to help your developers learn Java, or perhaps your code reviews were ineffective at helping programmers to improve their development skills.

6.2.1.4 Assessing Customer Involvement in the Project
The involvement, or lack of involvement, in your project of your customers should also be assessed. For the sake of our discussion, your customers include the user, operations, and support communities. You want to determine three things:

1. How, and how much, your customers were involved.
2. How, and how much, you actually needed the involvement of your customers.
3. How, and how much, your customers believed they should have been involved.

In an ideal world all three of those measurements are the same. Realistically, however, there will be great variances in the three answers. The variances arise for two reasons: (a) your customers rarely understand the software process well enough to determine

---

DEFINITIONS

mentor An experienced developer who transfers his or her skills to less experienced developers to aid in their education experience. This is a key role during all phases, but specifically during the Construct phase.

project auditor A professional who specializes in the review and assessment of projects. This is a key role during the Assess stage.

skills assessment (deliverable) A summary of the proficiencies of an individual, used for the purpose of developing a training plan for the individual and for identifying projects where their skills are needed.

skills assessment (process) A process in which the skills, both technical skills such as C++ programming and people skills such as eliciting requirements from users, of an individual are determined/measured.

skills database A database which records the skills and experiences of people within your organization. This information is both the input and the output of a skills assessment.

---

when and how they are needed, and (b) the development community rarely understands the software process well enough to determine when and how they need to work with their customers.

Consider user involvement. User involvement is obviously needed during the Initiate phase of a project to determine the initial requirements for an application and to determine the scope for your project. User involvement is also needed during the Construct phase to support your analysis efforts during the Model stage; and during the Test in the Small stage to review the user interface being developed. Users are also actively involved during the Deliver phase to perform user testing in the Test in the Large stage and are trained on your application during the Release stage. The point to be made is that user involvement is needed throughout your project.

User involvement is needed throughout your project.

An effective technique to obtain information from your customers is to hold focus group sessions, a meeting in which a group of people are brought together to discuss an issue informally. In our case, the issue to be discussed is how your customers believe they may be effectively involved in the software process. Depending on your environment, you may choose to hold a single focus group session for all of your customers, or one for each group (user, operations, and support). Second, I will often run the same sort of focus group session with a group of developers to discover when they believe their customers could have effectively been involved in the project. Also, when there is a large variance in the results of the two rounds of focus group sessions, I will get them together in a third focus group session to try to come to a consensus. The need for a third focus group session is often an indication that the relationship between your information technology (IT) department and your customers needs to be improved, and running these focus group sessions is a good start at building bridges.

6.2.2 Documenting the Assessment

Although the deliverables described in this section are worked on during your actual assessment efforts, described above, they are typically not finalized until after your assessment activities are complete. To document your assessment efforts, you must:

- Develop a learning history.
- Develop staff assessments.
- Develop a project assessment.
- Develop a plan to improve the software process.

6.2.2.1 Developing a Learning History

Kliener and Roth (1997) believe that an effective way to document the lessons learned on a project is to develop what they call a learning history, which in our case is a narrative describing your team's experience developing your application. An important aspect of a learning history is that it is written in such a way that individuals or groups are not directly identified, protecting the people who were involved in developing the learning history. A learning history for a project is developed from the information gathered by interviews with the people involved with the project—members of the development, user, operations, and support communities—because, when asked, individuals can always tell you what they believe went right or wrong on a project. When you combine these opinions, you can often distill what truly happened on a project.

Learning histories document what occurred on a project in a manner that does not directly identify individuals or groups.

Learning histories describe the mistakes that people made as well as the hidden logic and struggles that made breakthroughs possible. Learning histories are an excellent mechanism to transfer knowledge and lessons learned within an organization—because they are written in narrative form, they are interesting to read, and because they are relatively short, often less than 50 pages, they can be read in a few hours. Another advantage of learning histories is that they build trust within your organization because people who believe that their opinions were ignored are now given an opportunity to air them, helping to raise issues that people want to talk about but have not had the courage to discuss openly. Furthermore, they help to build a body of generalizable knowledge about the software process, about what works and what does not.

The learning history of your project should be made available to anyone in your organization involved with the development of software.

The customer of your learning history is anyone who is actively involved in the development of software. This includes senior management, who need to understand how to effectively manage future projects; developers, who need to learn how software is developed within your organization; users, who need a better understanding why it takes so long and is so expensive to develop software; and your operations and support staff, who need to determine when they should be involved in the development of software.

6.2.2.2 Developing Staff Assessments

A staff assessment, of which a skills assessment is an important part, describes the performance of an individual on your project. A staff assessment is basically a formalization of the information gathered during a staff assessment, and should include a training plan for the individual to promote their personal growth. The staff assessment, in particular the skills assessment, is an important input to the Define Infrastructure stage (Ambler, 1998) for future projects to select the appropriate individuals for a project team.

> **DEFINITION**
>
> **staff assessment** A summary of the performance with your organization of a single staff member. An assessment of the staff member's skills is included, as is a training plan for maintaining and improving those skills.

My experience is that staff assessments should always be performed at least at the end of a project (during this stage) and for longer projects they should be done at least once every six months. Staff assessments are a key deliverable of the People Management task, discussed in greater detail in Chapter 10, and should by used as an opportunity to ensure that the professional needs of your staff members are being fulfilled by your organization.

6.2.2.3 Developing a Project Assessment

A project assessment is a formal, two- or three-page document that summarizes the information contained in your project's learning history. The customer of your project assessment is typically senior management—a group that needs a summary of the

DEFINITION

project assessment
A two- or three-page document that summarizes what occurred on a project. This document is often used as introductory material to your learning history for the given project and for the process improvement plan that results from the lessons learned on the given project.

experiences of your project team, but that might not want to read the detailed information contained in your project's learning history. Your project assessment will often be used as the introductory material to your project's learning history and for its process improvement plan.

6.2.2.4 Developing a Software Process Improvement Plan

Assessing your project is of no value if you do not act on the results of your assessment. The implication is that you need to produce a plan to act on your suggested improvements to your organization's software process. Your plan should include a list of prioritized improvements, a description of the work required to act on the suggestion, a timeline for performing the work, and ideally an indication of who should be assigned to the work.

The advantage of having a plan for improving your organization's software process is that it increases the chance that the work will actually be done; without a plan, you run the risk that process improvement will be pushed aside in favor of application development work. Software process improvement is an investment in your organization's future, an investment that needs to be planned for.

6.3 Solution: Project Tasks

In this section I will discuss project task issues that are pertinent to the Assess stage.

6.3.1 Managing the Assess Stage

You need to address several key management issues during the Assess stage. First, you need to obtain support for assessing the project while your team members' memories of what occurred are still fresh. Senior management must be willing to invest in this effort and the people involved in the assessment must understand why this is important, both to them and to your organization. Second, not only must senior management support performing the assessment, they must also be willing to follow through on the suggested improvements to your software process. Third, you need to schedule both your project team and representatives from your customer groups (your users, your operations department,

---

TIP

Blame the Process, Not the People

For the things that went wrong on your project you want to put the blame on the process, not on the people working the process. Finger pointing, in other words blaming others for mistakes, is often of little value and will only build acrimony within your organization instead of building teamwork. The process will not get upset when you blame it for things that went wrong; on the other hand, people will.

---

and your support department) for interviews and focus group sessions. The Assess stage requires the input of a wide range of people, and these people need to be scheduled to provide that input.

6.3.2 People Management

People management is a major consideration of the Assess stage, because this is when you should be performing staff assessments. A key issue is to assure everyone that they can speak frankly about what went right and what went wrong on the project without fear of retribution. Having an outsider perform anonymous interviews of individuals is one way to do so, and another way is to reference past projects where assessments were performed without the people involved being punished.

6.3.3 Quality Assurance

In many ways the Assess stage is a major component of your quality assurance (QA) efforts. The entire stage focuses on reviewing your project efforts to learn from your experiences and reviewing your project team members to aid in their personal and professional growth. In other words, the goal of the Assess stage is to facilitate the improvement of your object-oriented software process (OOSP) and your staff to enhance the quality of the work that they produce.

The Assess stage is a major component of your quality assurance efforts.

6.3.4 Potential Risks While Assessing Your Efforts

Several risks are specific to the Assess stage:

1. **Developers are unwilling to participate in an assessment.** At this point in the software process your project team is likely

to be exhausted from overtime during the Construct phase, and the last thing that they want to do is talk about what happened on the project (unless, of course, your project has become a miserable failure and everyone is eager to point the finger at someone else). The good news is that by performing staff assessments as well as the project assessment during the Assess stage developers are more motivated to be involved.

2. **Senior management is unwilling to support an assessment at this time.** During the Deliver phase senior management is likely to be focused on getting the application in the hands of its users and, as a result, is unwilling to allow you to take the time to assess your project, at least not until after the application has been deployed. The issue is that the best time to assess the project, at least to assess what happened during the Construct phase, is during the Deliver phase while your memory is still fresh.

3. **Finger pointing.** As mentioned previously, finger pointing builds acrimony, not teams. The point of the Assess stage is to learn from your experiences, not to lay blame.

4. **Post-deployment issues may be missed.** This is why the Assess stage goes over into the Maintain and Support phase— you may often choose, or be forced for scheduling reasons, to finish your assessment after your application has been put into production. Furthermore, sometimes issues will crop up after an application has been released that weren't apparent until that point.

5. **The assessment is used against you.** No project is perfect; every project team has its successes and its blunders. Humphrey (1997) warns that the results of an assessment (in his case he refers to an assessment of your software process, but the issue is the same), may be used against your project team, either intentionally or unintentionally. To mitigate this risk, senior management must understand that the purpose of the Assess stage is for your organization to learn from its mistakes, not to provide the data needed to punish a project team that has gone astray.

6.3.5 Opportunities for Reuse

You have several opportunities for reuse during the Assess stage. First, template reuse for your learning history and staff assess-

---

DEFINITIONS

artifact reuse The reuse of previously created development artifacts: use cases, standards documents, domain-specific models, procedures and guidelines, and other applications.

template reuse The reuse of a common set of layouts for key development artifacts—documents, models, and source code—within your organization.

---

ments is an easy goal to attain. Second, and more importantly, you should consider either building or buying an application to analyze the metrics collected on your project. This application, an example of artifact reuse, will likely be composed of a series of common reports summarizing your collected metrics, and an ad-hoc reporting mechanism for extracting and/or calculating specific figures from your metrics.

6.3.6 Metrics

There are several metrics applicable to the Assess stage that you may consider collecting. These metrics are:

1. **Number of lessons learned.** This is a count of the number of suggested improvements to your object-oriented software process (OOSP) resulting from your assessment efforts. This metric is often reported by the priority of the improvement, and is important because it provides an indication of both how much work you need to do to improve your organization's OOSP and how serious your organization is about process improvement.

2. **Percentage of staff members assessed.** This metric provides an indication of the quality of your organization's people management processes. A low percentage indicates that your organization may not be investing the necessary resources to grow and sustain your staff.

6.4 Resulting Context: Exit Conditions for Assessing Your Efforts

The following conditions must be met before the Assess stage is considered complete:

1. **All staff assessments are finished.** Everyone on the project should have a staff assessment performed for them before they move on to their next project. A skills assessment should be performed for them and a training plan developed to support their personal and professional growth.
2. **The project assessment has been presented to senior management.** Your assessment of your project, including your learning history, should be presented to senior management so that they understand what has been learned by your project.
3. **The software process improvement plan has been accepted.** Your plan, or at least a subset of the plan, to improve your organization's software process based on the lessons learned on your project needs to be reviewed and accepted by senior management. There is little value in assessing a project if your organization does not act on the results of that assessment.

6.5   Secrets of Success

I would like to share with you a few tips and techniques for making your assessment efforts successful:

1. **Bring in an outsider.** By involving an outsider, someone with expertise assessing projects and/or people, you bring both a fresh outlook to your assessment and provide someone whom people can talk to in private without fear of retribution.
2. **Involve your customers.** It is critical to involve your customers—your user community, your support department, and your operations department—in your assessment because you want to ensure that your software process results in applications that meet their needs.
3. **Perform mini-assessments throughout the project.** Yourdon (1997) suggests that you should take the opportunity, especially during the Construct phase, to assess your project on a regular basis so that you may improve your software process while you are working it. A side benefit of this is that much of the work will be done for you when you begin the Assess stage.
4. **Celebrate your successes.** The Assess stage will reveal several things that your project team excelled at—things for which they should be publicly recognized to help reinforce positive

behaviors within your organization. Celebrating your successes increases the chance that they will be repeated again in the future. I'm also a fan of presenting your learning history as a success, even if the project wasn't one, because your organization has taken the opportunity to learn from its experiences.

6.6 Process Checklist

Use the following process checklist verify that you have completed the Assess stage.

ASSESS STAGE PROCESS CHECKLIST

Fulfillment of Entrance Conditions:
✔ Management support exists.
✔ Project members and key user representatives are available.
✔ Project deliverables, including the group memory and collected metrics, are available.
✔ Team members have been given the appropriate training for their part in this stage.

Processes Performed:
✔ Project deliverables were reviewed.
✔ Metrics collected during the project were analyzed.
✔ The performance of individual team members was assessed.
✔ The involvement of your user community was assessed.
✔ The involvement of your support community was assessed.
✔ The involvement of your operations community was assessed.
✔ The project assessment was documented.
✔ A learning history was developed.
✔ A software process improvement plan was developed.
✔ Artifacts that are potentially reusable by your project team during this stage have been identified and used where appropriate.

✔ Your risk assessment document has been updated where appropriate.

✔ Decisions made, and decisions forgone, have been documented in your group memory.

✔ Metrics have been collected.

Fulfillment of Exit Conditions:

✔ All staff assessments are complete.

✔ The project assessment has been presented to upper management.

✔ The software process improvement plan has been accepted.

6.7 What You Have Learned in This Chapter

In this chapter you discovered that there are two main goals for the Assess stage: (a) for your project team to learn from its experiences developing your application, and (b) to provide an opportunity to evaluate the members of your project team to support their personal growth. During the Assess stage you will develop a learning history for your project, a written narrative of your experiences and the lessons learned, a project assessment which summarizes your learning history, staff assessments for each team member that summarizes their skills and includes a training plan for them, and a software process improvement plan for incorporating the suggested improvements for your organization's object-oriented software process (OOSP).

6.8 References and Recommended Reading

Ambler, S. W. 1998. *Process Patterns—Building Large-Scale Systems Using Object Technology.* New York: SIGS Books/Cambridge University Press.

Kliener, A. and Roth, G. 1997. How to Make Experience Your Company's Best Teacher. *Harvard Business Review* 75(5), 172–178.

Humphrey, W. S. 1997. *Managing Technical People: Innovation, Teamwork, and the Software Process.* Reading, Massachusetts: Addison-Wesley Longman, Inc.

Maguire, S. 1994. *Debugging the Development Process*. Redmond, Washington: Microsoft Press.

Software Engineering Institute 1995. *The Capability Maturity Model: Guidelines for Improving the Software Process*. Reading Massachusetts: Addison-Wesley Publishing Company.

Yourdon, E. 1997. *Death March: The Complete Software Developer's Guide to Surviving "Mission Impossible" Projects*. Upper Saddle River, New Jersey: Prentice-Hall , Inc.

Part 2

Maintain and Support

████████████████████████

THE FOURTH SERIAL PHASE of the OOSP is the Maintain and Support phase, commonly referred to as maintenance and support in the structured world. This is where you keep the application running and as up-to-date as possible by:

- supporting the efforts of users by providing training, answering their questions, and fixing any problems that they may encounter.
- identifying any possible bugs with the application, prioritizing those bugs, and then addressing those bugs in a future release.
- identifying any possible enhancements that can be made to the application, prioritizing those enhancements, and then making those enhancements in a future release of the application.

Chapter 7

The Maintain and Support Phase

THE goal of the Maintain and Support phase, the fourth serial phase of the object-oriented software process (OOSP), is to keep your application running in production and to ensure that changes to the application are identified and acted on appropriately. Common forces applicable to this stage are the unwillingness of senior management to adequately fund maintenance and support efforts, the unwillingness of "hard-core" developers to perform maintenance activities (or to even recognize their importance), and the difficulty of finding and retaining support staff.

The process pattern depicted in Figure 7.1 shows that the Maintain and Support phase is comprised of two stages: the Support stage (Chapter 8) and the Identify Defects and Enhancements stage (Chapter 9). The Maintain and Support phase begins for an application after it has been successfully delivered to your customers—your user, support, and operations communities. The main output of this phase is a series of maintenance changes that have been allocated to the configuration items (CIs) that make up your application, changes that are accompanied by the software problem reports (SPRs), and software change requests (SCRs) from which they were generated.

The purpose of the Support stage is to respond to incoming support requests from users; to identify a resolution for the issue; and then to oversee the implementation of that resolution. The

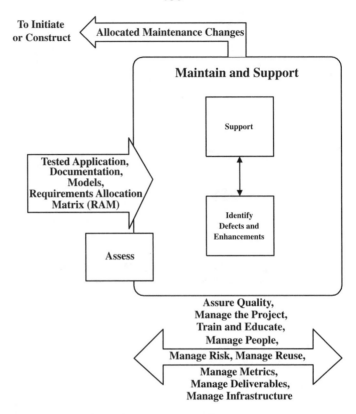

Figure 7.1.
The Maintain and Support process pattern

Support stage describes the processes that your support engineers will perform on a daily basis to support your application once it is in production. The purpose of the Identify Defects and Enhancements stage is to analyze SCRs that have been earmarked by the Support stage to describe potential changes to your application, to prioritize those potential changes, and then to allocate the changes to the appropriate CIs so they may be updated.

As you can see in Figure 7.1, the Assess stage (Chapter 6), part of the Deliver phase, may overlap into the Maintain and Support phase for one of several reasons. The most common reason is one of prioritization: the number one priority of the Deliver phase is to deploy the application to the user community, and as a result the Assess stage may be left to the end of the Deliver phase. A second reason is that you may choose to wait until your application is in production to include users in the assessment process who have had on-the-job experience with the application. Yes, you should at least start the Assess stage during the Deliver phase because your experiences on the project is still fresh in the minds of your project team, but you might decide to continue your assessment after the application has been deployed.

In many ways the name of this phase is a misnomer. It should really be called something like the "Support and Manage Maintenance Requests stage," due to the fact that your maintenance does not actually occur during this phase. I hold to the philosophy that maintenance is really just redevelopment and/or enhancement of an application, and this is reflected in the object-oriented software process (OOSP) by the arrow back to either the Initiate phase (Ambler, 1998b) or Construct phase (Ambler, 1998b). Depending on your organization and on the magnitude of the needed maintenance activities, you may choose to forgo the Initiate phase for a new release of your application (your project was previously initiated) and go straight to the Construct phase to begin work on the next release of your application. The reason this phase is called "Maintain and Support" is that I want to explicitly include both

The Assess stage often overlaps into the Maintain and Support phase.

W_{AR} S_{TORY}

What is Software Maintenance?

Chen and Chang (1994) define software maintenance as the activities required to keep a software system satisfactorily operational after it is placed into production. Boehm (1981) defines software maintenance as the process of modifying existing operational software while leaving its primary functionality intact. Although both of these definitions appear adequate at first, on deeper examination I believe they fall short of the needs of the OOSP. For example, the purpose of the Identify Defects and Enhancements stage is to analyze, prioritize, and allocate changes to configuration items. Nowhere in either of our definitions is the gist of this stage.

My definition of software maintenance is: "The update of configuration items (CIs) based on prioritized software change requests (SCRs) allocated in such a way as to retain and/or enhance the reusability and robustness of said CIs." The strengths of this definition are that it recognizes the fact that your organization builds software from collections of CIs, that all CIs must be maintained (a CI may be software, a model, a document, or other item), and that reusability and robustness are still important considerations.

maintenance and support efforts in the OOSP, to put them front and center when you are planning your project. Furthermore, as you saw in the Program stage (Ambler, 1998b), I am a firm believer that the needs of maintenance should drive your development efforts, and that including a phase called Maintain and Support as the end goal of the OOSP makes this philosophy more apparent.

In *Process Patterns* (Ambler, 1998b) we saw that a common way to develop object-oriented applications is to take an incremental approach. The basic idea is that instead of building an application all at once, producing a single "big-bang" release, you deliver the application in smaller releases, delivering portions of the overall required functionality in each release (releases are also referred to as product baselines). Each release is effectively a mini-project with all of the development components that a large project has, the only difference being that the scope is smaller. The required functionality is delivered to the user community; it's just that it's done in portions instead of all at once.

Incremental development results in getting portions of an application out sooner, and very often the entire application out sooner.

Figure 7.2 shows that you can choose between two basic strategies as to how you will release your application: either a large, single "big-bang" release or a series of smaller, incremental releases. Taking an incremental release strategy, notice how the first incremental release is the largest one. This is because for the first release you have to get a lot of basic infrastructure work done that is needed to support the application, such as development of the basic business classes needed by the application and the installation of any hardware, software, or middleware needed to support the application. Notice also how the overall effort needed to release the application is less than that for a single, big-bang release. Just as it is easier to eat your dinner by taking several bites than it is to try to consume it in a single bite, it is often easier to develop an application in several releases than it is to try to do it all at once.

Figure 7.2.
Comparing approaches to releasing software

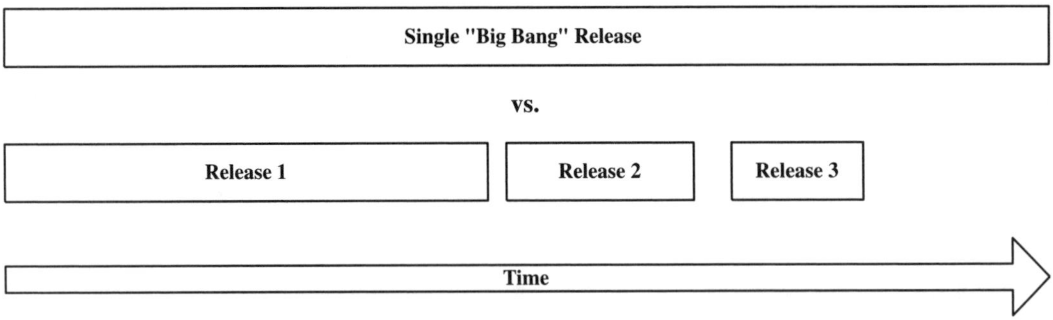

DEFINITIONS

big-bang development An approach to development where an application is released all at once in one, single project.

configuration item (CI) Any deliverable, or portion of a deliverable, that is subject to SCM procedures.

incremental development An approach to development where applications are released in several mini-projects, each delivering a portion of the required functionality for the overall application.

maintenance change A description of a modification to be made to one or more existing configuration items (CIs).

software change request (SCR) A description of a potential improvement to a software deliverable, often identified by users of that deliverable.

software problem report (SPR) A description of a potential software defect identified by someone who is not directly responsible for a given software deliverable.

Figure 7.3 shows a conservative approach to incremental development as it is best supported by the OOSP. Once an application enters the Maintain and Support phase, software change requests (SCRs) are gathered for it, prioritized, and then allocated to configuration items (CIs) so they may be implemented during the Construct phase of a future release for your software. In the OOSP traditional "maintenance efforts" are treated the same way as new development efforts are, following the same processes and procedures.

7.1 Initial Context: Entry Conditions to the Maintain and Support Phase

The main entry condition for this phase is that your application has been successfully delivered. The implies that your application

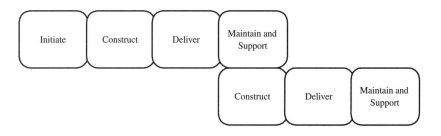

Figure 7.3.
A conservative approach to incremental development

Once your application is successfully delivered, it enters the Maintain and Support phase.

has been deployed to your user community, that the appropriate documentation has been delivered to your customers (your user, operations, and support communities), and that your customers have been trained appropriately in your application.

7.2 Solution: How Work Generally Proceeds During the Maintain and Support Phase

Figure 7.4 shows that the Support stage comprises the vast bulk of your efforts, between eighty and ninety percent, during this phase. The reason for this is simple—the Support stage runs continuously for an application once it is in production. The Identify Defects and Enhancements stage, although crucial to the success of future releases of your application, takes a very small portion of your time, between five and ten percent. As you'll see in Chapter 9 this stage is typically worked on a regular basis, perhaps once a month, by your configuration control board (CCB) often in a single afternoon. The management and documentation requirements for this phase are sparse, requiring between five and ten percent of your efforts, and for the most part are focused on the support of your application.

In Figure 7.5 you see that the Assess stage is comprised of one general task: assessing the project. The Assess stage, if it was not finished during the Deliver phase, generally runs at the start of the Maintain and Support phase to learn from your customer's experiences with your application once it is in production; but it

Figure 7.4
Organizing the Maintain and Support phase

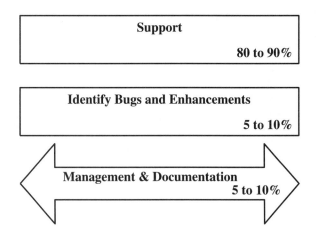

DEFINITIONS

configuration control board (CCB) The group responsible for approving proposed software changes. Also called a change control board or software configuration review board (SCRB).

support request A request for aid made by a user of an application. This request may be in the form of a phone call, an electronic mail (e-mail) message, a fax, or an entry into a support request database (likely via a Web page).

---

is quickly wrapped up so that the Deliver phase may be truly declared to be complete. You also see that the Support stage is composed of three sequential tasks: responding to a support request, determining a resolution for the support request, and then resolving the issue. The Support stage is invoked every time a support request is received by your support engineers, and finishes once your user is satisfied with the resolution to their issue. The Identify Defects and Enhancements stage contains three iterative steps—analyzing requests, prioritizing requests, and allocating changes—that result in new and/or modified requirements for a future release of your application.

7.3 Solution: Project Tasks

In this section I will discuss project task issues pertinent to the Maintain and Support phase.

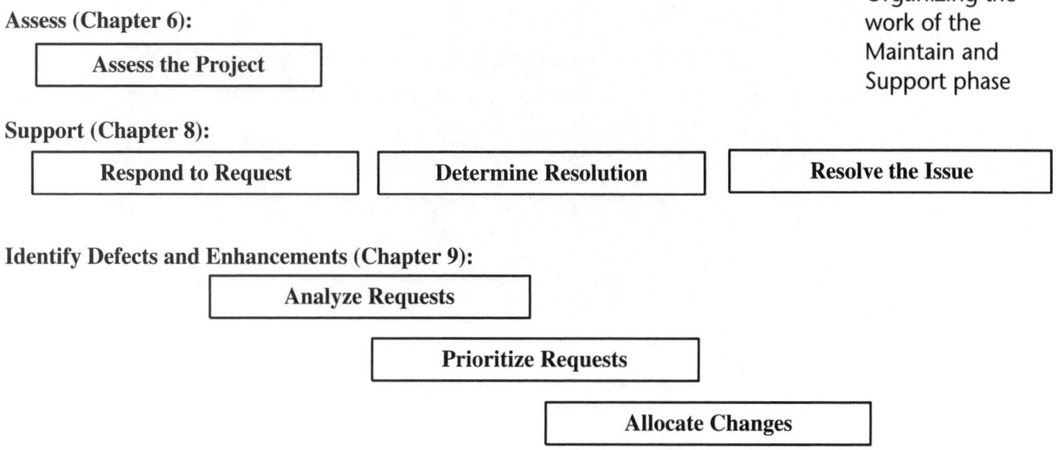

Figure 7.5.
Organizing the work of the Maintain and Support phase

Assess (Chapter 6):

| Assess the Project |

Support (Chapter 8):

| Respond to Request | | Determine Resolution | | Resolve the Issue |

Identify Defects and Enhancements (Chapter 9):

| Analyze Requests |

| Prioritize Requests |

| Allocate Changes |

7.3.1 Managing the Maintain and Support Phase

The management issues of the Support stage dominate this phase.

Because the Support stage (Chapter 8) constitutes the majority of this phase, its management issues dominate—issues that are discussed in detail in Chapter 8. A secondary management issue is the scheduling of the configuration control board (CCB) meetings, described in Chapter 9, to work the tasks of the Identify Defects and Enhancements stage. As noted previously, these meetings are typically held on a regular basis.

7.3.2 People Management

In this section I would like to describe the various roles fulfilled by people during the Maintain and Support phase. These roles are identified in Figure 7.6 and are described in Table 7.1.

The key roles during the Maintain and Support phase are the support and operations staff—the support manager, the operations manager, the support engineers, and the operations engineers—who work together to support and operate your application. The configuration control board (CCB) manager is a key player during the Identify Defects and Enhancements stage (this person effectively manages this process), as are the configuration item owners who work on the CCB and who are involved in the negotiation of changes to their CIs.

7.3.3 Potential Risks During the Maintain and Support Phase

Several potential risks are pertinent to the Maintain and Support phase:

1. **Allocated maintenance changes are not acted on.** The purpose of the Identify Defects and Enhancements stage is to

Figure 7.6.
Potential roles during the Maintain and Support phase

Support Manager	Operations Manager	Configuration Control Board Manager
Support Engineer	Operations Engineer	Configuration Item Owner

allocate needed changes to configuration items (CIs); if these changes are not acted on, then this stage provides no value to your organization. To mitigate this risk, your configuration control board (CCB) must allocate and track maintenance changes.

2. **Changes are made to the application without going through the software process.** Although this risk is endemic to software in general, it is a common problem for software that is currently in production—software that is being maintained and supported. Your software configuration management (SCM) procedures must be designed to manage this issue.

3. **The user community develops new versions of the application.** This risk is endemic to software that has not been updated to meet the current needs of its users, and to a lesser extent to software currently being developed for which users do not want to wait. To mitigate this risk you need to plan,

TABLE 7.1. Common Roles Held During the Maintain/Support Phase

Role	Description
Configuration control board (CCB) manager	The person responsible for managing the CCB.
Configuration item owner	The person or group responsible for developing and updating a given configuration item.
Operations engineer	A person responsible for operating one or more applications once they are placed in production.
Operations manager	The person responsible for managing your organization's operations department and operations engineers.
Support engineer	A person whose job is to collaborate with users needing help to use your software.
Support manager	The person responsible for managing your organization's support center and support engineers.

and then deliver, regular releases of your applications that implement new and improved features. Information technology (IT) departments that take an incremental approach to software development and that work closely with their users rarely experience this problem.

4. **There is no designated owner for a configuration item (CI).** This problem occurs when the original development team has been disbanded and the CI has not been reassigned to another group of developers. For CIs developed following the OOSP, this should not be a significant problem because the CI will be well documented and will have been developed following your organization's common development standards and guidelines. In other words, all of the information that another development team needs to pick up and modify a CI exists and is available to them. For CIs that were not developed following the OOSP, well, at least they'll provide a good example why it is important to follow the OOSP.

7.3.4 Training and Education Issues

Training and education issues are reasonably straightforward during the Maintain and Support phase. As new support and operations staff are hired by your organization, they will need to be trained on the applications that they are supporting and operating. These training and education requirements were described in detail by the Release stage (Chapter 5). Members of your configuration control board (CCB) will need to be trained in the pertinent software configuration management (SCM) procedures used by your organization.

> **DEFINITION**
>
> **software configuration management (SCM)** A set of engineering procedures for tracking and documenting software and its related deliverables throughout their life cycles to ensure that all changes are recorded and the current state of the software is known and reproducible.

7.4 Resulting Context: Exit Conditions from the Maintain and Support Phase

There are two ways for an application release to exit the Maintain and Support phase:

1. **The application is replaced with a new version.** The most common way for a given version of an application to exit the Maintain and Support phase is that it is replaced by a new version of the same application.

2. **The application is removed completely from production.** It is possible for an existing application to be removed from production, although this is a very rare occurrence. What usually happens is a new application is developed using new technology (yes, object-oriented technology will eventually be replaced by something even better) to replace the existing legacy system.

7.5 Secrets of Success

I'd like to share several tips and techniques that will help to make the Maintain and Support phase successful within your organization:

1. **Recognize that support is critical.** For the majority of your users your support engineers are your organization's information technology (IT) department. Users need help solving the problems that they experience using your application; otherwise, they will quickly become frustrated and will stop using it. Your support department is the key determinant of your application's success once it is in production.

2. **Rename your maintenance group.** If you choose to have a group of maintenance programmers (as I stated previously, I believe in treating maintenance the same as new development), then you should consider giving this group a positive name. Landsbaum and Glass (1992) point out that the term "maintenance" is loaded within the IT industry and often has negative connotations. They suggest the term "continuing support group" over "maintenance group" to help avoid an image problem for this team.

3. **Treat your support people with respect.** In the 1980s it became apparent that support engineers are key to the success of your application, that the skillset of a support engineer is a broad and complex one, and that support engineering provides a rich and fulfilling career path for many professionals.

4. **Your configuration control board (CCB) should meet regularly.** By having your CCB meet regularly, you guarantee that support requests which will potentially lead to new or improved features in your software are dealt with in a prompt manner.

7.6 Process Checklist

The following process checklist can be used to verify that you have completed the Maintain and Support phase.

MAINTAIN AND SUPPORT PHASE PROCESS CHECKLIST

Fulfillment of Entrance Conditions:
✔ The application has been successfully delivered.

Processes Performed:
✔ Support requests have been tracked.
✔ Operations issues have been tracked.

Fulfillment of Exit Conditions:
✔ The application has been replaced with a new version.
✔ The application has been removed from production (retired).

7.7 What You Have Learned in This Chapter

In this chapter you learned that the goal of the Maintain and Support phase is to keep your application running in production and to ensure that changes to your application are identified and acted on appropriately. The Maintain and Support phase is composed of two stages: the Support stage and the Identify Defects and Enhancements stage. The purpose of the Support stage is to respond to incoming support requests from users, to identify a resolution for the issue, and then to implement that resolution. The purpose of the Identify Defects and Enhancements stage is to analyze support requests that have been earmarked by the Support stage to describe potential maintenance changes to your application, to prioritize those potential changes, and then to allocate the changes to the appropriate configuration items (CIs) so they may be updated in future releases of your application. You also saw that the Assess stage will sometime overlap into the Maintain and Support phase, either because of scheduling conflicts or due to the desire to include lessons learned from users of your application once it is in production.

7.8 References and Recommended Reading

Ambler, S. W. 1998a. *Building Object Applications That Work—Your Step-By-Step Handbook for Developing Robust Systems with Object Technology.* New York: SIGS Books.

Ambler, S. W. 1998b. *Process Patterns—Building Large-Scale Systems Using Object Technology.* New York: SIGS Books/Cambridge University Press.

Boehm, B. W. 1981. *Software Engineering Economics.* Upper Saddle River, New Jersey: Prentice-Hall, Inc.

Chen, J. Y. and Chang, S. C. V. 1994. An Object-Oriented Method for Software Maintenance. *Journal of Object-Oriented Programming* 5(January) 46–51.

Landsbaum, J. B. and Glass, R.L. 1992. *Measuring and Motivating Maintenance Programmers.* Englewood Cliffs, New Jersey: Prentice-Hall Inc.

Pigoski, T. M. 1997. *Practical Software Maintenance: Best Practices for Managing Your Software Investment.* New York: John Wiley and Sons, Inc.

Tourniaire, F. and Farrell, R. 1997. *The Art of Software Support: Design and Operation of Support Centers and Help Desks.* Upper Saddle River, New Jersey: Prentice Hall PTR.

Chapter 8

The Support Stage

THE objective of the Support stage is to respond to incoming support requests from users, to identify a resolution for the request, and then to oversee the implementation of that resolution. The Support stage encapsulates the processes that your support engineers will perform on a continual, daily basis to support your application once it is in production. The Support stage is critical to the success of your application once it has been delivered to your user community; for many users your support engineers are your information technology (IT) department, because they are the only people that users interact with to help them work with your application. Developers put an application into production, but support engineers keep it in production.

Figure 8.1 shows that the input to the Support stage is a support request from a user, whom I will refer to in this chapter as a requester, in one of several forms (a phone call, an email message, and so on). The output of the Support stage is a solution, which is always provided to the requester, and potentially a software change request (SCR) which is sent to the Identify Defects and Enhancements stage (Chapter 9) so that potential maintenance changes may be identified. My experience is that your support process, and by implication your support staff, are key to the success of your application once it is in production. Think of it like this: your support engineers have a direct influence on the productivity of your users by helping them to solve problems with

Developers put an application into production. Support engineers keep it there.

The Support stage responds to user's requests, providing resolutions to the problems and SCRs which indicate potential maintenance changes to your application.

163

Figure 8.1.
The Support
stage

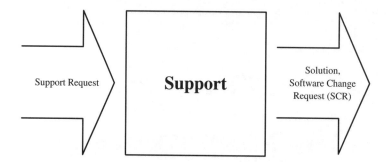

your organization's software. A productive user base is your organization's greatest asset.

8.1 Initial Context: Entry Conditions for Supporting Your Application

The entry condition for the Support stage is straightforward: a user initiates a support request. This request may be in the form of a phone call, an electronic mail (e-mail) message, a fax, or an entry into a support request database (likely via a Web page). Baudoin and Hollowell (1996) describe several types of support requests:

- A question ranging from how to use your application to how to obtain training for your application.
- A change request describing either a new application feature or a potential defect.
- A request for an environment change, such as a hardware upgrade or operating system upgrade.
- An indication that a software license has expired.

DEFINITIONS

support request A request for aid made by a user of an application. This request may be in the form of a phone call, an electronic mail (e-mail) message, a fax, or an entry into a support request database (likely via a Web page).

support request database An application built for the specific purpose of recording support requests. This database may be accessible to your users to allow them to submit support requests, perhaps via a Web page data entry screen.

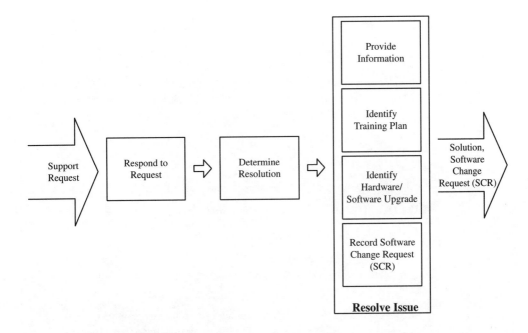

8.2 Solution: Supporting Your Application

Figure 8.2.
The Support
process pattern

The process pattern shown in Figure 8.2 indicates that there are three main tasks performed during the Support stage. The first task is to respond to the support request by communicating with the person making it. The second task is to gather sufficient information from the requester to determine a resolution, and the third task is to resolve the issue. There are four approaches to resolving a given issue: providing information to the requester; identifying a training plan for the requester; identifying a hardware and/or software upgrade for the requester; and recording a software change request (SCR) that describes a potential maintenance update for your application. Any given support request will be resolved using one or more of these approaches.

8.2.1 Responding to Support Requests

Whenever a support request is initially received by a support engineers it should be immediately acknowledged. Remember, you may decide to allow people to submit support requests via phone, fax, e-mail, or a support request database. The important thing is that the expectations of the person making the support request

---

TIP

Distribute a Support User's Guide

Tourniaire and Farrell (1997) suggest that you create a document called a *Support User's Guide* that describes the support process for your application from the point of view of your user community. This document will describe:

- The kind of services available and hours of availability.

- How to obtain support.

- Who is authorized to obtain support, and how often.

- The level of support (an indication of turnaround time by priority).

- A description of how support requests are resolved.

- Tips for obtaining the best service, including basic troubleshooting information, a list of information to have handy when you contact support, and the best times to call.

A support user's guide should be deployed to your user community during the Release stage (Chapter 5) as part of your overall application package. Many organizations choose to include this information as part of the application itself, either as a information screen built into the application or as a Web page on their internal network.

Respond quickly to a support request and set the requester's expectations appropriately.

are set: they should know that the request is being looked at and by whom, and be given either a solution on the spot or an estimate of when they will next hear back from the support staff. Never forget that your users will judge you on how fast, and how well, your support engineers respond to a support request. The best support engineers respond promptly, politely, and project the image that this problem is the most important thing they have to deal with.

8.2.2 Determining a Resolution

Once a support engineer has responded to a request they need to work with the requester to determine a resolution for it. There are four basic resolution strategies, described in detail in the next section, that support engineers will use to deal with a support request: providing information, identifying training for the requester, identifying hardware and/or software upgrades, and cre-

---

TIP

Support Engineers Need a Thick Skin

Many people are frustrated and angry by the time they make a support request, and will often take out their frustration and anger on the support engineer responding to them. The very first thing that a support engineer often needs to do is calm down the person making the request—a person who may be very abusive to the engineer. The secret is for the support engineers to not take the abuse personally, to remain calm themselves, to point out that there is no reason for the abuse, and that they are there to help them to solve the problem.

TIP

Minimizing Response Time

In the late 1980s I was involved in the development and design of a mainframe-based management information system (MIS) using a fourth-generation language (4GL). One of the interesting features of the language that we used was that it was able to recover gracefully from a run-time error, providing an indication of the error that occurred, the program module that it occurred in, and the line number of the statement within the module that was executing. I decided to put this feature to good use when an error occurred, I quickly displayed a message screen informing the user what happened and simultaneously displayed a similar message on the screen of the support engineer currently logged in to the system. The user was given the name and phone number of the support engineer assigned to the problem and the support engineer was given the name and phone number of the user who experienced the problem. It was a common occurrence for the support engineer to phone the user while they were still reading the error message, enabling the engineer to respond to the problem before the user could make a support request.

The result was that my application had the best support statistics within the entire organization, which at the time employed 55,000 people and had an information technology (IT) budget measured in the hundreds of millions of dollars. Our support resolution times (the total time to respond to and resolve a support request), were often measured in minutes, whereas most other applications had resolution times measured in hours and sometimes even in days.

ating an SCR report that potentially leads to a maintenance change to your application. To determine which combination of these four strategies to use to resolve an issue, the support engineers works with the requester to:

- Gather information and determine the request priority.
- Simulate the problem if necessary.
- Escalate the problem if necessary.

8.2.2.1 Gathering Information and Determining the Request Priority

When determining a resolution to a support request, the support engineer needs to gather enough information from the requester to determine the actual issue and the priority of the request. The support engineer usually begins by working through a series of questions with the requester to first determine basic information, such as their name and phone number and a description of what they believe the issue to be. If the issue is simply a request for information, the support engineer should be able to resolve the problem on the spot, either by directly answering the question or by pointing the user to the appropriate source of information. If the request is of a more serious nature, the support engineer will investigate the matter further through questions and/or simulating the problem that the user is experiencing—the topic of the next section.

The support engineer also needs to make an assessment of the priority of the request. Table 8.1 describes four common priorities for support requests.

8.2.2.2 Simulating the Problem

Support engineers will often need to have the user walk them through a problem while they simulate it on their own computer. For example, a user might make a support request describing a potential error on an editing screen. The support engineer would have the requester describe an example of where the error occurs, describing the steps that the support engineer needs to follow to simulate the error so that the support engineer may experience the problem. This is the purpose of the problem reproduction environment, a copy of the

---

DEFINITION

problem reproduction environment An environment in which a copy of your application runs in isolation. This environment is used by support engineers to simulate problems reported by your user community.

TABLE 8.1. Support request priorities

Level	Priority	Description
1	Emergency	The application cannot be operated without severe consequences to the user.
2	Urgent	There is a severe problem with the application but the effects aren't as devastating as level 1.
3	Regular	There is a slight problem with the application or the user has a "how-to" question.
4	Low	The user has identified a new feature or enhancement for the application.

TIP

Understand Common Categories of Problems Users Experience

Your users are likely to report several categories of problems. The first category is service issues, in which the user doesn't receive what she or he expected or was promised by the development/support organization. The second category is function issues, in which the application does not perform as expected; and the third category is technical issues, in which the application has a defect that prevents its proper functioning in ways that are not acceptable to the user. By understanding these categories, support engineers are able to better judge the appropriate response to a support request.

---

application that the support engineers uses to simulate problems that users are experiencing. By simulating a potential problem, the support engineer gains a better understanding of what the requester is describing to them, enabling the engineer to determine if there is a problem with the application, a problem with the requester's hardware/software configuration, or if the requester needs further training or information to use the application effectively. The problem reproduction environment should have been deployed to your support department during the Release stage (Chapter 5).

Support engineers use the problem reproduction environment to simulate the issue being described to them by the user/requester.

DEFINITION

support request escalation A process in which a support request is passed from the support engineer who initially responded to it to another person, potentially a more senior support engineer or developer, to be resolved.

8.2.2.3 Escalating the Support Request

Support engineers will occasionally encounter support requests that they do not know how to resolve or that they do not have the authority to resolve. When this occurs, the support engineer escalates the support request, a process in which they work with a more experienced support engineer, potentially their manager, and potentially a few developers to determine a resolution. When a support request is escalated, the support engineer should remain involved so that they expand their knowledge of the application, with the goal being to avoid a support request escalation the next time they encounter a similar issue.

Complex support requests may be escalated to more experienced personnel to be resolved.

Tourniaire and Farrell (1997) advise that once a support request escalation has been resolved that you should perform an escalation assessment to determine:

Perform an escalation assessment to learn from your experiences.

- Why the escalation occurred.
- What events were involved in the escalation.
- What went well with the escalation.
- What could have prevented the escalation.
- What recommendations could be made to improve the support process.

TIP

The Support Engineer Owns the Support Request

My experience is that the best support is given by organizations in which the support engineer who originally responds to the support request is responsible for it throughout the entire support process, including during any escalations that occur and during the resolution process itself. This provides a single point of contact for the requester and makes someone responsible for ensuring that the support request is resolved appropriately. The implication is that a requester isn't simply handed off by a support engineer if the request is escalated, or if the problem resolution strategy is to perform a maintenance change to the application something likely to take weeks or even months.

8.2.3 Resolving the Issue

Once the resolution strategy for a given support request has been determined, it then needs to be worked to resolve the actual issue. As mentioned previously, the resolution will typically be composed of a combination of the following strategies:

- The requester needs information.
- The requester needs training.
- The requester needs a software and/or hardware upgrade.
- There is a potential enhancement or problem with the application that needs to be reported.

8.2.3.1 Providing Information

Many support requests are resolved simply by providing information to the requester. Perhaps the requester needs to be told how to perform a specific task using your application, be given an answer to a common question, or be directed to a source of detailed information such as a manual, help file, or Web page. The implication is that your support engineers need to be knowledgeable about the applications that they support, about the business domain of your organization, about the information resources within your organization, and about your organization itself. Furthermore, support engineers should also have access to those information resources so that they can provide direct references to where specific information is to be found.

Support engineers must be knowledgeable in a wide range of issues.

8.2.3.2 Identifying a Training Plan

Users will often make support requests because they do not understand how to use your application, the computer, the mouse, the printer, and so on. It is important that support engineers realize that the user often does not realize what the actual problem is, and that what they really need is additional training. When a support engineer has determined that the user needs training, they should inform the user of this, and if possible, offer to schedule the training for them. This implies that the support engineer must be knowledgeable of the training resources of your organization and have access to your organization's training system to be able to schedule the training. If the support engineer does not have this knowledge an alternative approach would be for them to escalate the support request to your organization's training department to have the issue resolved that way.

Support engineers need the ability to assign users/ requesters to training courses.

8.2.3.3 *Identifying a Hardware/Software Upgrade*

Very often a person making a support request will not have the correct version of key software installed, or may not even have the software to begin with. Furthermore, they may not have adequate hardware to run the application and will require an upgrade. The minimum, as well as the recommended, hardware and software requirements must be defined for the application and made available to the support people so they may determine whether or not the user needs an upgrade in order to run the application. If the requester needs an upgrade they must be informed of this so they may obtain the appropriate approvals to have it done. Ideally the support engineer should be able to manage the process of an upgrade request, having the upgrade approved, scheduled, and performed without requiring the requester to do the necessary work.

Support engineers need the ability to manage upgrades to the hardware and/or software configurations of requesters.

When your application was deployed during the Release stage (Chapter 5) the computer configurations of each user should have been evaluated to determine whether the configurations were sufficient. If this was done, then you should expect to receive very few support requests generated by the need for an upgrade. In other words, by making necessary upgrades to the computer configurations of users during the Release stage, you will reduce the support costs for your application.

The necessary upgrades should have been made during the Release stage.

8.2.3.4 *Reporting Potential Changes to the Application*

Very often software contains defects and/or it doesn't meet the current, and always changing, needs of its users. As a result many support requests are actually descriptions of a defect or requests for either a new or updated feature. It is the responsibility of the support engineer to create a software change request (SCR) describing the issue so that it can be dealt with appropriately by the Identify Defects and Enhancements stage (Chapter 9). The support engineer should still be responsible for managing the sup-

---

DEFINITIONS

configuration control board (CCB) The group responsible for approving proposed software changes. Also called a change control board or software configuration review board (SCRB).

software change request (SCR) A description of a potential improvement to a software deliverable, often identified by users of that deliverable.

port request, even though it is now being worked by your organization's configuration control board (CCB) and potentially your development staff. The support engineer should regularly check the status of the SCR, ensure that the SCR is being actively worked, and keep the requester informed of the status of their request.

8.3 Solution: Project Tasks

In this section I will discuss project task issues pertinent to the Support stage.

8.3.1 Managing the Support Stage

To manage the Support stage effectively, you must determine:

- Your support-flow model.
- Your support toolset.
- Your hours of operation.
- Who should perform support.

8.3.1.1 Determining Your Support-Flow Model

Support flow, also know as call flow, is the process through which problems are received by support engineers from users, solutions are found, and answers are returned to the user. Tourniaire and Farrell (1997) believe that determining your support-flow model is the number one issue for setting up a support organization, of which you have two basic choices:

1. **Front-line/back-line model.** This approach is often called the tiered model, because the support staff are organized into two groups/tiers: a large group of less-experienced support engineers who take incoming support requests and try to resolve them within a short period of time, and a small group of experienced support staff who take difficult requests fielded to them by the front-line staff. The advantages of this model are that it provides an efficient manner for utilizing experienced staff; it provides a handy way for training new staff; it provides a career path for support engineers; and it provides a predictable model for users. The main disadvantage is that several people may touch the support request.

2. **Touch-and-hold model.** The support engineer who responds to the initial support request is responsible for handling it directly, sometimes requiring collaboration with experts for a given issue. The secret to this model is to get the right support request to the right support engineer, perhaps through an automated phone menu. The advantages are that there are fewer hand-offs so that the requester rarely has to start over making their request; that support engineers have greater opportunity to increase their skillset; and that throughput is higher due to fewer handoffs between support engineers. There are several disadvantages to this model: support engineers must have a reasonably high level of technical expertise; your organization needs a large pool of good support engineers; and service can be uneven because your support engineers will have different levels of expertise.

> **DEFINITION**
>
> **support flow** The process through which support requests are received by support engineers from users, solutions are found, and answers are returned to the user.

You need to take several issues into consideration when choosing a support-flow model for your support department. These issues are summarized in Table 8.2. Given the choice, I prefer to use the touch-and-hold support-flow model, as I believe it provides the greatest level of customer service to the person making the support request.

8.3.1.2 Determining Your Support Toolset

Tourniaire and Farrell (1997) point out that support work is process-oriented; therefore, tools can be found. The Support stage is a repetitive business wherein few support requests are truly unique; therefore, you should purchase a toolset that allows you to capture support request resolution information. Your support toolset (if your organization does not already have a sufficient support environment in place) should have been taken into consideration, and ideally selected, during the Define Infrastructure stage (Ambler, 1998). Table 8.3 summarizes the support tools that your organization will need to consider, tools which ideally are integrated.

8.3.1.3 Determining Your Hours of Operation

An important consideration for the management of the Support stage is the hours of operation for your support staff. Will support engineers be available from 9:00 a.m. to 5:00 p.m? Will they be

**TABLE 8.2. The Issues Involved with Choosing
a Support-Flow Model**

Issue	Front-Line/ Back-Line Model	Touch-and-Hold Model
Support request complexity	Simple, easy-to-resolve requests	Complex requests
Volume of complex support requests	Low volume	High volume
Ease of determining support request complexity	Easy	Difficult
Existence and quality of knowledge base	Knowledge base is required	Knowledge base is nice to have, but not necessary
User profile	Less sophisticated users will find this acceptable	Sophisticated users, users that demand good service
Staff expertise	Few experienced support engineers	Experienced support engineers are readily available

available on a seven-days-a-week, twenty-four-hours-a-day (7/24) basis? Something in between? The implication of operating your support center more than normal business hours, perhaps to support users in several time zones, is that you need to either stagger your support engineer's shifts or open several support centers in various time zones and direct your support requests appropriately. The issue is to not be excessive while still providing sufficient levels of service to your user community. Instead of operating a support center twenty-four hours a day, during off hours it may be adequate to simply use fax-back systems and Web sites, and perhaps one or two key support engineers available to be paged for emergencies.

TABLE 8.3. Potential Tools Needed by the Support Stage

Tool	Use
Automatic call distribution (ACD) system	An ACD is a phone system that distributes calls to support engineers in an efficient manner by requiring requesters to work through a menu of options. Usable menus are short (no more than three levels deep), provide a way to get to an operator, and provide basic information about non-phone-related support mechanisms such as a fax-back system or a Web site.
Customer tracking system	This application tracks basic information about the people submitting support requests, allowing you to maintain a support history for each requester. This application should be integrated with your support request tracking system.
Defect tracking system	This application maintains information about known defects, potential workarounds, and their current status as to when they will be fixed. This application should be integrated with your knowledge base, and is potentially a subset of it. This tool should also be integrated with the software configuration management (SCM) toolset.
Fax-back system	An application that allows users to call in and request information, such as solutions to common problems, to be faxed back to them. Fax-back systems are quickly being replaced by Web sites.
Knowledge base system	This is a collection of documents describing solutions to previously resolved problems. Support engineers will access this system when determining resolutions to new support requests to reuse previous solutions.
Problem reproduction environment	An environment in which a copy of your application runs in isolation. This environment is used by support engineers to simulate problems reported by your user community.

(continued)

TABLE 8.3. (continued)

Tool	Use
Support request tracking system	The key application used by support engineers, an application that is used to record information about support requests. This application should calculate many of the support metrics described in this chapter.
Web site	Online sources of information that people may access from their computers. Web sites can be used to provide users with access to your knowledge base so they may attempt to resolve their own issues; or they may provide access to your support request tracking system so they may submit a support request electronically instead of calling it in.

8.3.1.4 Determining Who Should Perform Support

The issue here is does your organization need professional support engineers for your application, can your developers support the application by themselves, or do you use a combination of the two? For large-scale, mission-critical applications, the development of which is the focus of this book, I think that it is likely that your developers alone cannot support the application effectively. Tourniaire and Farrell (1997) point out that the skills needed to be a good support engineer are different from those needed to be a good developer. Support engineers must have good technical, people, and organizational skills to be effective, whereas developers need good technical, cognitive, and organizational skills to be effective. Furthermore, developers must be given uninterrupted periods of time to do their work, something that they will not receive if they must respond to support requests. The implication is that there is an inherent conflict between developing software and supporting software. I believe that it is clear from the material covered by this chapter that software support is a profession, one that is different than the software development profession.

The skills to be a good support engineer are different than those to be a good developer.

8.3.2 People Management

The key people management issue during the Support stage is one of maintaining the morale of your support staff. Consider the nature of a support engineer's job: they deal with problems all day long, they are often verbally abused by the people that they are helping, and often the only feedback that they get is negative. Needless to say, your support manager must invest a portion of his or her time rallying the troops. Effective techniques that I have seen used include:

The challenge is to maintain the morale of support engineers.

- Publicly acknowledging support engineers who receive commendations from their customers.
- Group sports such as softball and football games.
- Online, multi-player software games played after hours over your organization's networks.
- Free movie passes to the support engineer of the week.

8.3.3 Training and Education

With respect to training and education, the basic issue is that support engineers need to constantly expand their depth of understanding of the business, of the application that they support, and of information technology in general. Although support engineers will naturally learn on the job, as we saw in the Release stage (Chapter 5) support engineers need to be extensively trained when they become responsible for supporting a new application and when they are initially required. Furthermore, earlier in this chapter you saw that support engineers may need an understanding of the training process within your organization to enroll users in training courses when appropriate.

Support engineers need to be constantly learning a wide range of new skills.

8.3.4 Quality Assurance

During the Support stage the main quality assurance issue is one of customer support: how do you ensure that your user community is receiving good service from your support staff? There are several ways to accomplish this. First, your support manager may choose to randomly monitor support calls, although this is an intrusive approach which many support engineers resent. When performed properly, however, monitoring can provide support engineers with productive feedback for improving their support skills. A second approach is to send questionnaires to, or to interview, requesters a few days after they made a support request to determine their level of satisfaction with the service that they received. Third, you may decide to analyze the information contained in your support request tracking system to determine whether the users that you are supporting are becoming independent of you. If you find that a given user is constantly making support requests, you know that his or her needs aren't being met (that person isn't learning from you). One measure of success is that your users do not require your services anymore.

8.3.5 Potential Risks While Supporting Your Application

There are two risks specific to the Support stage:

1. **Dissatisfied customers.** Because the Support stage is very customer-focused, a critical risk is that your user community becomes dissatisfied with the service they are receiving. Often, this may not be the fault of the support engineers; if the application that they are supporting has significant defects, the support department may be held responsible for the user community's dissatisfaction with the application. This risk is mitigated by ensuring that your application is well tested and fixed appropriately before being released to the user community, and by having a well-trained staff of professional support engineers to support your application once it is in production.

2. **Staff shortages.** It can be very difficult to hire and retain good support engineers. To avoid a staff shortage, support engineers must be treated with respect, be provided excellent training opportunities, be compensated fairly, and be provided with a good working environment so that you do not lose your existing staff. Organizations with staff departments that operate under these conditions often find that they are able to attract sufficient staff through their existing engineers simply by word of mouth.

8.3.6 Opportunities for Reuse

The primary source of reuse for the Support stage is to use a common set of support procedures and tools across all applications within your organization—an example of artifact reuse. The best way to achieve this goal is to have a support department responsible for working the processes of this stage.

> **DEFINITION**
>
> **artifact reuse** The reuse of previously created development artifacts: use cases, standards documents, domain-specific models, procedures and guidelines, and other applications.

8.3.7 Metrics

There are several metrics applicable to the Support stage, all of which may be taken for each specific application supported, by the type of support request (phone call, e-mail, or other), by the support request priority, and/or by the resolution strategy used.

1. **Average response time.** This is the average time between when a support request is submitted and when a support engineer begins working on it. This metric provides an indication of the delay that users may expect when requesting support.
2. **Average resolution time.** This is the average time between when a support request is reported and when the solution is accepted by the customer. This metric provides an indication of the length of time that users may expect to have their support requests resolved and can be used in combination with support request volume metrics to determine staffing requirements for your support center.
3. **Support request volume.** This is the number of support requests submitted, and the number closed, over a given period of time. This metric provides an indication of how busy a support center is and can be used to determine staffing requirements for your support center.
4. **Support backlog.** This is the number of support requests currently being worked, either by an individual support engineer or by your entire support department. Tourniaire and Farrell (1997) report that support engineers will typically have a backlog of between fifteen and twenty support requests with very little trouble at all. This metric provides an indication of the quality of the service being provided to your user community, and of the stress levels of your support staff (the greater the backlog, the lower the quality and the greater the stress).
5. **Support request aging.** This is the average age of the support requests in your backlog, measured from the time that the support request was first submitted. This metric provides an indication of the quality of service being provided to your user community.
6. **Support engineer efficiency.** This is a count of the number of support requests resolved by a support engineer over a given

period of time. For this metric to be effective, you need to perform a trend analysis—during some periods an engineer may "get lucky" and have a large number of simple requests to resolve, whereas other times they may "get stuck" with several difficult requests to resolve. As the name suggests, this metric provides an indication of the efficiency of your support staff.

7. **Reopened support requests.** This is a count, over a period of time, of the number of support requests that need to be reopened because they weren't truly resolved the first time. This metric provides an indication of the quality of service being provided to your user community.

8.4 Resulting Context: Exit Conditions for Supporting Your Application

The exit conditions for the Support stage are exactly those of the Maintain and Support phase: the current version of your application has replaced by a new version or your application has been taken out of production.

8.5 Secrets of Success

I would like to share with you a few tips and techniques for making your support efforts successful:

1. **Project the image that every support request is critical.** When you stop and think about it, every support request *is* critical, at least to the person making it. The most successful support engineers are the ones who recognize that from the point of view of a person making a support request, the only thing that the support engineer should be concentrating on is resolving their problem.

2. **Recognize that support engineers are the sales team for your application.** If your support engineers project a positive image of your application—if they teach users "neat tricks" to use it more effectively, and if they do their best to ensure that support requests are resolved quickly and efficiently—

then your users will become very satisfied with your application. On the other hand, if your support engineers have a bad attitude and bad-mouth your application, then your user community will quickly become disenchanted with it and with your support staff.

3. **Recognize that your objective is to support your user community.** The main objective of every information technology (IT) department should be to support their user community. As a result, support should be the first thing on your IT department's priority list.

4. **The support request is not resolved until the requester is satisfied.** This is a basic customer service issue, based on the precept that truncated service transactions result in unnecessary grief and frustration for the requester. To close a support request, you must first ask the person who made it whether they feel that the resolution meets their needs.

8.6 Process Checklist

The following process checklist can be used to verify that a support engineer has effectively fulfilled a support request.

SUPPORT STAGE PROCESS CHECKLIST

Conditions:
✔ The support request was responded to promptly.
✔ The support request was responded to politely.
✔ Information was collected about the support request.
✔ The support request priority was determined?
✔ The problem was simulated if necessary.
✔ If necessary, a training plan for the user was determined.
✔ If necessary, an upgrade for the requester was determined and scheduled.
✔ Potential defects/enhancements with the application were recorded.
✔ The support request was closed out with permission of the requester.

Escalations:

✔ The reason for escalation was recorded.

✔ The events surrounding the escalation were recorded.

✔ The requester was informed of the escalation and expectations were set.

✔ Lessons learned from the escalation were recorded.

8.7 What You Have Learned in This Chapter

In this chapter you saw that the objective of the Support stage is to respond to incoming support requests from users; to identify a resolution for the request; and then to oversee the implementation of that resolution. Resolution strategies include providing information to the requester, providing additional training to the requester, upgrading the requester's hardware and/or software configuration, and/or submitting a software change request (SCR) to the Identify Defects and Enhancements stage (Chapter 9) potentially to be resolved as a maintenance change to your application. The Support stage is critical to the success of your application once it has been delivered to your user community: for many users your support engineers are your information technology (IT) department, because these are the only people with whom users interact. The Support stage effectively describes the processes that your support engineers will perform on a continual, daily basis to support your application once it is in production.

8.8 References and Recommended Reading

Ambler, S. W. 1998. *Process Patterns—Building Large-Scale Systems Using Object Technology*. New York: SIGS Books/Cambridge University Press.

Baudoin, C. and Hollowell, G. 1996. *Realizing the Object-Oriented Life Cycle*. Upper Saddle River, New Jersey: Prentice-Hall, Inc.

Pigoski, T. M. 1997. *Practical Software Maintenance: Best Practices for Managing Your Software Investment*. New York: John Wiley and Sons, Inc.

Tourniaire, F. and Farrell, R. 1997. *The Art of Software Support: Design & Operation of Support Centers and Help Desks*. Upper Saddle River, New Jersey: Prentice Hall PTR.

Chapter 9

The Identify Defects and Enhancements Stage

THE purpose of the Identify Defects and Enhancements stage is to analyze software change requests (SCRs) defined during the Support stage (Chapter 8) so that maintenance changes to your application may be identified and allocated to the appropriate configuration items (CIs). This stage manages basic change control issues and identifies requirements for future releases of your application. The Identify Defects and Enhancements stage is worked on a regular basis, perhaps once a month, by your configuration control board (CCB).

No building is ever perfect.
—Christopher Alexander

Figure 9.1 shows that the main inputs into the Identify Defects and Enhancements stage are SCRs that describe potential changes to your application and the models and documentation that provide detailed information about the design of your application—required so your CCB may correctly allocate maintenance changes to configuration items. As you can see, this stage goes hand-in-hand with the Support stage. The output of this stage is a collection of maintenance changes, with accompanying software problem reports (SPRs) and SCRs that describe the original issue, that have been allocated to specific configuration items so they may be updated.

Figure 9.1.
The Identify
Defects and
Enhancements
stage

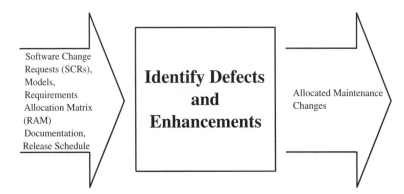

Software Change Requests (SCRs), Models, Requirements Allocation Matrix (RAM) Documentation, Release Schedule

Identify Defects and Enhancements

Allocated Maintenance Changes

9.1 Initial Context: Entry Conditions for Identification of Defects and Enhancements

The following conditions must be met before you may begin the Identify Defects and Enhancements stage:

1. **Software change requests (SCRs) have been identified.** For the Identify Defects and Enhancements stage to run, there must be at lease one SCR to be considered by your organization's CCB.
2. **Your configuration control board (CCB) is prepared to meet.** Because this stage is worked by your CCB, your CCB must be prepared to meet to review the pending SCRs. As we will see later in this chapter, the CCB meeting must be scheduled, and an agenda and information package must be distributed beforehand.

DEFINITIONS

configuration control board (CCB) The group responsible for approving proposed software changes. Also called a change control board or software configuration review board (SCRB).

configuration item (CI) Any deliverable, or portion of a deliverable, that is subject to SCM procedures.

maintenance change A description of a modification to be made to one or more existing configuration items (CIs).

software change request (SCR) A description of a potential improvement to a software deliverable, often identified by users of that deliverable.

3. **The application documentation, models, and requirements allocation matrix (RAM) are available.** Your application's documentation, models, and RAM must be available to the CCB so they may determine to which configuration items to allocate maintenance changes.
4. **Your application's release schedule is available.** Your CCB will need to know the release schedule for your application, originally developed during the Define Initial Management Documents stage (Ambler, 1998) and updated during the Release stage (Chapter 5), to be able to allocate specific maintenance changes to specific releases of your application.

> **DEFINITION**
>
> **requirements allocation matrix (RAM)** A mapping of requirements, defined in your requirements document, to the portions of your model(s) that implement them.

9.2 Solution: Identifying Defects and Enhancements

Your configuration control board (CCB), also called a change control board, is the group with the highest level of authority to allocate changes to configuration items. Your CCB performs the tasks of the Identify Defects and Enhancements stage to ensure that required maintenance changes are made in the future incremental releases of your application. Compton and Conner (1994) believe that the individuals on the CCB, which often include the configuration item (CI) owners, should have a stake in the project outcome and want to ensure that your organization's standards and guidelines are neither ignored nor applied so strictly that no revenue-producing product is

Figure 9.2.
The Identify Defects and Enhancements process pattern

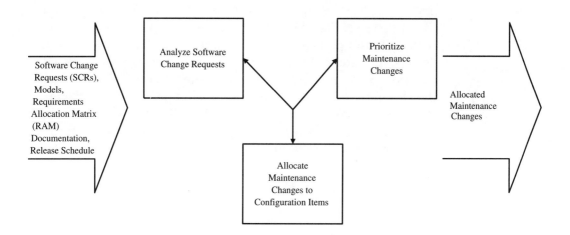

ever fielded. During this stage the CCB will follow your organization's configuration control board (CCB) procedures defined and selected during the Define Infrastructure stage (Ambler, 1998).

The process pattern shown in Figure 9.2 indicates that there are three iterative tasks performed during the Identify Defects and Enhancements stage. First, the software change requests (SCRs) generated by the Support stage (Chapter 8) must by analyzed to determine whether they describe defects or enhancements. Second, the priority of the maintenance changes must be identified so they may be worked in an appropriate order. Third, an impact analysis is performed to allocate the maintenance changes to the specific configuration items (CIs) that will need to be updated. Although these three tasks are likely to be performed in a serial manner for any given SCR, the tasks are likely to be performed iteratively for the collection of SCRs being reviewed at any given time.

Let's discuss the three iterative tasks of the Identify Defects and Enhancements stage in detail:

- Receive and acknowledge software change requests (SCRs).
- Prioritize maintenance changes.
- Allocate maintenance changes to configuration items.

9.2.1 Analyzing Software Change Requests (SCRs)

The first step is for your configuration control board (CCB) to review a software change request (SCR) to determine whether the SCR describes a defect within your application or an enhancement for it. Table 9.1 describes four basic categories of maintenance changes: adaptive, corrective, perfective, and preventive (Boehm, 1981; Pigoski, 1997). For the purpose of our discussion, corrective and preventive maintenance changes will be considered defects, and adaptive and perfective maintenance changes will be considered enhancements. It is important to differentiate between the different types of maintenance changes so you can manage your maintenance efforts effectively. For example, it's a completely different matter to have 200 outstanding enhancements for your application than it is to have 200 outstanding defects within your application.

If an SCR describes a defect, then the source of the defect needs to be determined, if possible. For example, the defect may be the result of missing or misunderstood requirements; it may be a

TABLE 9.1. Maintenance Categories

Category	Description	Example
Adaptive maintenance	Enhancements necessitated by changes in technical environment.	An application is updated to work on a new version of an operating system.
Corrective maintenance	Changes necessitated by actual errors.	A calculation in a report is discovered to be wrong.
Perfective maintenance	Enhancements necessitated by changes in the business environment.	A report to support new government legislation must be developed.
Preventive maintenance	Changes necessitated by the desire to prevent problems before they occur.	Your application source code must be updated before January 1st, 2000 to support four digit years.

design flaw; or it may be a coding error. It is at this point that the SCR becomes a software problem report (SPR)—effectively a specialized SCR that includes additional information pertinent to defects, such as the source or cause of the defect. Grady (1992) reports that you are likely to find, for well-tested applications, one defect after your application is released for every ten defects that you found before release.

If the software change request (SCR) describes a defect, then the SCR becomes a software problem report (SPR).

Tourniaire and Farrell (1997) point out that users are likely to require a workaround for a given defect until the time the defect is fixed. This workaround will need to be communicated through the appropriate support engineer to the user who made the original support request. The workaround should also be recorded in your support department's knowledge base so that the workaround may be shared with other users experiencing the same problem.

DEFINITION

software problem report (SPR) A description of a potential software defect identified by someone who is not directly responsible for a given software deliverable.

9.2.2 Prioritizing Maintenance Changes

Once a software change request (SCR) has been identified as either a defect or an enhancement, the next step is to assign

Maintenance changes must be assigned priorities so they are worked on at the appropriate times.

it a priority. There are several ways to prioritize maintenance changes: using an emergency/urgent/regular rating scheme similar to the one used by the Support stage to prioritize software problem reports (SPRs); simply assigning the maintenance change to a specific release of your application; or indicating the expected turnaround time for the change, such as immediate, twenty-four hours, one week, one month, and so on. Your configuration control board (CCB) procedures, defined and selected during the Define Infrastructure stage (Ambler, 1998), should define how maintenance changes should be prioritized within your organization.

The Software Engineering Institute (1995) points out that an important feature of a mature software process is the effective negotiation and management of requirements between your information technology (IT) department and your user community. This is a goal of the Level 2 Requirements Management key process area (KPA) of the Capability Maturity Model (CMM), a goal that is supported by involving your user community, represented by subject matter experts (SMEs), in your prioritization efforts. This makes a lot of sense: very often the people who are best suited to prioritize software change requests (SCRs) are your SMEs. Don't forget that they are the experts, not you; therefore they are likely the ones with the background needed to prioritize SCRs effectively.

9.2.3 Allocating Maintenance Changes to Configuration Items

The next step is to allocate a maintenance change to a specific release of one or more configuration items (CIs) so that the

---

DEFINITIONS

Capability Maturity Model (CMM) A strategy defined by the Software Engineering Institute (SEI) that describes the key elements of an effective software process.

key process area (KPA) An issue that must be addressed to achieve a specific Capability Maturity Model (CMM) maturity level.

subject matter expert (SME) A person who is responsible for providing pertinent information about the problem and/or technical domain, either from personal knowledge or from research. This is a key role during the Define and Validate Initial Requirements stage and the Model stage.

change is put into production. To do so, work through the following steps:

1. **Identify the configuration items(CIs) potentially affected by the maintenance change.** Your configuration board (CCB) must trace through your application's CIs to identify which ones are likely to be affected by a given maintenance change. This is one of the reasons why CI owners are members of your CCB: the people who are familiar with your CIs are the ones best suited to determine which CIs may be affected by a given change.

2. **Determine the impact of the maintenance change.** Once you have identified the CIs that potentially will be affected, you must then determine exactly how they will be affected so that an estimate of the required work can be made. Your requirements allocation matrix (RAM) is key to determining the impact of a maintenance change because it maps requirements into your models, which in turn trace to the code that implements your application. The Software Engineering Institute (1995) points out that it is critical that you maintain the integrity of your deliverables, which is why it is critical that an impact analysis be performed. Maintaining the integrity of deliverables is a goal of the Level 2 Software Configuration Management key process area (KPA) of the Capability Maturity Model (CMM).

3. **Determine if the maintenance change is feasible.** Once you understand the full impact of the change, you must then decide whether you still want to make the change. Some changes are very easy to make, whereas others are very difficult and expensive to perform. You need to compare the assigned priority to the change to the impact of the change to determine whether the change is feasible.

4. **Schedule the maintenance change.** This is a complex process that takes the priority of the change, your existing application release schedule, and the dependencies between both CIs and between changes themselves (sometimes you need to make a change to support another one) into consideration. An advantage of scheduling maintenance changes to specific releases of a CI is that when the CI is updated during the Construct phase, you are able to make the modifications

required for that CI at the same time, increasing the efficiency of your development/maintenance efforts.

5. **Inform the person who initiated the support request.** At this point the support request that generated the software change request (SCR) is still considered open, and will be until the maintenance change has been implemented and put into production. The user that submitted the original support request should be informed of the status by the support engineer responsible.

9.3 Solution: Project Tasks

In this section I will discuss project task issues pertinent to the Identify Defects and Enhancements stage.

9.3.1 Managing the Identify Defects and Enhancements Stage

The one basic management issue during the Identify Defects and Enhancements stage is to manage the configuration control board (CCB) meeting. To do so, you begin by preparing an agenda for the meeting that indicates who should attend, what their roles and responsibilities are, and what they should bring with them. The software change requests (SCRs) to be reviewed at the meeting should be packaged together and distributed, along with the *The CCB meetings* agenda, to the meeting attendees so they may prepare for the *must be properly* meeting. The CCB meeting will be held and the SCRs will be *managed to ensure* worked through so that maintenance changes may be identified *their effectiveness.* and allocated appropriately. Meeting minutes for the CCB should be prepared after the meeting to summarize the identified maintenance changes. The meeting minutes should be distributed to all attendees and be made available to others as appropriate.

9.3.2 People Management

People need to understand that the Identify Defects and Enhancements stage needs to be managed—that it is not simply an ad-hoc process. The configuration control board (CCB) manager is a key player during this stage for the simple reason that he or she manages it. The configuration item (CI) owners are also important because they are active members of the CCB, negotiating and managing changes to their respective CIs.

9.3.3 Training and Education

The members of your configuration control board (CCB) will need training in: your organization's software configuration management (SCM) procedures; the analysis and prioritization of software configuration requests (SCRs); and object-oriented (OO) development techniques so they understand how to allocate maintenance changes to the configuration items (CIs) that make up your OO application.

9.3.4 Quality Assurance

There is one basic quality assurance (QA) issue for the Identify Defects and Enhancements stage: you want to ensure that the priorities given to maintenance changes are being followed. For example, everything being equal, this implies that high-priority changes should be made before low-priority changes. The implication is that maintenance changes must be tracked through development by the configuration control board (CCB) until they are put in production.

> **DEFINITION**
>
> **software configuration management (SCM)** A set of engineering procedures for tracking and documenting software and its related deliverables throughout their life cycles to ensure that all changes are recorded and the current state of the software is known and reproducible.

The CCB must track maintenance changes through the development process to ensure that they are being worked in priority order.

9.3.5 Potential Risks While Identifying Defects and Enhancements

There are several risks specific to the Identify Defects and Enhancements stage:

1. **There is a lack of management support.** When there is little or no management support for this stage your maintenance efforts quickly get out of control, resulting in the wrong maintenance changes being made, the right changes not being made, and changes being made in the wrong order. The quality of your organization's software quickly erodes because inappropriate modifications are made to configuration items, because there was little or no analysis made to determine the impact of maintenance changes.
2. **Maintenance changes are not prioritized.** When no priorities are assigned, then everything becomes the number one prior-

> **DEFINITIONS**
>
> **artifact reuse** The reuse of previously created development artifacts: use cases, standards documents, domain-specific models, procedures and guidelines, and other applications.
>
> **template reuse** The reuse of a common set of layouts for key development artifacts—documents, models, and source code—within your organization.

ity. There is always a backlog of maintenance changes, and the only way to determine which ones need to be made first is to prioritize them.

3. **The configuration control board (CCB) meeting schedule is too rigid.** Sometimes critical software change requests (SCRs) are identified that cannot wait for the next CCB meeting to be considered. Your CCB must be flexible enough so that occasional emergency sessions can be held.

9.3.6 Opportunities for Reuse

There are two opportunities for reuse during the Identify Defects and Enhancements stage. First, template reuse for software change requests (SCRs) and software problem reports (SPRs) is easy to achieve. Second, artifact reuse can be achieved by developing and then modifying (where appropriate) a common agenda for your configuration control board (CCB) meetings. These meetings are likely to involve the same people following the same procedures month after month; plan the meeting once and then reuse the plan.

9.3.7 Metrics

Two metrics are commonly collected during the Identify Defects and Enhancements stage:

1. **Mean time between failures.** This is the average amount of time that a user can expect between experiencing severe problems with your application. This metric provides an indication of the quality of your application.
2. **Software change requests (SCRs) opened and closed.** This metric is taken over a given period of time, likely for a given calendar month, and is a simple count of the number of SCRs worked on. It is likely that you will wish to distinguish between SCRs and software problem reports (SPRs), as well as

collect this metric for various types of deliverable (the application, user documentation, operations documentation, and so on). Trend analysis of this metric provides an indication as to the effectiveness of your maintenance efforts (the number of SPRs should reduce as your application matures).

9.4 Resulting Context: Exit Conditions for Identification of Defects and Enhancements

The primary exit condition for this stage is that maintenance changes have been allocated to appropriate configuration items and your application release schedule has been updated to reflect this fact.

9.5 Secrets of Success

I would like to share with you a few tips and techniques to make the Identify Defects and Enhancements stage successful:

1. **There must be room for exceptions and emergencies, but you still need the rules.** The difference between a good configuration control board (CCB) manager and a bad one is that a good one knows when to hold fast and when to compromise; a bad one doesn't (Compton and Conner, 1994). Sometimes critical software change requests (SCRs) must be dealt with by emergency CCB meetings, but this should occur very infrequently.
2. **Recognize that difficulties identifying the affected configuration items (CIs) imply future difficulties making the maintenance change.** Problems analyzing the impact of a given maintenance change indicate either that your CCB doesn't understand the change, it doesn't understand your application, your application is poorly designed, or your application is poorly documented. In any case, if you do not have the ability to determine the impact of a change, it is highly unlikely that you can make that change successfully.
3. **Track and manage all maintenance changes.** Track all problems during and after software development to ensure that the most important problems are closed first. Also, it is

important to track and report on maintenance changes to help manage the expectations of both senior management and your user community. Grady (1992) reports that it takes four to ten times longer to fix defects in large mature software systems than to make fixes before, or shortly after, initial release of a system. The implication is that people will likely have to wait a much longer time to have a change made once your application is in production than the time they became accustomed to during development; therefore, their expectations will need to be managed appropriately.

9.6 Process Checklist

The following process checklist can be used to verify that you have completed the Identify Defects and Enhancements stage.

IDENTIFY DEFECTS AND ENHANCEMENTS STAGE PROCESS CHECKLIST

Fulfillment of Entrance Conditions:
✔ Software change requests (SCRs) have been identified.
✔ Your configuration control board (CCB) is prepared to meet.
✔ The current versions of Construct phase deliverables are available.
✔ The application release schedule is available.
✔ Team members have been given the appropriate training for their part in this stage.

Processes Performed:
✔ The type of each SCR was determined.
✔ Each SCR was prioritized.
✔ Maintenance changes were allocated to configuration items.
✔ The impact of each maintenance change was determined.
✔ Each maintenance change was scheduled.
✔ The initiator of each SCR was notified of the status.

✔ Artifacts that are potentially reusable by your project team during this stage have been identified and used where appropriate.

✔ Your risk assessment document has been updated where appropriate.

✔ Decisions made, and decisions forgone, have been documented in your group memory.

✔ Metrics have been collected.

Fulfillment of Exit Conditions:

✔ The maintenance changes have been allocated and scheduled accordingly.

9.7 What You Have Learned in This Chapter

In this chapter you saw that software change requests (SCRs) are analyzed during this stage: that maintenance changes are then identified and allocated to the appropriate configuration items (CIs) so that the changes will be implemented in a future release of your application. The main inputs into the Identify Defects and Enhancements stage are SCRs identified by the Support stage (Chapter 8) that describe potential changes to your application, and the models and documentation that provide detailed information about the design of your application—information required to correctly allocate maintenance changes to configuration items. The output of this stage is a collection of maintenance changes that have been allocated to specific CIs.

9.8 References and Recommended Reading

Ambler, S. W. 1998. *Process Patterns—Building Large-Scale Systems Using Object Technology.* New York: SIGS Books/Cambridge University Press.

Boehm, B. W. 1981. *Software Engineering Economics.* Upper Saddle River, New Jersey: Prentice-Hall, Inc.

Chen, J. Y. and Chang, S. C. V. 1994. An Object-Oriented Method for Software Maintenance. *Journal of Object-Oriented Programming* 5 (January), 46–51.

Compton, S. B. and Conner, G. R. 1994. *Configuration Management for Software*. New York: Van Nostrand Reinhold.

Pigoski, T. M. 1997. *Practical Software Maintenance: Best Practices for Managing Your Software Investment*. New York: John Wiley and Sons, Inc.

Software Engineering Institute. 1995. *The Capability Maturity Model: Guidelines for Improving the Software Process*. Reading Massachusetts: Addison-Wesley Publishing Company.

Tourniaire, F. and Farrell, R. 1997. *The Art of Software Support: Design & Operation of Support Centers and Help Desks*. Upper Saddle River, New Jersey: Prentice Hall PTR.

Part 3

Tying Up
Loose Ends

THE OBJECT-ORIENTED SOFTWARE PROCESS (OOSP) is held together by a collection of project and cross-project tasks that support your organization's efforts to develop software. Although I have touched on them throughout this book, I have yet to specifically focus our attention on them. Until now. Furthermore, I have yet to discuss the means through which you can successfully introduce process patterns into your organization.

Chapter 10: The Project and Cross-Project Tasks of the OOSP

Chapter 11: Introducing the OOSP Into Your Organization

Chapter 12: Parting Words

Chapter 10

The Project and Cross-Project Tasks of the OOSP

███████████████████

THIS chapter focuses on the "big arrow" portion of the Object-Oriented Software Process (OOSP): the project and cross-project tasks shown in Figure 10.1. These tasks apply across all project phases and stages, and although I have touched on them, I have not addressed these tasks in detail—until now.

The projects and cross-projects tasks of the OOSP are:

- Managing projects
- Managing people
- Training and Education
- Quality assurance
- Managing risk
- Managing reuse
- Managing metrics
- Managing deliverables
- Managing your organization's infrastructure

10.1 Managing Projects

Project management is the act of organizing, monitoring, and directing a project. A running joke among project managers is that there are really six phases to a project: exaltation, disenchant-

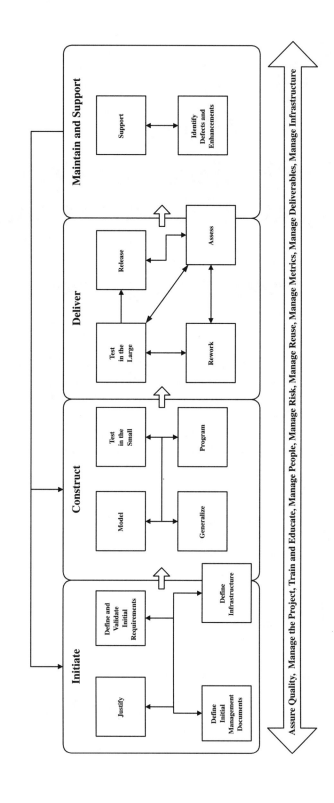

Figure 10.1.
The Object-
Oriented Software
Process (OOSP)

ment, confusion, search for the guilty, punishment of the innocent, and distinction for the uninvolved. I can't help but think that this belief reflects an antipattern, one that you can avoid by managing your projects effectively. In this section I will discuss the factors associated with successful project management.

DEFINITION

project management The process of organizing, monitoring, and directing a project.

First, the best way to ensure that a project will be managed successfully is to select a good project manager. The key thing that I look for in a project manager is experience with similar projects. Has this person managed a project of similar size? Using similar technology? Using a similar approach? Within your business domain? Within your organization? I also look for project managers who understand that, although the mechanics of project management is important, the true key to project management is actually people management, the topic of Section 10.2.

Select a good, experienced project manager.

10.1.1 The Mechanics of Project Management

The mechanics of project management comprise a fairly basic set of tasks. The Capability Maturity Model (CMM) includes three key process areas (KPAs) that directly address the mechanics of project management: Software Project Planning, Software Project Tracking and Oversight, and Software Quality Management (SEI, 1995). The Software Project Planning KPA focuses on the development and negotiation of estimates for work to be performed, establishing the necessary commitments, and defining the plan to perform the work. The Software Project Tracking and Oversight KPA concentrates on providing visibility into the actual progress of a project so that management can take effective actions whenever the performance on the project deviates from the plan. Finally, the Software Quality Management KPA involves the definition of quality goals for software products and the establishment of plans to achieve these goals. It also includes the monitoring and adjustment of the software plans, software work products, activities, and quality goals to satisfy the needs and desires of your user community for high-quality products.

Your project plan is central to the mechanics of project management. Humphrey (1997) believes that by working to the project plan, you learn where your plan was in error and you do the job the way that you planned to. Experience shows that many of the problems in

*Plan your project
in appropriate
detail and then
work to your plan.*

software development are actually the result of ill-considered short-cuts, carelessness, and inattention to detail—in other words, to not creating and then following a plan. Brown, Malveau, McCormick, and Mowbray (1998), however, warn with the Death By Planning antipattern that it is often a fatal mistake to take overly-detailed plans seriously. As I suggested in *Process Patterns* (Ambler, 1998b), you want to plan the long term "in the large" (not in too much detail) and plan the short term "in the small" (in greater detail).

*There are infinitely
many ways to
waste a day, but
not one to get
it back.*
—Tom DeMarco

Your schedule, a key component of your project plan, needs to be developed during the Initiate phase and then updated throughout your project. Many project managers make the mistake of committing to an unrealistic schedule and/or sticking to a schedule once it becomes apparent that it is unrealistic. DeMarco (1997) has an interesting point about the use of overtime and pressure to meet a schedule—its real purpose may be to make everyone look good when the project fails. The secret is to set a realistic schedule based on input from the people who will be doing the work and then to empower them to meet that schedule.

The Project Mismanagement (Brown, Malveau, McCormick, Mowbray, 1998) process antipattern describes the common mistakes made in the mechanics of running a project day-to-day. They point out that common mistakes include inadequate architecture definition, insufficient technical reviews, inadequate testing, and ineffective risk management.

10.1.2 Milestones

One of the most difficult concepts for people new to large-scale development using object-oriented techniques is the difficulty of identifying clear milestones for your project. The problem is that large-scale object-oriented development is fundamentally serial in the large and iterative in the small, as can be seen in Figure 10.1, which depicts the OOSP. The serial nature of the OOSP makes it

---

DEFINITIONS

Capability Maturity Model (CMM) A strategy, defined by the Software Engineering Institute (SEI), that describes the key elements of an effective software process.

key process area (KPA) An issue that must be addressed to achieve a specific Capability Maturity Model (CMM) maturity level.

easy to identify three milestones—one at the end of each of the Initiate, Construct, and Deliver phases, and arguably a fourth at the end of the Maintain and Support phase that would represent either the start of the development of a new release or the removing of your application from active service. To identify more detailed milestones, however, becomes problematic because of the iterative nature of the project stages. Iterative development simply doesn't lend itself to legacy concepts such as milestones.

It is easy to identify milestones for serial development and very difficult for iterative development.

So what do you do? You could decide to tailor the OOSP to have project stages that occur in a serial manner instead of an iterative manner, but I would hope by now that it is obvious that this idea simply will not work. It didn't work for the structured paradigm, which started out from a serial mindset; and it certainly will not work for the object-oriented (OO) paradigm, which started from an iterative mindset. The concept that the OOSP is serial in the large is radical enough for many developers, but trying to artificially force OO development techniques to be serial in the small simply is not feasible.

Forcing the OOSP to be serial in the small, as well as serial in the large, is not a viable approach.

Luckily, senior management is generally interested in midphase milestones for the Construct phase, and sometimes for the Deliver phase. One alternative is for you to define your milestones as the completion of each timebox. Timeboxing (Ambler, 1998b) is an approach to construction in which work is performed in a defined period of time in which the scope of what you are building is modified to meet the schedule. For the Deliver phase, the successful completion of the Test in the Large stage is usually the key mid-phase milestone. With a little bit of creativity, the need to have milestones in your project schedule doesn't need to become a millstone around your neck.

The completion of a timebox can become your new milestones.

DEFINITIONS

milestone A significant event in a project, usually the completion of a major deliverable: a point where upper management is traditionally informed of the status of the project. Because the OOSP is serial in the large and iterative in the small, the only clear milestones occur at the completion of project phases.

timebox A defined period of time, from several days to several months, in which a team of developers is assigned to produced a given deliverable. With a timebox the end date is actually a fixed deadline; if the team needs to, it will cut features out of the deliverable. The team will not extend the delivery date.

10.1.3 Secrets of Success

I would like to share a few tips and techniques I have picked up over the years that will help you to manage your projects successfully.

1. **Make your project status known, good or bad.** Many project managers mistakenly believe that they should only report good news—that bad news such as schedule slippage should not be communicated unless absolutely necessary. My experience is that if you are behind schedule and/or overbudget, it will likely get worse; therefore, it is your responsibility as project manager to make this information available to senior management so that they may either give you the aid that you require or cancel your project before losses become too great.

2. **Allow people to report both good news and bad.** I want to hear news, good or bad, as early as possible. The more information that you have about the issues affecting your project, the better you will be able to make decisions. To ensure that you get news in a timely manner, you must not shoot the messenger (punish the person bringing you the news). My experience is that many project managers do not follow this advice—I am riddled with the bullet holes to prove it.

3. **Manage your interface to other groups.** Among the biggest risks to your project are external teams that your project depends on, but that you do not control. This includes subcontractors, partners, your support department, your operations department, and your user community. You need to manage your relationship with these groups, both to keep abreast of their status and to keep them advised of what you need from them and when.

4. **Ruthlessly focus on your deliverables.** Booch (1996) believes that successful project managers focus on the development of a system that provides a well-understood collection of essential, minimal characteristics.

5. **Manage to the goals and objectives of your project.** Goldberg and Rubin (1995) advise that all project management decisions should relate to your project's stated goals and objectives: if a decision doesn't directly address a goal or objective, why are you making it?

6. **Manage to the big picture.** Booch (1995) points out that no one factor of a software project can ever drag it to a success-

ful closure. Focusing on programming may result in some of the best source code that your organization has ever produced, but if it doesn't meet the needs of your users, then what value does your source code really have? The obsessive focus on any one particular success factor (language, tool, method, process) is a clear sign of organizational immaturity and is a good predictor of failure.

7. **Produce regular status reports.** My experience is that the single most important project management deliverable, after your project plan, is your regular status report, which is often prepared weekly. Your status report should provide an indication of where you are in your schedule, where you should be in your schedule, any updates to risk assessment, an indication of the decisions made since your last status report, and an indication of any decisions deferred. Although this sounds like an onerous burden at first, if you maintain a group memory during your project as suggested in Chapter 6 in *Process Patterns*, then this status report is merely an extract of information that you are already collecting.

8. **Have a gatekeeper.** Coplien (1995) describes the Gatekeeper organizational pattern, a person on your project team who is responsible for disseminating relevant, leading edge, and fringe information from outside the project. Gatekeepers are often tasked with "leaking" information to the outside world and with managing the project's interfaces to other key groups within your organization such as marketing and senior management.

9. **Recognize that different development approaches require different management approaches.** You've seen in this book that object-oriented development is serial in the large, iterative in the small, delivering incremental releases over time.

DEFINITIONS

group memory A record of what your project team accomplished, decisions made by your team and the reasoning behind them, deferred decisions, and the lessons learned on your project. A group memory provides a mechanism to record this information when it is first recognized so that it is not lost.

organizational pattern A pattern that describes a common management technique or a structure appropriate to a software organization.

Each of these approaches, and in general all of the process patterns presented in this book, has its own unique requirements and needs to be managed appropriately. With project management, one size does not fit all.

10. **Build checkpoints into your schedule.** You should always include defined points, also called milestones, in your schedule where you assess the current status of your project. This provides an opportunity—actually, it forces an opportunity—for you to step back and evaluate where you are, what is going right, and what is going wrong on your project.

10.2 People Management

> **DEFINITION**
>
> **people management**
> The process of organizing, monitoring, coaching, and motivating people in such a manner to ensure that they work together effectively and contribute to a project/organization positively.

People management is the act of organizing, monitoring, coaching, and motivating people in a manner to ensure that they work together effectively and contribute to a project/organization positively. My experience is that one of the most important lessons that you can learn is that people aren't interchangeable parts. Every single person has a different set of skills, a different set of experiences, a different set of strengths, and a different set of weaknesses.

In this section I will discuss several issues associated with people management:

> *Good software comes from people. So does bad software.*
> *—Larry Constantine*

- Working together.
- Reward systems.
- Politics and power struggles.
- Staffing an object-oriented project.
- The secrets of success.

10.2.1 Working Together

There are several issues that you need to address to ensure that your project team will work together effectively. First, important decisions should be made by the entire team, not just the manager, to promote ownership of the decision and to improve the quality of the decision. However, recognize that the project manager will need to rule with an iron fist sometimes—rarely, I hope—so that the decision can be made in a timely manner. One of the hardest things for project managers to accept is that they do not have all the answers, nor are they expected to, and that they need to work together with their staff to make the right choices.

The only way that people can work together is if they can communicate with one another effectively. Most projects will use a combination of meetings, electronic mail, shared documents, and possible groupware tools to support communication between team members. Good communication leads to a common vision among your team members, a vision that you need to define early and nurture throughout the project, which in turn helps you to motivate your team members and to keep your project on track.

An important aspect of working together effectively is to manage the inevitable conflicts that arise between team members. Maguire (1994) believes that waiting will only allow the problem to get worse and potentially become so ingrained that it is difficult to deal with later. My experience is that few problems between people are so big that they cannot be worked out by talking through them, and in the worst case you may need to transfer one or more person to another project.

Many people are worried about the deleterious effects that "superstar" developers can have on the overall morale of a team, but I believe that the real issue is that the superstars simply have to be managed properly and have their egos kept in check. Superstars are important because they help your project teams solve difficult problems, and they can be an excellent source of expertise to aid in the training and education process. The important thing is that you have your superstars work together as part of your team, not just on their own, and have them follow the processes, standards, and guidelines chosen by your project team. Even your superstars have to follow the rules.

DEFINITION

groupware A form of software that allows several users to work together on common information, often simultaneously from different physical locations.

10.2.2 Reward Systems

Your organization's reward system is also a key people management issue. The first issue is always pay—if you stop paying your people, they will quickly find work elsewhere—and there are several factors unique to the information technology (IT) industry that you need to be aware of. First, you need to pay people the going market rate, and with IT professionals the market is a global one because there are few countries in the world today who aren't desperate for technology workers. I am acutely aware of this issue as a Canadian: I do most of my consulting work in the United States because I am paid much better there. Second, your organization needs to maintain a separate pay scale for IT professionals, and more realistically a collection of separate pay scales. Junior developers with one or two years of experience are often paid significantly more, and their salaries will rise significantly faster, than junior employees in other parts of your organization: developers are often in more demand than other people with only one or two years of experience. To increase the complexity of your pay scales, the pay rate for developers is also dependent on the types of skills they have; at the time of this writing, a Java programmer with two years of experience is worth nearly fifty percent more than a C++ programmer with similar experience.

The market for systems professionals is global; pay your people what they are worth.

Coplien's (1995) Compensate Success organizational pattern advises that you should establish lavish rewards for individuals contributing to make or break projects and that the entire team should receive comparable rewards to avoid demoralizing individuals on the team. Yourdon (1997) supports this approach, advising that you should reward people handsomely, but that you should not dangle extravagant bonuses in front of them all through the project because it will only distract them. For a bonus to work, team members must believe that they will actually receive it and that management will not find some devious excuse to withhold it. Yourdon also believes that if people are going to do overtime, then the best way to reward them is by compensating them in their next paycheck.

Bonuses, when mismanaged, are often ineffective and nonmotivating.

I am also a firm believer in nonmonetary rewards such as flex time (the ability of people to set their own schedules) including allowing people to work from home several days a week—being able to avoid a long commute to work several times a week is reward enough for many people. Sending people to professional conferences and to training is often an effective reward which also benefits your organization because your staff improves their skillsets.

Use nonmonetary rewards such as flex-time and training to motivate your staff.

10.2.3 Politics, Power Struggles, and Other Realities

A key responsibility of a project manager is to ensure that team members do not become innocent victims in political battles and power struggles between senior managers and/or between groups within your organization. Although I would like to advise you to strive to isolate your staff from political issues, the fact remains that this goal not only is not possible, it is not even a very good idea. Savvy politicos will often pounce on your unsuspecting team members, asking them for information that they will later use against you. The best strategy is to make your staff aware of the political realities of your project, to identify who your friends and foes are, and then try to protect them as best you can from the politics so that they can concentrate on getting their jobs done.

Ensure that your staff is aware of political realities but not unduly hampered by them.

One of the most damaging forms of politics that a development team can experience is to have clashing consultants. Consultants are brought into a project because of their expertise in a given technology or technique, and can often have very strong opinions about how things should be done. They are also in a position where they can be easily let go, and as a result are motivated to make themselves as indispensable as possible. When you have several consultants with strong opinions trying to make themselves indispensable and, even worse, to grow their business, it is likely that conflict will arise. Sides will often form between members of your project team, increasing the damage caused by the conflict. The point to be made is that you need to be aware of this potential source of political difficulties and to deal with it appropriately.

Another common political problem that I have seen in several organizations is the situation when someone, or a group of peo-

WAR STORY

Politics and Rumors Distract You from the Real Work

I once worked on a development team of about fifteen people, and we were about half-way into a six month project when someone overheard two senior managers arguing about the programming language that we were using. It was a well-known fact that these two managers didn't agree on technology issues: one was in favor of a popular fourth generation language (4GL) and the other supported the language that we were using. Word quickly spread among the team—we were going to be shut down because we were using the wrong language. Motivation plummeted, people started updating their resumes, and for the most part we lost a solid week of work. Eventually cooler heads prevailed, not mine, and our project manager obtained a reaffirmation from senior management that we would continue on the same path as before.

DEFINITION

fourth-generation language (4GL)
A category of computer languages in which the development environment includes tools that generate some or all of the source code for your application.

ple, whose main job responsibilities pertain to the "back end" work (often toward the end of the Construct Phase or during the Deliver Phase) have undue influence over key decisions during the "front end" work. This is something that I call the Tail Wags Dog antipattern. Examples that I have seen in practice include: having a testing group dictate the format of requirements documents to meet their specific needs while disregarding the needs of the modelers who are in fact the primary customers of the documents; a repository manager that reduced the breadth of products developed during the Model Stage instead of modifying his tool to support the "new" object-oriented models; and a database administration group that chose the programming environment for an organization simply because it came from the same vendor as their chosen database (disregarding the actual needs of the projects). The solution to this antipattern is to recognize when someone should be allowed to make a decision and when they should only be allowed input into a decision. In all three examples the people involved should have had input into the relevant decisions, but none of them should have been permitted to make the decisions, because the scope of the decision was out of their domains.

10.2.4 Staffing an Object-Oriented Project

A prominent issue with respect to people management is how to staff a project. Figure 10.2 shows the relative staffing for an object-oriented project following the process patterns of the OOSP. Black bars represent the relative effort of a given role/position for a project stage of the OOSP. For example, when we read the chart horizontally, we see that infrastructure engineers are most prominent during the Define Infrastructure stage and have a minor role during the Justify stage, the Construct phase, and for most stages of the Deliver phase. Reading the chart vertically, we see during the Program stage that development engineers (i.e., programmers, team leads) hold the most prominent role, that project managers have an important role, and that modelers, configuration management staff, infrastructure engineers, and technical writers play smaller roles.

The chart presented in Figure 10.2 is important because it provides insight into how to schedule people on a project, and more importantly, indicates what type of people you need and when

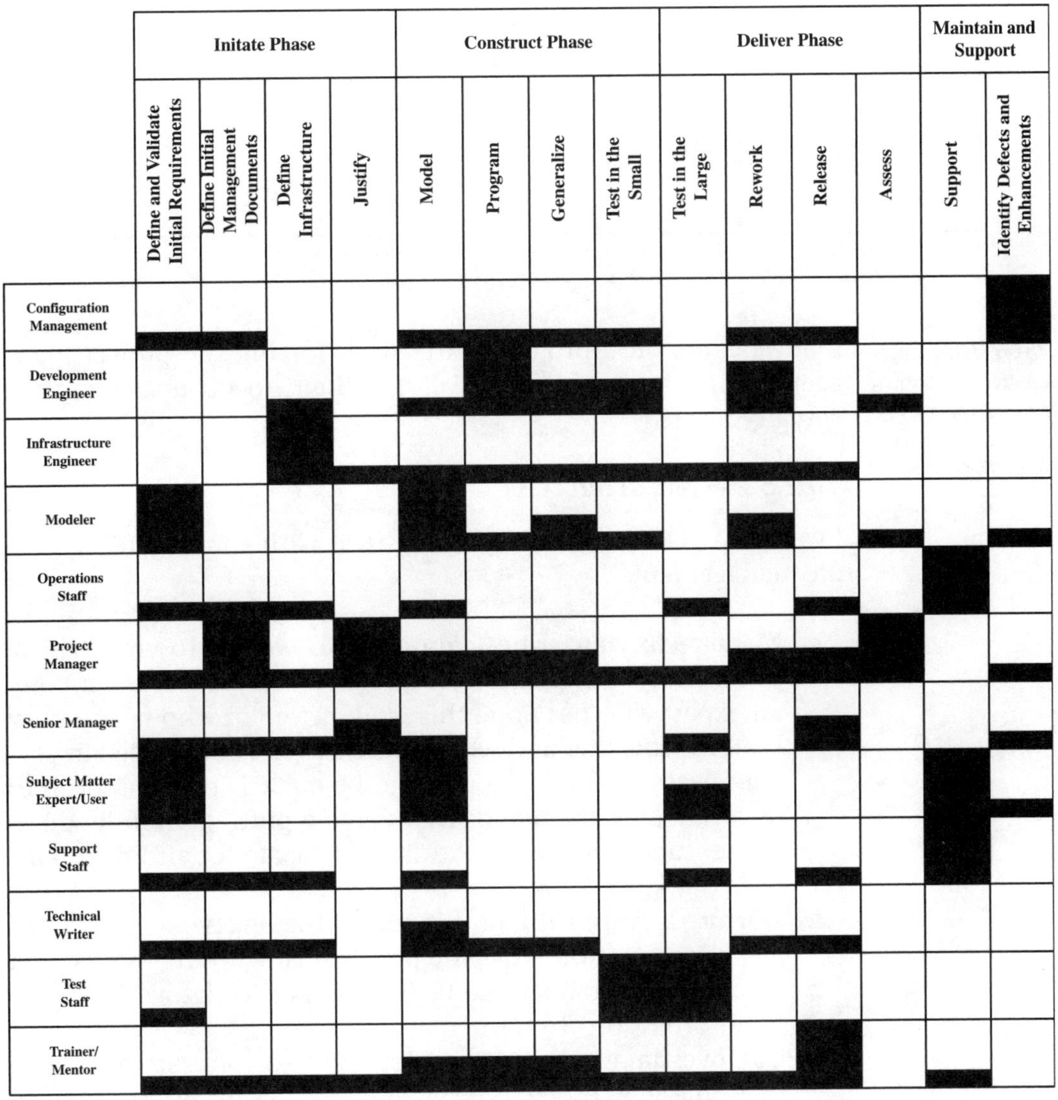

	Initate Phase				Construct Phase				Deliver Phase				Maintain and Support	
	Define and Validate Initial Requirements	Define Initial Management Documents	Define Infrastructure	Justify	Model	Program	Generalize	Test in the Small	Test in the Large	Rework	Release	Assess	Support	Identify Defects and Enhancements
Configuration Management														
Development Engineer														
Infrastructure Engineer														
Modeler														
Operations Staff														
Project Manager														
Senior Manager														
Subject Matter Expert/User														
Support Staff														
Technical Writer														
Test Staff														
Trainer/ Mentor														

Figure 10.2. Relative staffing requirements, by project stage, for an object-oriented project

you'll need them. Ideally, as Figure 10.3 shows, you want to have a small project staff during the Initiate phase, perhaps only two or three people; a larger number of people during the Construct phase, which begins with a large percentage of modelers at first and transitions to a majority of programmers at the end of the phase; a smaller number of people during the Deliver phase; and a small number of people during the Maintenance and Support phase. A common mistake that organizations make is to put too

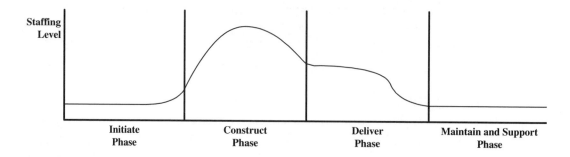

Staffing Level

Initiate Phase

Construct Phase

Deliver Phase

Maintain and Support Phase

Figure 10.3.
Relative staffing levels during the phases of an object-oriented project

many people on a project at the start, forcing the project manager to find "something useful" for them to do until they are actually needed.

10.2.5 Secrets of Success

I would like to share a few tips and tricks with your regarding people management.

1. **Manage to your critical resources as well as to your critical path.** Every project has one or two critical resources: usually an expert who has done this work before or who knows how it all fits together and who always seems to be needed in several places at once. The point to be made is that you need to be aware of the demands that you are putting on individuals and ensure that they are realistic; you cannot afford to burn out your key people.
2. **Nurture a shared vision.** It is critical that everyone have a single, clear focus on what the problem is, who the user is, and what the solution should be for them to work together effectively (Yourdon, 1997).
3. **Use overtime judiciously.** Short bursts of pressure and even overtime may prove to be effective tactics for increasing productivity for a short time, but over the long term they are productivity-reduction factors (DeMarco, 1997).
4. **Provide challenging work and opportunities for growth.** Developers are motivated by challenging work and opportunities to learn new technologies. When the future is open, when people see possibilities for personal growth, their morale goes up.
5. **Be aware of your "truck number."** Harrison (1996) describes the concept of a truck number, the number of critical people

on a project such that if any of them were to be hit by a truck (were to leave) the project would lose essential knowledge and not be able to continue. The greater your truck number, potentially an important management metric, the greater the risk to your project.

5. **It is easier to retain good people than to hire good people.** The current market for information technology (IT) professionals is fiercely competitive, and is likely to remain so for years to come; and many organizations are finding it difficult if not impossible to find the people that they need. To retain your current staff, you must reward them appropriately, provide them with challenging work, and keep them happy with their work environment. My experience is that the one-year and two-year anniversaries are the points in time that many developers will decide whether they want to remain with your organization, as the completion dates of projects.

6. **Do not overstaff your project early.** DeMarco (1997) correctly points out that early overstaffing on a project (project managers are often given more programmers than they need at the beginning of a project) often results in cutting the key activity of the Construct phase, modeling, to give everyone something to do. Figure 10.3 depicts a suggested approach to staffing an object-oriented project.

10.3 Training and Education

The third project/cross-project task is training and education (T&E), a task whose scope includes both information technology (IT) workers and your customers: support staff, operations staff, and members of your user community. The training and education of your customers was covered in detail in the Release stage (Chapter 15) so in this section I will concentrate on T&E of IT staff.

Humphrey (1997) observes that the job of a software engineer is to deliver high-quality software products on budget and on schedule. In other fields professionals are required to demonstrate basic competence before they are permitted to do even the simplest procedures, but in the software industry engineers must learn on the job. This has significant implications for your organization; in particular, it points to the need to invest significantly in the training and education of its IT professionals.

Your organization must make a significant investment in the training and education of its IT staff.

In this section I will discuss the following issues pertaining to training and education:

- The expected lifespan of skills.
- How to get people started with objects.
- Successful approaches to classroom training.
- Successful approaches to mentoring.
- Supporting the learning experience.
- The secrets of success.

10.3.1 The Expected Lifespan of Skills

In the early 1990s I spent a lot of time mentoring and training people in object technology, and in fact I still spend a portion of my time doing so. One of the realizations that I've come to, depicted in Figure 10.4, is that any given skill has an expected period of time for which it is in demand. My experience is that programming skills, such as C++ or Java programming skills, will be in high demand over a period of three to five years and then will dwindle in popularity. These two languages are in fact perfect examples. In the early 1990s, C++ programmers were the most sought-after developer; five years later as I am writing this, the most sought-after people are programmers with Java experience. Five years from now I expect that another language will have replaced Java (perhaps Java++). Similarly, modeling skills, such as use-case development or object-oriented design, have an expected lifespan of ten to fifteen years. The skills with the greatest longevity in the information technology (IT) industry, it appears, are project management and people/communication skills, which have an expected lifespan of thirty to forty years.

Figure 10.4 has several implications. First, the more technical a skill is, the shorter the period of its usefulness to you. This should not be a surprise; the rapid rate of change in the technology field necessitates an equally rapid change in the skills of technologists. Second, if you choose to specialize in programming, and many developers do, then you need to be prepared to overhaul your skillset every five years or so. Yes, you might be able to stay with a single language for fifteen or twenty years (look at COBOL and C programmers), but then again, look at the sparse employment opportunities for APL, BASIC, and FORTRAN programmers. Third, if you choose to stick to skills with greater longevity—for exam-

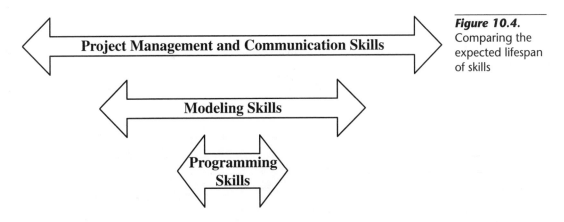

Figure 10.4.
Comparing the
expected lifespan
of skills

ple, project management—you still need to be prepared to keep current with new technologies. In many ways project managers have an even greater need than programmers for training—programmers specializing in a single language need to gain detailed skills in a reasonably narrow topic, whereas project managers need to gain a shallow knowledge of a broad range of skills.

Understanding when and why to retrain is critical to your career success.

10.3.2 Getting People Started With Objects

Organizations that want their object-oriented training and education programs to be successful must carefully consider two important issues. First, it takes from six to nine months for a person to gain a working knowledge of OO, and potentially another year or two for them to become truly expert at it. OO is a whole new development paradigm, one that you cannot pickup overnight. Compounding this issue is the fact that the more experience that a person has in structured development, the harder it is for them to learn OO—they have more to unlearn than people with less experience.

Your most experienced people have the hardest time learning OO development skills.

A second issue is that people learn differently. Sometimes people respond best to hands-on training, while others prefer lecture-style instruction. Some people like computer-based training (CBT) and others work best in learning teams. Successful training and education (T&E) programs are flexible enough to support various learning styles. We'll discuss these T&E techniques later in this section.

How do you train people in object-oriented technology? Figure 10.5 depicts an approach to object-oriented training and education, composed of six tasks:

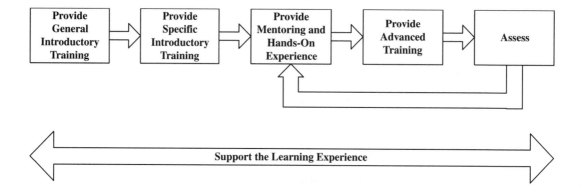

Figure 10.5.
Object-oriented
training and
education

1. Provide general introductory training.
2. Provide introductory training specific to their position.
3. Provide mentoring and hands-on experience.
4. Provide advanced training.
5. Assess and iterate.
6. Provide support for training and education efforts.

10.3.2.1 *Provide General Introductory Training*

Have you ever noticed that the people who come prepared to a course, who know something about the material before attending it, tend to get a lot more out of it than people who go into it cold? My advice is to take advantage of this observation and help your staff to prepare before taking a course. Begin the object-oriented learning experience by distributing an introductory book—I always suggest *The Object Primer* (Ambler, 1995)—and ask each staff member to read it before taking a one-day introductory course a week later. This initial course should cover the fundamental concepts of OO development and provide an overview of the OOSP.

Distribute books ahead of time to enhance the learning process in the classroom.

Immediately after this first course, distribute another book—preferably something like my second book, *Building Object Applications That Work* (Ambler, 1998a), which describes many of the fundamental development techniques of object-oriented development. Four or five weeks later, send everyone on a one-day refresher course, a slightly more advanced version of the introductory course, providing people the opportunity to get any questions that they may have from their initial learning efforts.

10.3.2.2 *Provide Introductory Training Specific to Their Position*

Immediately after the refresher course, you should distribute one or more books to each staff member—this time, books specific to each person's job. For example, test engineers would be given books about object-oriented testing and modelers would be given books about object-oriented modeling. I maintain a reading list of object-oriented development books at my Web site, *http://www.ambysoft.com*, so please feel free to refer to it.

Once again, after allowing each individual sufficient time to read their books, send them on another course or series of courses, this time specific to their jobs. It is important that people get detailed training in what they do as well as at least cursory training in the jobs of the people that they work with. For example, a programmer might be given five days of training in the object-oriented (OO) programming language that they will work in, and two days of training in each of OO modeling and OO testing. By giving programmers training in the skills of modelers and testers, you give them a better appreciation for what their teammates do and what their needs are.

Give people detailed training in their jobs and overviews of the jobs of the people that they interact with.

10.3.2.3 *Provide Mentoring and Hands-On Experience*

Once the initial training is complete—something that may take as long as two or three months—your staff is ready to begin applying their new skills. It is at this point that many organizations run into trouble because they mistakenly believe that their staff now has the skills necessary to build object-oriented software on their own. Nothing could be further from the truth. Would you send somebody to a couple of accounting courses and give them control of your organization's finances? Would you send somebody to a couple of marketing courses and put them in charge of your advertising campaign? Would you send somebody to a couple of law courses and then have them defend you in court? Of course not. Therefore, why would you send somebody to a couple of OO development courses and expect them to develop mission-critical software with their new-found skills?

A couple of weeks of training in OO is only a couple of weeks of training in OO.

After the initial training is complete, developers are now qualified to be mentored by someone experienced in OO development. The objective of mentoring is to have someone who is experienced with object technology guide novices through the learning process, showing them how to use OO development techniques. The mentoring effort should be performed on a development project, one in which the trainee is given the opportunity to apply and evolve the skills that they received during training. The best mentors have several years of experience in object technology, have mentoring experience, and have good communication skills. Mentoring success factors are discussed in detail in section 10.3.5.

DEFINITIONS

analysis pattern A modeling pattern that describes a solution to a business/domain problem.

design pattern A modeling pattern that describes a solution to a design problem.

10.3.2.4 Provide Advanced Training

After several months of hands-on experience under the tutelage of an experienced mentor, developers should return to the classroom for advanced training in their specific job. The experience that developers have gained gives them the knowledge that they need to understand and absorb the material presented in the advanced courses. For example, an advanced modeling course is likely to concentrate on analysis and design patterns, and an advanced programming course will convey a series of programming tips and tricks.

10.3.2.5 Assess and Iterate

The next step is to assess the progress of each person to determine whether they are ready to fly on their own without a mentor. Few people will be ready to do so after only a few months of mentoring, so do not be alarmed. The vast majority of developers need six to nine months of mentoring, if not more, to learn object-oriented development techniques.

10.3.2.6 Support the Learning Experience

There is far more to the object-oriented training and education process than formal classroom training. Learning teams, bag-lunch training, self-paced training, mentoring, and computer-based training (CBT) can all be used to enhance the OO learning process.

An effective way to train people in OO is to put them into learning teams, small groups of people who are given the task of working together to learn a particular aspect of OO. Learning teams are often asked to produce a small application for the company, perhaps something for the human resources or marketing departments. They are usually asked to spend between twenty and fifty percent of their working hours on the mini-project, devoting the rest of their time to their current responsibilities.

The best learning teams are made up of people from separate areas in your systems department who have different skills sets. Perhaps one is a manager, another is a systems programmer, another an analyst, and so on. This wide range of skills and backgrounds enables the team to approach the learning process from several directions, increasing their learning opportunities.

Learning teams should have a heterogeneous membership.

For learning teams to be successful, the team members need training in OO to give them the base skills; they need access to OO development tools; and they need access to OO literature to gain a better understanding of the development process. Unfortunately, the one flaw with learning teams is that they have a tendency to flounder without the guidance of an experienced mentor.

Another excellent way to enhance the object-oriented T&E process is bag-lunch training sessions. These are one-hour mini-lessons held during the daily lunch break. The sessions are typically given by OO development experts, usually your mentors, and will cover a wide range of OO development topics. One day the lesson may be about Smalltalk Collection classes and the next day about managing an OO development team. Successful bag-lunch training programs typically involve 2 or 3 sessions a week with each individual session being given several times so that everyone has an opportunity to attend. Bag-lunch sessions are easy to do and really give a boost to the learning process.

Short training sessions can be held during lunch to enhance the learning process.

Computer-based training (CBT) is also a valid T&E approach, especially when combined with formal training and mentoring. Many organizations provide their employees access to introductory CBT courses before sending them on formal training courses, giving them a head-start on learning. Unfortunately, CBT by itself is of minimal value for teaching people OO development skills. OO development is simply too complex and evolves too fast to be captured in a CBT course. Furthermore, when you have questions about something, you need to talk to an expert to get them answered. A computer cannot do that for you, although a mentor can (mentoring and CBT are a powerful combination). In short, CBT is only part of the OO learning picture.

Computer-based training (CBT) can be used to support the OO learning process.

I cannot stress enough that for OO training and education

> **DEFINITIONS**
>
> **computer-based training (CBT)** A program designed for the purpose of training users in a specific topic. CBT programs often use multimedia features such as animated graphics and sound.
>
> **learning team** A small group of people assigned the task of working together to learn a particular subject.

(T&E) to be successful, your organization must supply access to OO development tools and to OO literature. Most developers learn by playing, reading, and then playing some more. This means they need access to OO programming languages, OO modeling tools, and OO testing tools. You should also buy everyone several OO books, ranging from OO introductions to OO programming to OO analysis and design, and subscriptions to magazines such as *Software Development, Object Magazine, Journal of Object-Oriented Programming,* and *Java Developer's Journal.*

10.3.3 Successful Approaches to Classroom Training and Education

Instructors must have expertise in what they are teaching, and students need training in all aspects of the OOSP.

You can do many things to ensure that classroom training and education is successful. Lilly (1995) stresses that the instructor needs expertise in the subject matter. My experience is that the best instructors work at what they teach an average of three weeks a month and teach one week a month. Lilly also believes that even at the introductory level, it is important to expose students to analysis and design; and I go even further to suggest that exposure to the complete Object-Oriented Software Process (OOSP) is necessary. Furthermore, you need to train everybody, not just your programmers and not just your best people. Finally, as indicated earlier, you should put students to work right away after training, otherwise you run the risk that they will forget everything that they have learned.

It is not enough to do your best: you must know what to do, and THEN do your best.
—W. Edwards Deming

Lato (1997) suggests that the training should be focused on what is in it for "me," at both an organizational and an individual level. Everyone should be made aware of the benefits of OO. Lato stresses that senior management must be trained in the deliverables, the processes, the resources needed, the differences compared to the old way of doing things, and the risks associated with transitioning to object technology.

10.3.4 Successful Approaches to Mentoring

For mentoring to be successful, your mentors must be qualified to do the job. Did you ever take a college course where the instructor was ahead of the students in reading the textbook by only a chapter or two? Wasn't a very good learning experience, was it? The same thing applies to mentors. Mentors must have experience in what they are teaching. The bottom line is that good mentors have communication skills and several years of experience in what they are mentoring. If you do not have people with the skills (and many organizations still do not), you'll need to hire from the outside.

Mentors must be experienced in object technology and have good communication skills.

Mentors should participate as active members of your project team, not just as teachers. For a mentor to be a productive member of the team, you will need a ratio of one mentor for every two or three novices; anything more and the mentor will be too busy mentoring to get anything done on your project. There is nothing wrong with this, as long as there are other experienced people available to develop the complex portions of your application. Project teams consisting of one expert and a large number of novices are likely to fail.

Schedlbauer (1997) points out that mentoring is in addition to training and education, not a replacement for it. One of the roles of a mentor is to help your project team see the big picture, and the mentor will need to refocus the team occasionally by explaining how new methods can be applied to solve development problems. Schedlbauer stresses that mentors should play a key advisory role on your project, but should not be the project leader or chief designer because those roles should be filled, if possible, by permanent employees. Finally, Schedlbauer believes that mentors should be involved throughout the entire project, especially at the early stages of it, so that the learning process gets off on the right track.

Your goal is to wean yourself from your mentors gradually.

My experience is that the mentoring process typically takes between six and twelve months, with the mentor being needed full-time at the beginning of a project and then only a day or two a week towards the end, when your development staff become self-sufficient. The trick is to slowly wean yourself off your mentor by having them transfer their skills to your staff. Good mentors make you independent of them; bad mentors do not.

10.3.5 Secrets of Success

I would like to share several tips and techniques that lead to success in training and education:

1. **Get your staff into the habit of learning.** The rate of change in the information technology (IT) industry is simply too fast to allow someone to train once and then sit on their laurels.

2. **Just-in-time (JIT) training is critical.** Give your people training when they need it, not several months before or several months after. People will forget the majority of what they have learned less than a month later unless they apply their new skills immediately after training.

3. **Expect to train in skills other than object-orientation.** Do not forget that you may also need to give your staff skills in related topics such as graphical user interface (GUI) design, client/server development, and personal computer skills, to name a few. Very often the move to OO development was precipitated by a move to a new hardware/software platform. Perhaps your organization is moving from a mainframe-based environment to a client/server environment using personal computers with GUI front-ends. This move to a new environment means you'll need to give your staff the skills to work in and develop for this new environment.

4. **Perform skills assessments for everyone.** Compare the skills assessments from the beginning of the project, taken during the Define Infrastructure stage (Ambler, 1998b), and at the end of the project, taken during the Assess stage (Chapter 6). You need to understand someone's current skills before you can develop an effective training plan for them.

5. **Recognize that not everyone learns the same way.** Some people learn best in the classroom, while others learn best by sitting down and working with a language, and others learn best by working with others. Because no training and education plan is perfect for everyone, you will want to create an approach that can be modified to meet the needs of individual students. Flexibility is a key success factor in OO training and education.

6. **Motivate everybody.** Motivating developers to learn about object-oriented development is typically no problem: They are usually chomping at the bit to get into this stuff. Unfor-

tunately, some experienced developers aren't so eager; perhaps they are afraid they will not be able to pick it up as fast as others. Given time and a flexible learning environment, everyone can learn OO; they just have to *want* to learn. A great carrot to dangle is the fact that object-oriented developers are typically assigned to the most interesting projects and are paid better than non-OO developers. If you know of better motivators for developers than interesting work and good money, I would be interested in hearing about them.

7. **Expect to deal with bruised egos.** A significant problem with transitioning experienced developers into OO is the fact that overnight, they go from being a recognized expert to a recognized novice. This hurts. Developers need to realize that if they apply themselves, they can become experts once again; it just takes awhile.

8. **Expect the "I've done it before" syndrome.** It is quite common for experienced structured developers, especially the really good ones, to initially convince themselves that they have been doing OO all along. This is because OO includes many important structured software engineering principles that the best developers typically use. Familiarity with some of the underlying principles of OO, the ones that are usually taught in introductory OO classes, makes it easy to convince yourself that you've been doing OO all along. This problem is usually self-correcting, because as soon as someone starts to work on a real project with good mentors, they realize quickly that there is a lot more to OO than they originally thought.

9. **Recognize that you cannot retrain everyone at once.** Never forget that on the first few OO projects, many of the developers on your staff will not be involved. You need these people to keep your existing legacy systems up and running, but at the same time they want to be involved in the exciting new projects. My advice is to keep them up-to-date on what's being learned on the project; let them know when and how they will be brought on to it; give them access to the tools on off-hours so they can learn on their own; invite them to bag-lunch training sessions; and give them access to OO books and magazines. Not everyone can be on the first project, but they can still be involved in the OO learning process. If you do not involve them, you risk losing them—forcing you to move people from your OO projects to support your legacy applications.

10. **Recognize that some colleges and universities are still not familiar with object orientation.** Although this problem is quickly being addressed, it can still be difficult to find high-quality OO courses at your local college or university. Object orientation has caught many computer science departments off-guard; if they weren't actively involved in OO research, then chances are they didn't have an OO curriculum in place until just recently. Avoid OO courses that are being taught for the first time, because they are still in the process of evolving and you run the risk of the instructor being only a chapter or two ahead of the students.

11. **Get people into training quickly.** Once you have made the decision to get into OO, get training as soon as possible. Although it is a very good idea to do some reading on your own, the bottom line is that it is too easy to misunderstand an issue and not realize it. Professional instructors can help you to learn OO properly and avoid gaining bad habits.

12. **Understand that many things are different with OO.** Although the OO development paradigm is based on many tried-and-true principles that we learned from structured development, there are also a lot of things about the OO paradigm that make it unique. Because OO is a combination of both new and old techniques, it is not always obvious what still works and what does not. Many of the things that you have been doing for years simply aren't applicable anymore in the OO development world.

13. **Educate as well as train.** Training gives you the skills to do your job; education gives you the knowledge to understand your job. The most important thing that an educational program can do is to explain the interrelationships between the concepts and techniques.

14. **Teach from experience.** Goldberg and Rubin (1995) point out that good instructors practice what they preach, and that their hands-on experience gives them the confidence and the ability to address tough questions.

15. **Recognize that people do not quit because they are trained.** Developers quit because the money is not good enough, the work is not interesting enough, or because they do not like the people they're working with. OO developers are paid more than non-OO developers, and any organization that

enters into OO development had better be prepared to pay their people what they're worth after training them. OO developers are in demand, and your competition would love to poach your newly trained OO developers. Treat your people well.

10.4 Quality Assurance

Quality assurance (QA) is the act of reviewing and auditing the project deliverables and activities to verify that they comply with the applicable standards, guidelines, and processes adopted by your organization. The Capability Maturity Model (CMM) includes a key process area (KPA) called Software Quality Assurance, which directly addresses the needs of quality assurance for a software project. Software Quality Assurance is a Level 2 KPA, indicating that quality assurance is considered a fundamental task of a mature software process.

The CMM defines two other KPAs that are included in the QA project/cross-project task: The Level 3 Peer Reviews KPA and the Level 4 Software Quality Management KPA. The Peer Review KPA describes how to conduct a methodical examination of the deliverables of a developer by her or his peers to identify potential defects and areas where changes are needed. The Software Quality Management KPA focuses on the definition of quality goals for software products and the establishment of plans to achieve these goals. It also involves the monitoring and adjustment of the software plans, software work products, activities, and quality goals to satisfy the needs and desires of the user community for high-quality products.

A key concept in quality assurance is that quality is often in the eye of the beholder. This indicates that there are many aspects to software quality, including:

- Does it meet the needs of its users?
- Is it on time?
- Is it on budget?
- Does it follow standards?
- Is it easy to use?
- Is it reasonably free of defects?

TIP

Quality is Everyone's Job

Looking for quality after the fact in a technical review is a part of the solution, but it definitely is not enough. Quality is a way of life for professional developers, who strive to create high-quality deliverables the first time every time. Developers who do this focus for their deliverable on the customers, the people who will use their products downstream in the development process. Your best developers actively look for new and better ways to do things, constantly trying to improve the quality of their work. Quality is everyone's job, not just the quality assurance department's.

Quality is in the eye of the beholder.

- Is it easy to maintain and to enhance?
- How easy will it integrate into the current technical environment?

10.4.1 Quality Assurance Throughout Your Project

The Engage QA (Coplien, 1995) organizational pattern correctly suggests that quality assurance should play a central role in your software development efforts, advice that I have taken to heart in the OOSP. Table 10.1 summarizes by project stage the quality assurance techniques that your team may choose to employ throughout your project. Notice the predominance of peer reviews, inspections, and walkthroughs, all implementations of the Technical Review task process pattern of Figure 10.6.

DEFINITIONS

Capability Maturity Model (CMM) A strategy, defined by the Software Engineering Institute (SEI), that describes the key elements of an effective software process.

key process area (KPA) An issue that must be addressed to achieve a specific Capability Maturity Model (CMM) maturity level.

quality assurance (QA) The process of ensuring that the efforts of a project meet or exceed the standards expected of them.

technical review A testing technique in which the design of your application is examined critically by a group of your peers. A review will typically focus on accuracy, quality, usability, and completeness. This process is often referred to as a walkthrough or a peer review.

TABLE 10.1. Quality Assurance Throughout the OOSP

Project Stage	Quality Assurance Techniques and Issues
Initiate: Define and Validate Initial Requirements	• Perform requirements and prototype walkthroughs. • Perform use-case scenario testing.
Initiate: Define Initial Management Documents	• Peer review the project plan, schedule, and estimate. • Walkthrough the initial risk assessment.
Initiate: Justify	• Review the technical feasibility study with technical experts. • Review the economic feasibility study with accounting and finance staff. • Review the operational feasibility study with your operations staff.
Initiate: Define Infrastructure	• Peer review the project infrastructure with members of former OO projects if possible.
Construct: Model	• Peer review models for consistency, traceability, and maintainability. • Review models with experienced developers, including the programming team that will implement the models.
Construct: Program	• Peer review source code. Everyone, including experienced programmers, should have their code reviewed.
Construct: Generalize	• Peer review all reusable items, including any documentation, models, and source code. The original items should have already been peer reviewed, but will need to be re-reviewed.
Construct: Test in the Small	• Peer review all testing deliverables, including your test plan, test scripts, and test cases.
Deliver: Test in the Large	• Peer review all testing deliverables, including your test plan, test scripts, and test cases.
Deliver: Rework	• Follow the same quality assurance processes as you would for the Construct phase.

(continued)

TABLE 10.1. (continued)

Project Stage	Quality Assurance Techniques and Issues
Deliver: Release	• Ensure that your training efforts were effective by testing the trainees. • Ensure that your application deployment goes smoothly by first deploying it to a small group of users to validate your deployment procedures.
Deliver: Assess	• Review your project to determine how your object-oriented software process (OOSP) may be improved. • Review the members of your team to help them to manage their personal and professional growth.
Maintain and Support: Support	• The goal is to ensure that your user community is receiving good service from your support staff. • The support manager may choose to randomly monitor support calls. • Send questionnaires to, or to interview, users a few days after they made a support request to determine their level of satisfaction with the service that they received. • Analyze the information contained in your support request tracking system to determine whether the users that you are supporting becoming independent of you.
Maintain and Support: Identify Defects and Enhancements	• The goal is to ensure that the priorities given to maintenance changes are being followed. • Track maintenance changes through until they are put in production.

10.4.2 A Few Words About ISO 9000

ISO (International Standards Organization) 9003 is the component of the ISO 9000 collection of quality standards that deals specifically with how organizations should manage their software quality assurance programs. In a many ways ISO 9003 is seen as a subset of the ISO 9001 standard, because it defines how organizations should manage their entire quality assurance programs, not just software quality assurance.

A simplistic view of ISO 9000 is that it is a definition of how

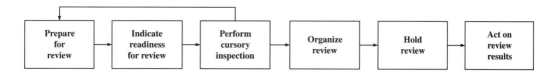

| Prepare for review | Indicate readiness for review | Perform cursory inspection | Organize review | Hold review | Act on review results |

Figure 10.6.
The Technical Review process pattern

your organization produces the products and services that it sells to its customers, as well as the definition of how the customers can complain about what they have received. In a nutshell, ISO 9000 defines quality standards for the processes by which your company operates. I believe that there is much value in the ISO 9000 standards, and ISO 9003 in particular, for software developers. If you are serious about improving the software-testing process in your organization I highly suggest you look into both of them.

10.4.3 Secrets of Success

I would like to share with you several tips and techniques about quality assurance (QA) that I have picked up over the years:

1. **Strive to discover defects early.** A goal of quality assurance is to discover defects when they are made, or soon afterward, so that they do not infect other portions of your work. The earlier that you detect a defect, the easier and less expensive it is to fix.
2. **Quality assurance is an organization-level task.** All efforts within your organization should be governed by quality constraints. From a software project point of view, consistent quality standards must be applied for all projects: if each project sets and meets its own quality standards there is little

---

DEFINITIONS

International Standards Organization (ISO) A nonprofit organization promoting the development and support of internationally accepted standards.

ISO 9001 A standard defined by the International Standards Organization (ISO) that defines how organizations should manage their quality-assurance programs.

ISO 9003 The standards defining how organizations should manage their software-quality assurance programs.

> ## *Scott's Soapbox*
>
> ### ISO 9000 Says Nothing About the Quality of a Product
>
> Although ISO 9000 guarantees a quality process, it doesn't guarantee a quality product. To explain my point, a company that makes parachutes out of lead (instead of light-weight parachute silk) could gain their ISO 9000 certification as long as they define how they build the parachutes and how their customers can complain if they are unhappy with them. ISO 9000 certification only guarantees a quality process, not a quality product.

---

    value if as a whole the projects are inconsistent.

3. **Review everything.** It is too easy to look at something quickly and assume that it is right. My experience is that you should review all major deliverables, often several times, to identify defects with them as early as possible.

4. **Define quality.** Landsbaum and Glass (1992) point out that if employees have no definition of quality, and no numerical target to strive for, it is difficult to motivate them to achieve quality. There are several potential quality factors—functionality, reliability, integrity, efficiency, maintainability, enhanceability, ease of use, flexibility, and user satisfaction—which you can prioritize as part of your definition of quality. Yourdon (1997) goes further, suggesting that you define your quality factors specific quality factors for each part of the OOSP, and then redefine them as necessary throughout the project when practice shows that you have chosen the wrong quality factors.

5. **Recognize that quality is in the eye of the beholder.** Technical people often have different definitions of quality from users, whose definitions differ from support staff, whose definitions differ from operations staff.

6. **Recognize that software can be good enough.** Yourdon (1997) points out that few applications need to be perfect; therefore, you should define what is "good enough," not what is ideal.

7. **Recognize that invisibility is the enemy of quality.** If you know that nobody is going to look at your work, what is your motivation to do a good job? While at first you might strive

to produce the best work that you can, it is human nature to eventually put less effort into something that you know only you will look at. If you want to ensure quality on your software projects, you have to make all work products visible for others to review and evaluate.

8. **Recognize that quality is not free, but it is very profitable.** It is harder to produce high-quality software than it is to simply hack out some code. However, high-quality software is significantly easier to maintain and to enhance than software that has been hacked out. Experience shows time and again that developers who invest the time to build quality software are significantly more productive in the long term, and often in the short term as well, than developers who take shortcuts during development and ignore quality assurance issues.

10.5 Risk Management

Risk management is the process of identifying, monitoring, and mitigating the risks faced by a project team. A fundamental motivation of risk management is that by the time problems become apparent, the damage has already been done and it is probably too late to do anything about it. Karolak (1995) believes that software risk management must be viewed holistically throughout the entire development effort, and that it requires rigor and discipline to identify, calculate, determine, plan, collect, and report software risk items.

Perform risk management throughout all phases of the OOSP.

One of the realities of risk management is that different groups of people define risks in different manners, their definition being driven by their experiences and by their job focus. Karolak (1995) observes that software developers define risk in terms of technologies: perhaps two technologies will not work together or a given technology is likely to be replaced by another. Management, on the other hand, often defines risk in terms of performance and profit, and your user community defines risk in terms of usability, functionality, and delivery dates. As you would imagine, your operations and support staff define risk in terms of the operational capability and supportability of your application. Different groups of people have different definitions of risk.

Technologists, managers, and users will each focus on different risks.

In this section I will discuss the following topics:

> ### DEFINITION
>
> **risk management** The process of identifying, monitoring, and mitigating the risks faced by a project team. These risks may typically be strategic, technical, and/or political.

- The sources of risk.
- The Risk Management process pattern.
- The potential risks throughout your project.
- The secrets of success.

10.5.1 The Sources of Risk

Fundamentally, there are three determinants of risk: lack of control, lack of information, and lack of time (Karolak, 1995). With respect to software, these three determinants can be seen in the potential sources of software risk: cost risk, organizational risk, schedule risk, and technical risk. Table 10.2 describes each type of risk.

Many organizations are still struggling internally with whether they should migrate, at a large scale, to object technology. Most organizations by now have at least invested in one or more pilot projects to test the viability of object technology, but due to being distracted by the Year 2000 (Y2K) crisis, they have not had the resources to truly move to object technology. Until now. Table 10.3 compares the risks associated with moving to object technology with those of not moving to object technology. It is very difficult to make the decision to make such a significant change because the risks associated with not changing have been slowly building over the years, often unbeknownst to you. Just as the proverbial frog in the frying pan that doesn't notice the slowly rising temperature will eventually boil to death instead of jumping

> ### DEFINITIONS
>
> **pilot project** A small project whose purpose is to prove the viability of a new technology.
>
> **Year 2000 (Y2K) problem** A common problem in which dates within software and databases have been recorded with a two-digit year (for example, 05) instead of a four-digit year (for example 2005). This problem results in software not recognizing dates on or after January 1st, 2000, believing that they represent dates on or after January 1st, 1900 instead.

TABLE 10.2. The Sources/Types of Risk

Type of Risk	Description
Cost	The focus of cost risk is whether your project is economically feasible. Karolak (1995) indicates that you need to manage several sources of cost risk: the budget, nonrecurring costs, recurring costs, fixed costs, variable costs, and your desired profit/loss margin.
Organizational	The focus organizational risk is whether your organizational environment will permit your project to succeed. You will need to be aware of and possibly manage several sources of organizational risk: politics, power struggles, mergers with other organizations or departments, reorganization of your existing organizational structure, and changing management priorities.
Schedule	The focus of schedule risk is whether your project can deliver the desired products on the dates that they are required. You need to actively manage several sources of schedule risk: availability of key technologies such as hardware and development tools; dependencies on external groups such as subcontractors and your user community; availability of funding for your project; availability of training; and availability of software professionals.
Technical	The focus of technical risk is whether a given technology meets the needs of your project. Karolak (1995) indicates that you need to manage several sources of technical risk: functionality, quality, reliability, usability, timeliness, maintainability, and reusability.

TABLE 10.3. The Potential Risks of (Not) Using Object Technology

The Risks of Using Object Technology	The Risks of Not Using Object Technology
• The misperception persists that object technology is not yet proven. • Many developers still do not have sufficient experience building software with object technology. • There are many tools, techniques, and methods to choose from.	• Your organization is locked into legacy technology that is no longer supported by vendors. • It is difficult to hire people experienced in your legacy technology. • It is difficult to motivate developers to work with legacy technologies.

out of the pan, many organizations are having difficulty recognizing that the structured/procedural development paradigm is slowly ending, causing your existing development environment to slowly come to a boil. Can you afford not to make the jump to object technology?

10.5.2 The Risk Management Process Pattern

The Risk Management pattern depicts the process to manage a single risk and to continually report the current status of all outstanding risks.

Figure 10.7 depicts the Risk Management task process pattern, which is comprised of five tasks: identify a risk, assess the risk, develop mitigation strategies, mitigate the risks, and report risks. There are two aspects to this process pattern; the serial boxes represent the serial tasks that you need to perform to manage a single risk, and the "big arrow" task represents the need to constantly report the status of all outstanding risks to management.

Let's discuss the five tasks of the Risk Management process pattern in detail:

1. **Identify a risk.** The first step to manage a risk is to identify it. In the previous section we described several types and sources of risk—sources that you must monitor continually to detect potential threats to your project. Furthermore, it is likely that your teammates will also identify potential risks,

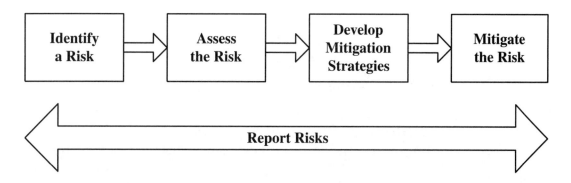

implying that you need to be open to listening to and then acting on their concerns.

Figure 10.7.
The Risk Management task process pattern

2. **Assess the risk.** Your risk assessment should include the following information: a description of the risk, the probability that it will occur, its priority, its severity, the consequences of not mitigating it, and the potential delay to your project. Yourdon (1997) advises that a risk assessment should include several different organization perspectives; you saw previously that people define risks differently and balance them accordingly. DeMarco (1997) also advises that you should describe the events that potentially indicate that a risk will materialize to enable you to avoid the frog-in-the-pan syndrome of not noticing a series of minor changes.

3. **Develop mitigation strategies.** Once a risk has been assessed, contingency plans to mitigate the risk should be developed. Is there an alternate product or technology that can be used to mitigate a technical risk? Can you obtain an alternate source of funding or reduce costs somehow to mitigate a cost risk? Are you willing to simply accept the consequences if the risk does occur; and if so, have you included a reserve in your project plan for it?

4. **Mitigate the risk.** To mitigate the risk, you must choose one of the strategies identified in the previous step and work it.

5. **Report risks.** An important aspect of the Risk Management process pattern is the reporting of the current standing of all outstanding potential risks. Your report is often presented to senior management on a regular basis, often weekly or monthly, and should include an indication of the number of risks that have been closed out by priority, the number of

risks still pending by priority, and an indication of the risks that your user community understands and agrees to.

10.5.3 Potential Risks Throughout Your Project

Table 10.4 summarizes by project phase and stage the potential risks that your project may experience. These risks and potential mitigation strategies were described in detail in the appropriate chapters.

10.5.4 Secrets of Success

I would like to share with you several tips and techniques for successfully managing risk on your project:

1. **Appoint a risk officer.** DeMarco (1997) advises that your organization appoint a risk officer: someone responsible for supporting and overseeing risk management within your organization. Risk officers should not be expected to always maintain a can-do attitude and should be willing, and expected, to deliver both good and bad news to senior management.
2. **Prevent risks, do not manage them.** When you stop and think about it, your real goal should be to prevent risks from occurring, not to manage them after they have occurred.
3. **Maintain a risk database.** Your organization should maintain a risk database, perhaps a subset of your group memory, in which all risks are tracked.
4. **Use objective criteria to identify, evaluate, and manage risks.** Many organizations either choose to not manage risks, or if they do, they choose to not manage them properly. I've worked in many organizations where senior management simply didn't want to hear about actual risks to a project, even when the risk had already manifested itself (I am always amazed at management's ability to deny the fact that a project that has already missed its delivery date). My advice is to not stick your head in the sand just because the head honcho does—risks rarely go away by management decree.
5. **Reward people for identifying and managing risks.** You should recognize developers at all levels for identifying and

**TABLE 10.4. Potential Risks, by Project Stage,
Throughout Your Project**

Project Stage/Phase	Potential Risks
Initiate phase	• Pressure from senior management to start construction too early. • Pressure to bring people onto the project too early. • Beware the new toy/fad syndrome. • Resistance to change.
Define and Validate Initial Requirements stage	• Lack of support for defining and validating initial requirements. • Not analyzing requirements for their viability.
Define Initial Management Documents stage	• Unreasonable estimates and/or schedules. • Inaccurate estimates. • Lack of management support.
Justify stage	• Politics. • Skipping the stage. • Not looking at all three aspects of feasibility. • Unqualified people performing the assessment.
Define Infrastructure stage	• Choosing inappropriate infrastructure artifacts.
Construct phase	• Coding starting too soon.
Model stage	• Myopia toward business and/or technical issues. • Lack of a common architecture.
Program stage	• Cowboy coders. • Lack of training in the infrastructure. • Premature release. • Not following your models. • Lack of documentation. • Overly focused on optimization issues.
Generalize stage	• Leaving generalization to future projects. • Lack of management support. • Thinking that the Generalize stage is the sole reuse task.

(continued)

TABLE 10.4. (continued)

Project Stage/Phase	Potential Risks
Test in the Small stage	• Lack of testing knowledge. • Testing in the small not seen as a continuous process. • Developers testing their own work. • Not performing code reviews. • Lack of development standards/guidelines. • Lack of time. • The "you can only test code" attitude. • The belief that object-oriented testing is just like structured testing. • Underestimating the importance of regression testing. • Lack of management support.
Deliver phase	• Testing is cut short. • Rework has not been planned for. • Your developers quit. • Resources to assess your project have not been allocated. • The needs of operations and support are not adequately considered. • The data conversion task has been underestimated. • Training has been poorly planned.
Test in the Large stage	• No testing standards/guidelines. • Lack of resources. • Underestimating the importance of regression testing.
Rework stage	• The temptation to rush. • The temptation to reduce testing. • The temptation to only update the source code. • The temptation to not fix known defects.
Release stage	• Pressure to forgo training of your users, operations staff, and support staff. • Pressure to accept poor documentation. • Your data conversion effort is late and/or fails.

(continued)

dealing with risks; this will increase their motivation to aid your risk management efforts.

6. **Recognize that you cannot identify all risks.** Two main risks are associated with risk management itself: first, that you will not identify a risk; and second, that you will misidentify a risk. DeMarco (1997) believes that the greatest risks to your project fall into the second category, that what you know that is not so is often much more damaging than what you simply do not know.

7. **Recognize that risk management is an organizational issue.** Risk must be addressed not only from a project viewpoint, but from an organizational viewpoint—you've seen that

TABLE 10.4. (continued)

Project Stage/Phase	Potential Risks
Assess stage	• Developers unwilling to participate in an assessment. • Senior management unwilling to support an assessment at this time. • Finger pointing. • Post-deployment issues being missed. • The assessment being used against you.
Maintain and Support phase	• Allocated maintenance changes are not acted on. • Changes are made to the application without going through the software process. • The user community develops new versions of the application.
Support stage	• There is no designated owner for a configuration item (CI). • Dissatisfied customers.
Identify Defects and Enhancements	• Staff shortages. • There is a lack of management support.

many of the risks associated with software projects, particularly organizational and cost risk, are partially out of your control.

8. **Recognize that you will always have risk.** The reality is that profit and risk coexist: you will always have some risk on a software project.

10.6 Reuse Management

Reuse management is the process of organizing, monitoring, and directing the efforts of a project team that will lead to reuse on a project—of either existing or purchased items. It is possible to achieve reuse throughout the entire OOSP, but it is not free and it is not automatic. You have to work at it. Furthermore, although we have a project stage, Generalize (Ambler, 1998b), dedicated specifically to building reusable components during the Construct phase, this is only a start. You can reuse your project plans, your estimates, your risk analysis, your test strategies, your construction standards, and your documentation templates—but only if you decide to. Reuse management is the key to reducing the overall cost of application development.

Reuse is not free and it is not automatic; you have to actively work at it throughout the entire OOSP.

There are two main approaches to reuse: opportunistic reuse, in which you harvest reusable items from projects after-the-fact; and systematic reuse, in which reusable artifacts are identified via architectural and enterprise modeling (Ambler, 1998b) and are designed to be reusable from the very start. The Develop Reusable Artifacts task process pattern, depicted in Figure 10.8, shows that systematic reuse is a top-down approach to reuse, whereas opportunistic reuse is bottom-up. You need both approaches to reuse: systematic reuse to achieve reuse of large-scale domain compo-

---

DEFINITIONS

group memory A record of what your project team accomplished, decisions made by your team and the reasoning behind them, deferred decisions, and the lessons learned on your project. A group memory provides a mechanism to record this information when it is first recognized so that it is not lost.

risk officer Someone in your organization who is responsible for supporting and overseeing risk management.

SCOTT'S SOAPBOX

The NIH Syndrome is a Myth

Very often you will have to combat the "not invented here" (NIH) syndrome held by other members of your team, a problem that could prevent you from trying to spread the reuse attitude among your team. According to the NIH syndrome, developers will not reuse the work of other developers because they didn't create it themselves. Pure hogwash. Professional developers constantly seek to reuse the work of others because it frees them up to work on the domain-specific portions of their own applications. My experience is that professional developers will readily reuse the work of others as long as it meets their needs, is of high quality, and is well documented and easy to understand. The NIH syndrome is a myth, an excuse cooked up by people who do not want to admit to themselves that other developers aren't interested in reusing their shabby work. If the NIH syndrome were true, then object-oriented development environments wouldn't come with class libraries, and the hundreds of companies selling reusable components and frameworks wouldn't exist.

You need to take both systematic and opportunistic approaches to reuse.

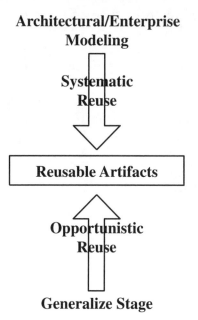

Architectural/Enterprise Modeling

Systematic Reuse

Reusable Artifacts

Opportunistic Reuse

Generalize Stage

Figure 10.8.
The Develop Reusable Artifacts process pattern

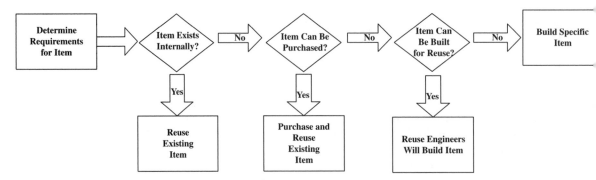

Figure 10.9.
The Reuse First
process pattern

nents and common frameworks; opportunistic reuse to achieve reuse of smaller-scale artifacts such as class hierarchies, user interface widgets, and common documentation templates.

Figure 10.9 depicts the Reuse First task process pattern, a fundamental enabler of Reuse Management within your organization. The Reuse First process pattern shows the basic steps of achieving reuse throughout your project: you determine the requirements for the item that you need; you determine if the item already exists within your organization; if not, you attempt to purchase the item; if this fails, you attempt to build the item to be as reusable as possible if resources permit, or at worst build a version of the item that is specific to the task at hand.

The advantages of the Reuse First process pattern are that it reduces both the development time and cost for the software that you are building, and that it is applicable to any type of deliverable—this process pattern can be applied to the reuse of standards, of documentation, of models, and of source code. In many ways this process pattern shows that reuse is really an attitude; the only way that your organization will achieve high levels of reuse is to actively attempt to reuse or purchase items instead of building them.

*Build things only
as a last resort.*

In this section I will discuss the following topics:

- Types of reuse.
- Potential reuse throughout your project.
- The Reuse Capability Model.
- Reuse tools.
- The secrets of success.

10.6.1 Types of Reuse

Part of not "reinventing the wheel" is to first understand that you have more than one wheel at your disposal to reuse. You can reuse

DEFINITIONS

architectural modeling High-level modeling, either of the business or technical domain, whose goal is to provide a common, overall vision of your domain. Architectural models provide a base from which detailed modeling will begin.

enterprise modeling The act of modeling an organization and its external environment from a business, not an information system, viewpoint.

opportunistic reuse A reuse approach in which reusable items are harvested from project deliverables after the fact.

reuse management The process of organizing, monitoring, and directing the efforts of a project team that lead to reuse on a project—of either existing or purchased items.

systematic reuse An approach to reuse that involves modeling techniques whose purpose is to define high-leverage, reusable components.

source code, components, development artifacts, patterns, and templates. If there's one lesson to take away, it is this: Your work is not reusable simply because it is object-oriented; instead, it is reusable because you have taken the time to make it so.

Figure 10.10 compares the effectiveness of the eight categories of reuse described in this book: code reuse, inheritance reuse, template reuse, component reuse, framework reuse, artifact reuse, pattern reuse, and domain-component reuse. For example, component

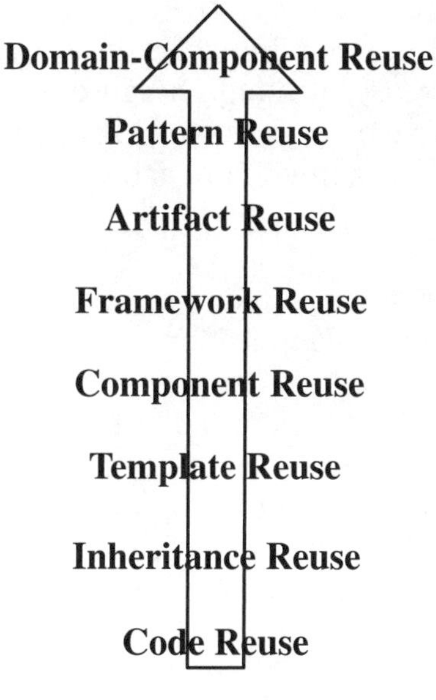

Reuse is not free and it is not automatic. You need to manage the reuse process.

Domain-Component Reuse

Pattern Reuse

Artifact Reuse

Framework Reuse

Component Reuse

Template Reuse

Inheritance Reuse

Code Reuse

Figure 10.10.
The effectiveness of the various approaches to reuse

DEFINITIONS

artifact reuse The reuse of previously created development artifacts: use cases, standards documents, domain-specific models, procedures and guidelines, and other applications.

code reuse The reuse of source code within sections of an application and potentially across multiple applications.

component reuse The reuse of pre-built, fully encapsulated components in the development of your application.

domain-component reuse The reuse of pre-built, large-scale domain components that encapsulate cohesive portions of your business domain.

framework reuse The reuse of collections of classes that together implement the basic functionality of a common technical or business domain.

inheritance reuse The use of inheritance in your application to take advantage of behavior implemented in existing classes.

pattern reuse The reuse of publicly documented approaches, called patterns, to solving common problems.

template reuse The reuse of a common set of layouts for key development artifacts—documents, models, and source code—within your organization.

---

reuse is generally more effective than template reuse. An interesting point that Figure 10.10 shows is that the least productive type of reuse is code reuse; in fact, code reuse can even provide a negative productivity rate when defective code is copied several times. Figure 10.10 also shows that domain-component reuse is the most productive form of reuse, although because it is based on an architecture-driven approach to modeling (Ambler, 1998b), it is also the most difficult reuse approach to achieve.

10.6.1.1 Code Reuse

Code reuse, the most common kind of reuse, is the reuse of source code within sections of an application and potentially across multiple applications. At its best, code reuse is accomplished through the sharing of common classes and/or collections of functions and procedures. At worst, code reuse is accomplished by copying and then modifying existing code. A sad reality of our industry is that code copying is often the only form of reuse practiced by developers.

Code reuse is often the only form of reuse practiced by developers.

A key aspect of code reuse is that you have access to the source code—if necessary, you either modify it yourself or have someone else modify it for you. This is both good and bad; by looking at the code you can determine, albeit often slowly, whether or not you want to use it. At the same time, by releasing the full source code to you, the original developer is less motivated to document it properly (see below), increasing the time that it takes you to understand it and consequently decreasing the benefit of it to you. The main advantage of code reuse is that it reduces the amount of actual source code that you need to write, potentially decreasing both development and maintenance costs. The disadvantages are that its scope of effect is limited to programming, and that it often increases the coupling within an application.

10.6.1.2 Inheritance Reuse

Inheritance reuse refers to the use of inheritance in your application to take advantage of behavior implemented in existing classes. Inheritance is one of the fundamental concepts of object orientation, allowing you to model *is a*, *is like*, and/or *is kind of* relationships. For example, to develop a CheckingAccount class you start by having it inherit from SavingsAccount, directly reusing all of the behavior implemented in SavingsAccount.

The practice of using the inheritance relationship in your designs is referred to as inheritance reuse.

The advantage of inheritance reuse is that you take advantage of previously developed behavior, decreasing both the development time and the cost of your application. Unfortunately, inheritance reuse has several disadvantages. First, the misuse of inheritance will often result in developers missing an opportunity for component reuse, which, you will see, offers a much higher level of reuse. Second, novice developers will often skimp on inheritance regression testing (the running of superclass test cases on a subclass), resulting in a fragile class hierarchy that is difficult to maintain and enhance. As you can see, this is reuse; but at a prohibitive cost.

10.6.1.3 Template Reuse

Template reuse is the practice of using a common set of layouts for key deliverables—documents, models, and source code— within your organization. For example, you may choose to adopt common documentation templates for use cases, status reports, developer time sheets, change requests, user requirements, class files, and method documentation headers. The main advantage of documentation templates is that they increase the consistency and quality of your development artifacts, and the main disadvan-

The practice of reusing common layouts for deliverables is called template reuse.

tage is that developers have a tendency to modify templates for their own use and not share their changes with their coworkers.

10.6.1.4 Component Reuse

Component reuse is the use of pre-built, fully encapsulated components in the development of your application. Components are typically self-sufficient and encapsulate only one concept. Component reuse differs from code reuse in that you do not have access to the source code, and it differs from inheritance reuse in that it doesn't use subclassing. Common examples of components are Java beans and Microsoft's ActiveX™ components.

Third-party vendors develop and sell reusable components.

Component reuse has several advantages. First, component reuse offers a greater scope of reusability than either code or inheritance reuse because components are self sufficient, you literally plug them in and they work. Second, the widespread use of common platforms such as the Win32 operating system and the Java virtual machine provides a market that is large enough for third-party vendors to create and sell components to you at a low cost. The main disadvantage to component reuse is that, because components are small and encapsulate only one concept, you need a large library of them.

To start with components the easiest way is to start out with user interface widgets—slide bars, graphing components, and graphical buttons to name a few. But do not forget that there

DEFINITIONS

ActiveX An approach to developing reusable components defined by Microsoft.

Java bean A well-defined approach to developing reusable components with the Java programming language.

is more to an application than the user interface; you can get components that encapsulate operating system features, such as network access, and persistence features, such as access components to a relational database. If you are building your own components, make sure they do one thing only. For example, a user interface component for editing surface addresses is very reusable; you can use that on many editing screens. A component that edits a surface address, an email address, and a phone number is not as reusable; there are not as many opportunities where you will want all three of those features simultaneously. Instead, it would be better to build three reusable components and reuse each one where it is needed. When a component encapsulates one concept, we say that it is cohesive.

10.6.1.5 Framework Reuse

Framework reuse is the use of collections of classes that together implement the basic behavior of a common technical or business domain. Bassett (1997) advises that developers should use frameworks as the foundation from which they build an application; because the common eighty percent is in place already, they just need to add the remaining twenty percent specific to their application. Frameworks that implement the basic components of a graphical user interface are very common; frameworks for insurance, human resources, manufacturing, banking, and electronic commerce are now available. In fact, IBM (Lazar, 1998) now offers several frameworks written in Java for common business domains. Framework reuse represents a high level of reuse at the problem domain level.

The main advantages of frameworks are that they provide a good start at developing a solution for a problem domain and often encapsulate complex logic that would take years to develop from scratch. Unfortunately, framework reuse suffers from several disadvantages. The complexity of frameworks makes them difficult to master, requiring a lengthy learning process on the part of developers. Frameworks are often platform-specific and tie you into a single vendor, increasing the risk for your application. Although frameworks implement eighty percent of the required logic, it is often the easiest eighty percent; and the hard stuff, the business logic and processes that are unique to your organization, is still left for you to do. Frameworks rarely work together, unless they come from a common vendor or consortium of vendors, and often require you to change your business to fit the framework instead of the other way around.

> **DEFINITION**
>
> **framework** A reusable, almost-complete application that can be extended to produce custom applications.

10.6.1.6 Artifact Reuse

Artifact reuse is the use of previously created development artifacts—use cases, standards documents, domain-specific models, procedures and guidelines, and other applications—to give you a kick-start on a new project. There are several levels of artifact reuse, ranging from one-hundred-percent-pure reuse, wherein you take the artifact as is and use it on a new project, to "example reuse," wherein you look at the artifact to give you an idea about

The reuse of deliverables from previous projects is called artifact reuse.

how to proceed. For example, standards documents such as coding and user interface design standards are valuable artifacts to reuse between projects, as are modeling notation documents and methodology overview documents. It is also possible to reuse existing applications, either via a common data interface or by putting an object-oriented "wrapper" around them to make them look like normal classes.

Artifact reuse promotes consistency between projects, and it reduces the project management burden for your new project. Another advantage is that you can often purchase many artifacts or find them online: User interface standards are common for most platforms, coding standards for leading languages are often available, and standard object-oriented methodologies and modeling notations have been available for years. The main disadvantage of artifact reuse is that it is often perceived as "overhead reuse" by hard-core programmers; they simply move the standards and procedures binders from one desk to another and ignore them. The bottom line is that artifact reuse is an important and viable technique that should not be ignored.

> **DEFINITION**
>
> **wrapper** A collection of one or more classes that encapsulates access to non-OO technology to make it appear as if it is OO.

10.6.1.7 *Pattern Reuse*

Pattern reuse is the use of publicly documented approaches to solving common problems. Analysis and design patterns are often documented by a single class diagram, and are typically composed of one to five classes, whereas process patterns are depicted as a collection of tasks to be performed to solve a common process problem. With pattern reuse you're not reusing code; instead, you are reusing the thinking that goes behind the pattern. Patterns are a very high form of reuse that will prove to have a long life span, at least beyond the computer languages that you are currently using, and in the case of process patterns potentially even beyond the object-oriented paradigm itself.

The reuse of documented solutions to common problems is called pattern reuse.

Pattern reuse provides a high level of reuse that can be implemented across multiple languages and multiple platforms. Patterns encapsulate the most important aspect of development: the thinking that goes into the solution. Patterns increase the maintainability and enhanceability of your application by using common approaches to problems that are recognizable by any experienced object-oriented developer. The disadvantage of pattern reuse is that patterns do not provide an immediate solution; you still have to write the code that implements the pattern.

10.6.1.8 *Domain-Component Reuse*

Domain-component reuse is the identification and development of large-scale, reusable business components. A domain component is a collection of related domain/business classes that work together to support a cohesive set of responsibilities. For example, Figure 10.11 is a component diagram for a telecommunications firm that shows several domain components, each encapsulating many classes. The Service Offerings component encapsulates over a hundred classes, ranging from a collection of classes modeling long-distance calling plans to cable television packages to Internet

Figure 10.11.
A component model for a telecommunications firm

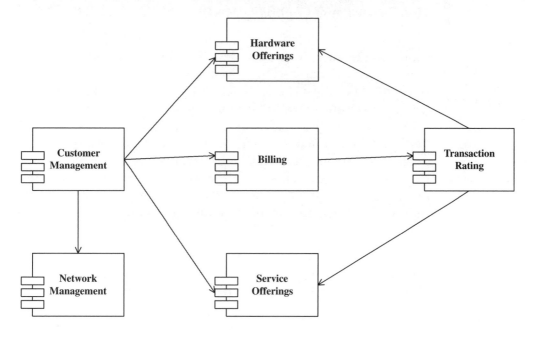

service packages. Domain components are initially identified by taking an architecture-driven approach to modeling (Chapter 8 in *Process Patterns*), and modified and enhanced in the course of developing new applications for your organization.

Domain components provide the greatest potential for reuse because they represent large-scale, cohesive bundles of business behaviors that are common to many applications. The component diagram shown in Figure 10.11, in combination with the corresponding specifications that describe the purpose and public interface of each component, provides a strategy for how application developers should organize their efforts so that any new domain development is performed in such a way as to be reusable by future applications. Domain components are effectively "architectural bins" into which business behaviors are organized and then later reused.

10.6.2 Reuse Throughout Your Project

There are many opportunities for reuse within the OOSP.

As you have seen, there are many potential sources of reuse throughout the Object-Oriented Software Process (OOSP). These opportunities are summarized by reuse approach and project phase in Table 10.5. The important lesson to take away from Table 10.5 is that you have a wide range of opportunities for reuse on your project—opportunities that you should take advantage of whenever possible.

10.6.3 The Reuse Capability Model

The Reuse Capability Model (RCM) provides a basis from which to develop a realistic Strategic Reuse Plan for your organization.

McClure (1997) describes the Reuse Capability Model (RCM), shown in Figure 10.12, which describes the various maturity levels at which your organization may stand with respect to reuse management. Like the Capability Maturity Model (CMM), the RCM describes maturity levels that your organization will need to work through to achieve the level of reuse that it desires. To successfully implement reuse management within your organization, McClure suggests that you first assess your organization to determine the maturity level at which it stands, and then, based on your assessment, develop a Strategic Reuse Plan describing how your organization intends to implement its reuse management strategy.

10.6.4 Reuse Tools

Although the success of your reuse efforts depends more on cultural issues, such as changing the mindset of your developers to

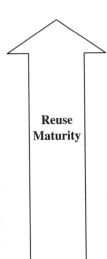

Reuse Maturity

Level 5. Optimized
Reuse is practiced across the enterprise, including systematic reuse driven by architectural/enterprise modeling.

Level 4. Planned
A reuse library exists and analysis is performed by projects to identify opportunities for reuse.

Level 3. Managed
Reuse is practiced at the domain level and is a business goal of your organization.

Level 2. Monitored
Reuse is practiced at a project level and management is aware of the reuse efforts.

Level 1. Initial
Reuse is resisted and/or practiced at an individual level.

Figure 10.12.
The Reuse Capability Model (RCM)

reuse the work of others, the technical issue of having adequate tools to support reuse is still important. McClure (1997) points out that developers need access to the following tools:

1. **A reuse repository.** This repository contains high-quality items that developers can reuse. Your reuse repository will contain items that were developed in house and items purchased off the shelf from a third party vendor.
2. **A configuration management system.** Your reuse repository will likely need to support projects using different hardware

---

DEFINITIONS

maturity level A well-defined evolutionary plateau toward achieving a mature software process. According to the Capability Maturity Model (CMM), for an organization to achieve a specific maturity level it must satisfy and institutionalize all of the key process areas (KPAs) for that level and the levels below.

Reuse Capability Model (RCM) A model which describes five maturity levels at which your organization may operate with respect to reuse.

strategic reuse plan Your organization's plan for implementing its reuse management approach, including a description of its reuse goals, its schedule, and its commitment to supporting reuse management.

TABLE 10.5. Opportunities for Reuse Throughout the OOSP

Reuse Approach	Initiate	Construct	Deliver	Maintain and Support
Artifact	• Previously defined requirements and use cases • Infrastructure artifacts • Skills evaluations • Research performed during technical assessments • Research performed about your organization's operations and support organizations	• Modeling standards and procedures • Testing standards, guidelines, and procedures • Peer review checklists • Coding standards • Software configuration management (SCM) procedures	• Testing standards, guidelines, and procedures • Installation procedures • Metrics analysis and reporting application • Support procedures	• Support procedures • Support tools • Agenda for configuration control board (CCB) meetings
Code		• Sharing of common classes and/or collections of functions and procedures • Copying and modifying existing code		

Reuse Approach	Initiate	Construct	Deliver and Support
Component	• Use of reusable components during user interface prototyping	• Inclusion of reusable components in design models • Use of reusable components during programming	
Domain-Component		• Domain-components are modeled by architectural modeling and reused during detailed modeling	
Framework	• Use of reusable frameworks during user interface prototyping	• Frameworks are used by programmers to increase their productivity • Frameworks are used during detailed analysis and design	

(continued)

TABLE 10.5. (continued)

Reuse Approach	Initiate	Construct	Deliver	Maintain and Support
Inheritance		• Inheritance is used during modeling and programming		
Pattern		• Analysis patterns • Design patterns		
Template	• Feasibility study • Project plan • Requirements documents • Risk assessment • Test plan • Use case specifications	• Modeling notations • Model documents and specifications	• Learning history • Operations documentation • Software problem reports (SPRs) • Staff assessments • Support documentation • User documentation	• Software change requests (SCRs) • Software problem reports (SPRs)

and software configurations, projects that will need to use different versions of the same component. The reuse repository is likely to incorporate archiving and version control qualities to support the needs of applications using different versions or configurations of the same item.

3. **A browser/search tool.** Developers need to be able to find the items that are available for reuse.

4. **A catalog.** Your browser/search tool will access your reuse catalog to find appropriate reusable items based on their descriptions. These descriptions, often indicating key words, are stored in the catalog.

10.6.5 Secrets of Success

I would like to share with you several tips and techniques for improving your reuse efforts:

1. **Recognize that reuse requires patience and investment.** Not all developers conceptualize reuse well, therefore your organization will need to do some education and training in reuse techniques.

2. **Recognize that reuse is performed across projects.** The real benefits of reuse are achieved across several projects, not just on a single one. Your problem domain requires many different applications to meet its needs, not just one. Many organizations fail at reuse because they do not understand its scope; reuse between projects is where you get your payback, not reuse within a single project. Many organizations prematurely give up on reuse when they do not achieve it on their first project, which is foolish when you consider that there is nothing to reuse to start with. This is why an architecture-driven approach to development is important: because it looks beyond the needs of a single project to the needs of the entire organization, and an important organizational need is to reuse existing work wherever possible.

3. **Recognize that you need to be a reuse consumer before you can become an effective reuse producer.** Reifer (1997) and McClure (1997) both advise that the developers best suited to become reuse producers are developers with several years of experience on a wide range of applications who have been reuse consumers on those projects. Until you have experi-

ence reusing the work of other people, how can you possibly know what how to develop something that is reusable?

4. **Recognize that there are many interrelated keys to reuse success.** Most organizations fail in their reuse efforts because they are looking for a quick fix, a silver bullet, to increase their inability to achieve the levels of reuse that they desire. The fact is that there is no quick fix; you need to develop an infrastructure that this able to support reuse. This infrastructure includes a common architecture to which all projects develop; common development standards; a common software process; a group of reuse producers/engineers; a reuse repository; and commitment from both management and developers to support reuse within your organization.

5. **Reuse requires a change in mindset.** Developers must be willing to work together, to reuse each other's work, to help the reuse efforts of your organization, and to plan to reuse items wherever possible. When you begin a project, the first thing you should do is determine what portions of your application can be reused from elsewhere. Perhaps someone else has built what you need, or perhaps you can purchase them. The second side of the coin is that you must be willing to share your work with other people so that they can reuse it. A good team lead will constantly be on the lookout for opportunities for reuse, and will promote and reward reuse within their team. An excellent approach is to look for reuse during inspections: During a model walkthrough, look for opportunities for inheritance and pattern reuse, and during code walkthroughs, look for component and code reuse. Reuse is an attitude, not a technology.

6. **Document reusable items.** You cannot reuse something if you do not know how to reuse it. Reusable items must be well documented and include one or more real-world examples of how to use them. In addition, the documentation should indicate when and when not to reuse an item, so that other developers understand the context in which it is to be used.

7. **It is not reusable until it has been reused.** My rule of thumb is that something is not reusable until it has been reused at least three times on three separate projects by three separate teams. You can attempt to design something for reuse, but you cannot claim success until it has actually been reused. Reusability is in the eye of the beholder, not in the eye of the creator.

<table>
<tr><td colspan="1">DEFINITIONS</td></tr>
</table>

DEFINITIONS

not-invented-here (NIH) syndrome A common myth in the information technology (IT) industry that states that developers are unwilling to reuse the work of others. The reality is that developers will only reuse high-quality work of other developers.

reuse consumer A developer who reuses the work of other developers.

reuse producer A developer who creates reusable items.

8. **Plan for reuse.** The only way you will get reuse is if you plan for it—you need to allocate the time and resources necessary to make your work reusable. If you do not step back and take the time to generalize your work, then it will never happen; project pressures will motivate you to put that work aside until you have the time to do it. The bottom line is that if reuse management is not part of your development process, then reuse likely will not happen.

9. **Understand the impediments to reuse.** McClure (1997) provides a list of common reasons for the failure of reuse management within organizations: The not-invented-here (NIH) syndrome, a lack of understanding of how to practice reuse, a belief that reuse is counter-creative, a lack of commitment, no reuse champion, no methodology to support reuse, a corporate culture and/or reward system that punishes reuse efforts, no training in reuse, an unwillingness to change the current way of working, a lack of management understanding of the value of reuse, a view of reuse as a high-risk technology, a lack of tools to support reuse, and having nothing to reuse. Your reuse management strategy will need to address these concerns.

10. **Recognize that word of mouth is often the way that people find reusable items.** Yes, you need a reuse repository, but in many ways a reuse repository is similar to the official chain of command in your organization—sometimes things get done through "official channels" and sometimes things get done through your informal network of contacts; similarly you sometimes find reusable items in the repository and you sometimes get them from your friends.

11. **Build systems from scratch only as a last resort.** My experience (Ambler, 1998a) is that source code is the root of all evil

in the software industry: think how easy maintenance would be without source code! McClure (1997) advises that your organization should strive to reuse as many things as possible, to avoid developing software unless it is absolutely necessary.

10.7 Metrics Management

Metrics management is the process of collecting, summarizing, and acting on measurements (metrics) to potentially improve both the quality of the software that your organization develops and the actual software process of your organization. As the old saying goes, "You cannot improve it if you cannot measure it." Metrics management provides the information critical to understanding the quality of the work that your project team has performed, and how effectively that work was performed. Metrics range from simple measurements of work effort, such as the number of hours invested to develop a model, to code quality measurements, such as the percentage of comments within your code.

In this section I will discuss the following topics:

- Why should you collect metrics?
- Collecting metrics throughout your project
- Metric categories
- Metrics applicable to the entire OOSP
- Establishing a metrics program
- The secrets of success

10.7.1 Why Should You Collect Metrics?

Landsbaum and Glass (1992) describe a host of reasons for collecting metrics:

- To support greater predictability and accuracy of schedules and estimates
- To support quality assurance efforts by identifying the techniques that work best and the areas that need more work
- To support productivity and process improvement efforts by measuring how efficient you are and by indicating where you need to improve
- To improve management control by tracking both projects and people

- To improve the motivation of developers by making them aware of what works and what doesn't
- To improve communications by describing accurately what is happening, and by identifying trends early on

There are many reasons to collect metrics.

10.7.2 Collecting Metrics Throughout Your Project

As you can see in Table 10.6, there is a wide range of potential metrics, described in the chapters for the projects stages in which they are taken, that you may decide to collect throughout your project. In fact, there are so many that you need to narrow the list down to the handful that are important to you—a topic discussed below.

10.7.3 Metric Categories

An interesting observation about the metrics listed in Table 10.6 is that there are clearly several different types to collect. In fact, by understanding the types of metrics available, you are able to make better-informed decisions as to which ones you wish to collect. Table 10.7 describes several categories of metrics.

10.7.4 Metrics Applicable to the Entire OOSP

Looking at the categories described in the previous section it becomes clear that we may be missing a few metrics in Table 10.6. The reason for this is simple: when I described each project phase and project stage, I chose to identify only specific metrics for that process pattern. What I have yet to do is describe metrics common to all phases and stages of the Object-Oriented Software Process (OOSP). Table 10.8 describes several metrics applicable to all of the project phases and project stages of the OOSP.

DEFINITIONS

calendar time The overall time that it takes to complete a project, measured from the start of a project to its end. A project that starts on May 1st, then ends on May 24th of the same year, has a calendar time of twenty-four days.

work day A standard amount of time, measured in hours, that your organization considers a day. Most organizations define a standard work day as being seven, seven-and-a-half, or eight hours.

work month A standard amount of time corresponding to the average number of work days in an average month. Also known as a man month, person month, staff month, or engineering month.

TABLE 10.6. Potential Metrics to Collect Throughout the OOSP

Stage	Potential Metrics
Initiate: Define and Validate Initial Requirements	• Number of use cases • Function/feature points
Initiate: Define Initial Management Documents	• Level of risk • Project size
Initiate: Justify	• Cost/benefit breakpoint
Initiate: Define Infrastructure	• Number of reused infrastructure artifacts • Number of introduced infrastructure artifacts
Construct: Model	• Requirements instability • Method count of a class • Number of instance attributes of a class • Inheritance tree depth • Number of children of a class • Number of class attributes • Number of ignored methods within a subclass
Construct: Program	• Requirements instability • Method size • Method response • Comments per method • Percentage of commented methods • Global usage
Construct: Generalize	• Number of candidate items for generalization • Percentage of items generalized • Effort required to generalize an item
Construct: Test in the Small	• Percentage of deliverables reviewed • Time to fix defects • Defect recurrence • Defect type recurrence

(continued)

10.7.5 Establishing a Metrics Program

To establish a metrics program within your organization, you must begin by defining what you wish to measure, which in turn should be based on your organization's goals and objectives. Henderson-Sellers (1995) suggests several possible goals for your metrics program, including: cost and schedule estimation from your requirements analysis; predicting likely maintenance cost from your source code; evaluating the reusability of designs, frame-

TABLE 10.6. (continued)

Stage	Potential Metrics
Deliver: Test in the Large	• Time to fix defects • Defect recurrence • Defect type recurrence • Defect severity count • Defect source count
Deliver: Rework	• Work effort to fix a defect • Percentage of SPRs reworked
Deliver: Release	• Enhancements implemented per application release • Problems closed per release • Percentage of customers trained • Average training time per person
Deliver: Assess	• Number of lessons learned • Percentage of staff members assessed
Maintain and Support: Support	• Average response time • Average resolution time • Support request volume • Support backlog • Support request aging • Support engineer efficiency • Reopened support requests
Maintain and Support: Identify Defects and Enhancements	• Mean time between failures • Software change requests (SCRs) opened and closed

Table 10.7. Metric categories

Categories	Description
Cost	Cost metrics measure the amount of the money invested in a project. Examples of cost metrics include effort expended and your investment in training.
Productivity	Productivity metrics measure the effectiveness of your organization's infrastructure. Examples of productivity metrics include the number of reused infrastructure items and trend analysis of effort expended over given periods of time.
Quality	Quality metrics measure the effectiveness of your quality assurance efforts. Examples of quality metrics include the percentage of deliverables reviewed and defect type recurrence.
Requirements	Requirements metrics measure the effectiveness of your requirements definition and validation efforts. Examples of requirements metrics include requirements instability and number of use cases.
Schedule	Schedule metrics measure the accuracy of your proposed schedule to your actual schedule. Examples of schedule metrics include the calendar time expended to perform a task or project phase.
Size	Size metrics measure, as the name suggests, the size of your development efforts. Examples of size metrics include the number of methods of a class and the function/feature point count.
Testing	Testing metrics measure the effectiveness of your testing efforts. Examples of testing metrics include the defect severity count and the defect source count.

works, and source code; and allocating resources effectively to project teams.

Start by defining your goals.

The next step is to assign responsibility for your metrics program to someone who, based on the defined goals, will research potential metrics that reflect those goals. Although this book suggests many metrics, I highly recommend several books (Grady, 1992; Lorenz and Kidd, 1994; Goldberg and Rubin, 1995; Booch,

TABLE 10.8. Metrics Applicable to All of the Phases and Stages of the OOSP

Metric	Description
Calendar time expended	This schedule metric is a measure of the calendar time to complete a task, where a task may be as small as the creation of a deliverable or as large as a project phase or an entire project.
Overtime	This cost metric is a measure of the amount of overtime for a project and can be collected as either an amount of work days or a percentage of overall effort. This metric is often subdivided by overtime for work directly related to development, such as programming or testing, and by indirect effort, such as training or team coordination.
Staff turnover	This productivity metric is a measure of the number of people gained and lost over a defined period of time, typically a calendar month. This metric is often collected by position/role and can be used to help define human resources requirements and the growth rate of your information technology (IT) department.
Work effort expended	This cost metric is a measure of the amount of work expended to complete a task, typically measured in work days or work months. This metric is often collected by task (see above).

Research and select a small handful of metrics that support your goals.

1996; Ambler, 1998) that describe in detail a wide range of metrics. Once you have researched the potential metrics, you then need to select a small handful to collect. The best metrics programs start small and grow, if needed, from there.

You need to sell your metrics program and provide tools for collecting and analyzing metrics.

The next step is to sell your metrics program to the people who will be collecting them. A key selling point to a metrics program is the ease of collecting metrics; metrics that are difficult to collect will likely not be. The implication is that you need to purchase tools to automatically collect, and potentially analyze, your chosen metrics. An important tool is a metrics database that allows you to store and then report on the metrics that you collect.

Train developers and management in metrics.

The final step to establishing a metrics program within your organization is to train and educate both developers and management. Developers need to understand why the metrics are being collected and why they need to be collected, and management needs to understand how to use the information effectively.

Small is beautiful.

Grady (1992) warns that over ninety percent of all metrics programs fail in the first year because of the decision to collect too many metrics. The implication: start small. A good rule of thumb is that if you cannot remember the values of the metrics that you are collecting then you are likely collecting too many.

10.7.6 Secrets of Success

This section describes a collection of tips and techniques for improving your metrics efforts:

1. **Keep it simple.** Effective metrics programs start with a few key metrics that are easy to collect, often automatically. The important thing is to not burden your developers.
2. **Collect metrics in a timely fashion.** Metrics have value only if you have sufficient time to understand and act on them.
3. **Do not allow the bureaucrats to get involved.** The quickest way to have a metrics program fail is to put it in the hands of your accounting department. Accountants will often focus on obtaining precise, accurate measurements, a virtue in the accounting world, whereas the true value of metrics is their indication of general trends, not their precision (Landsbaum and Glass, 1992).
4. **Understand that measuring something is likely to improve it.** When people know that something is being measured, any-

thing at all, they will strive to improve it. This is simply human nature.

5. **Do not use metrics against developers.** Another way to ensure the failure of your metrics program, either through people stopping their efforts to collect metrics or the reporting of false metrics, is to begin measuring people based on the metrics collected. You can use metrics to criticize the process followed and the products developed, but not the people following the processes to develop the products.

6. **Make metrics available to developers.** Although you should not use metrics against people, you should still make them available to them. As a developer I would like to know the number of defects found in the code that I write, and the effort required to fix them, so that I can improve the way that I work. I would like to know my personal productivity levels compared to the average within my organization to know where I stand. Yes, you should not use metrics against your staff, but you should still allow them to benefit from the metrics if they so desire.

7. **Combine metrics.** A common mistake is to use a single metric to measure the effectiveness of a process or tool. For example, a new technique may reduce the time that you take to develop an application, which sounds really good; but when you combine that metric test metrics, you discover that you have increased the number of defects in your software, resulting in a greater overall cost to your organization when maintenance is taken into consideration. The lesson to be learned is that you should not use one metric to the exclusion of others.

8. **Train everyone in metrics.** You need to train both developers and management in the collection and use of metrics. If people do not understand your metrics program, they likely will not support it.

9. **Understand the criteria for success.** Henderson-Sellers (1995) indicates that your metrics program should be considered successful when metrics are actively used in decision making, they are communicated and accepted outside your information technology (IT) department, and your program lasts longer than two years

10.8 Managing Deliverables

Deliverable management is key to the management of a project, to the successful operation of an application, and to the successful maintenance and support of an application. A deliverable is any information, either printed or electronic, that describes all or part of an application or system. Deliverables may be internal, used only by members of the project team, or external, delivered as part of the application. Deliverables may be for developers, for users, for support staff, or for operations staff. The review and update of deliverables is a fundamental part of quality assurance, discussed in Section 10.4, and the existence of accurate and complete documentation is a fundamental part of risk management. Deliverables are created and updated by all members of a project team throughout the entire project.

Many deliverables—models, source code, documents, and plans for example—are created throughout the OOSP. Therefore they need to be managed appropriately. A key concept of deliverables management is that if it is not written down, dated, distributed, and then agreed to, then it is not real. Another key concept for managing deliverables effectively is that every deliverable, including models and documents, should be placed under configuration control.

10.8.1 Software Configuration Management

Any deliverable worth creating is worth putting under SCM control.

A critical issue for the successful management of deliverables is its use of software configuration management (SCM) techniques. Compton and Conner (1994) define SCM as a set of engineering procedures for tracking and documenting software, including its related deliverables, throughout their life cycles to ensure that all changes are recorded and the current state of the software is known and reproducible. My experience is that any deliverable worth creating is worth putting under SCM control; if I am going to invest my time building something, then I should also invest the time to ensure that it is accurately tracked and documented. SCM was covered in detail in the description of the Construct phase (Ambler, 1998b).

10.8.2 The Qualities of Good Deliverables

Steinman and Yates (1995) believe that there are four principles which define a good deliverable. The first is conceptual integrity, which is when a deliverable describes an item on the same conceptual level as that item. For example, a class specification describes a single class and a class model describes a collection of classes; we do not have a single deliverable that attempts to document both the classes of an application and the details of those classes all on "one page." The second principle is constant accuracy, the quality that the deliverable is in synch with the item that it describes. For example, a class specification should accurately describe the source code that implements the class specified. The third principle is that of accessibility, the concept that everyone has access to the deliverables that they need to do their jobs, and that the right people are able to modify the documentation. The fourth principle is measurability, the concept that all deliverables should be reviewed and accepted by the project team and/or the users of the application being built.

Deliverables should have conceptual integrity, be in synch with the items that they describe, be accessible, and be measurable.

Booch (1995) believes that a good deliverable should further an understanding of your application's desired and actual behavior and structure. A deliverable should also serve to communicate the application's architectural vision, and is likely to provide a description of details that cannot be directly inferred from the software itself or from executable artifacts. My experience is that good deliverables are like good code: they are cohesive, loosely coupled, maintainable, extensible, and understandable.

10.8.3 Deliverables Throughout Your Project

Table 10.9 summarizes the major deliverables that are input into, created by, and then output from each serial project phase. This table was created based on the process pattern for each phase; as a result, several deliverables that are created during a given phase are "rolled up" into a single deliverable that is output from the phase. For example, during the Initiate phase, the Group Memory, Project Plan, Master Test/QA, and Risk Assessment are all included in the Management Documents deliverable. However, it should be noted that some deliverables are created and then "consumed" within a single project phase. For example, a feasibility study is created during the Initiate phase, but is not output from the phase, as it is used to obtain the funding for a project. The deliverables that are consumed within the same phase as they are created are labeled with an asterisk (*).

TABLE 10.9. The Key Deliverables for Each Project Phase

Phase	Input	Creates	Outputs
Initiate	• Maintenance Changes	• Feasibility Study * • Group Memory • Master Test/QA Plan • Project Funding • Project Plan • Project Scope • Recommendation * • Requirements Document • Risk Assessment • Tailored Software Process • Team Definition • Tool Selection	• Initial Requirements • Management Documents • Project Charter • Project Funding • Project Infrastructure
Construct	• Initial Requirements • Maintenance Changes • Management Documents • Project Charter • Project Funding • Project Infrastructure	• Packaged Application • Source Code • Test Results • Tested Artifacts • Reusable Items • Models • Requirements Allocation Matrix (RAM)	• Initial Plans • Management Documents • Models • Packaged Application • Requirements Allocation Matrix (RAM) • Source Code

Phase	Input	Creates	Outputs
Deliver	• Initial Plans • Management Documents • Models • Packaged Application • Requirements Allocation Matrix (RAM) • Source Code	• Learning History * • Operations Procedures • Process Improvement Plan • Project Assessment • Requirements Allocation Matrix (RAM) • Staff Assessments • Support Procedures • Test Results * • Tested Application • User Documentation	• Models • Operations Procedures • Requirements Allocation Matrix (RAM) • Support Procedures • Tested Application • User Documentation
Maintain and Support	• Models • Operations Procedures • Requirements Allocation Matrix (RAM) • Support Procedures • Tested Application • User Documentation	• Maintenance changes • Software change requests (SCRs) • Solutions to support requests *	• Maintenance Changes

> **DEFINITIONS**
>
> **group memory** A record of what your project team accomplished, decisions made by your team and the reasoning behind them, deferred decisions, and the lessons learned on your project. A group memory provides a mechanism to record this information when it is first recognized so that it is not lost.
>
> **master test/quality assurance (QA) plan** A document that describes your testing and quality assurance policies and procedures, as well as the detailed test plans for each portion of your application.
>
> **project plan** A collection of several project management deliverables, including but not limited to a project overview, a project schedule, a project estimate, a team definition, and a risk assessment. Project plans are a deliverable of the Initiate phase and are updated regularly throughout a project.
>
> **project phase** The large components of the OOSP that are performed in a serial manner. The four project phases are Initiate, Construct, Deliver, and Maintain and Support. A project phase is depicted by a process pattern.
>
> **risk assessment** A document indicating potential factors, called risks, that would harm the project if they were to occur. A risk assessment is used to identify risks so that they may be dealt with appropriately. Risk assessments are a deliverable of the Initiate phase and are updated regularly throughout a project.

10.8.4 Secrets of Success

I would like to share with you several tips and techniques to improve your deliverable management efforts:

1. **Place key deliverables under configuration management control.** If you do not use configuration management (CM) techniques to manage your deliverables, you will soon discover that some have been lost, some have been overwritten by previous versions, and some have been updated by people who were not authorized to do so. You can and should place all deliverables under CM control, not just your source code.
2. **Every deliverable has a quality gate.** My experience is that if you can build something, then you can test/validate it. The implication is that every deliverable should go through a quality gate, a process such as a peer review in which it is validated as being of sufficient quality for your organization.
3. **Every deliverable should be worth it.** Maguire (1994) suggests that each deliverable that you produce have positive value,

that every deliverable asked for is worth the resources spent to produce it.

4. **Document key information.** A basic fundamental of science is that if you didn't write it down, then it did not happen. We have all worked on legacy systems where there was little or no documentation, or even worse, the documentation was inaccurate. If it is important, document it.

5. **Document both what you did and did not do.** Constantine (1995) points out that it is just as important to know what alternatives you considered and why you didn't take them—a key reason why project teams should maintain a group memory.

10.9 Managing Infrastructure

Infrastructure management is a cross-project effort that includes the architectural and enterprise modeling efforts of the Model stage (Ambler, 1998b), and the definition and support of your organization's processes, standards, guidelines, and chosen toolsets. The Define Infrastructure stage (Ambler, 1998b) is a key function of infrastructure management because it defines and/or selects the infrastructure for a single project. However, from the point of view of your organization the Define Infrastructure stage is not sufficient to promote a common infrastructure between projects, hence the need for infrastructure management.

There are four key process areas (KPAs) of the Capability Maturity Model (CMM) applicable to infrastructure management. The first KPA is called Organization Process Definition, which focuses on developing and maintaining your organization's standard software process, along with related process assets such as descriptions of software life cycles, process tailoring guidelines and criteria, your organization's software process database, and a library of software process-related documentation. The second KPA is Integrated Software Management, which involves the integration of both software engineering and management activities into a coherent, defined process for each project that is tailored from the standard software process of your organization. This includes developing the project's defined software process and

managing the software project based on this process. The third KPA is Organization Process Focus, which involves developing and maintaining an understanding of your organization's and project's software processes and coordinating the activities to assess, develop, maintain, and improve these processes. The fourth KPA is Quantitative Process Management, which is the act of establishing goals for, and then measuring, the performance of a project's defined software process.

10.9.1 Infrastructure Throughout Your Project

Infrastructure management is a major component of several stages of the OOSP. First, the Define Infrastructure stage (Ambler, 1998b) was specifically included in the OOSP to provide an explicit mechanism for tailoring your organization's infrastructure to meet the specific needs of a project. Second, the architectural and enterprise modeling aspects of the Model stage (Ambler, 1998b) specifically address the need to create a set of common, high-level enterprise/architectural models for your organization. Third, the Generalize

The Define Infrastructure, Model, Generalize, and Assess stages explicitly grow and evolve your organization's infrastructure.

stage (Chapter 10 in *Process Patterns*) addresses the need to evolve your organization's infrastructure through the opportunistic reuse and improvement of the deliverables of your project. Finally, the Assess stage (Chapter 6) is an explicit process pattern for improving your software process through learning from your experiences.

Your organization's infrastructure is used implicitly during all project stages and phases, including but not limited to the use of standard processes, guidelines, standards, and tools.

10.9.2 Secrets of Success

Here are several tips and techniques that lead to successful management of your infrastructure:

1. **Your infrastructure group is not an ivory tower.** The infrastructure group is there to support and enhance the efforts of the project teams; it is not there to develop white papers simply for the sake of developing white papers, or to develop "really cool" software components that nobody will ever use.
2. **Your infrastructure efforts must be separately financed.** Infrastructure management, for the most part, is a cross-project effort that must have its own source of funding beyond that of single projects. Many organizations have experimented

DEFINITIONS

architectural modeling High-level modeling, either of the business or technical domain, whose goal is to provide a common, overall vision of your domain. Architectural models provide a base from which detailed modeling will begin.

domain architecture A collection of high-level models that describe the problem domain. Domain architectures are typically documented by high-level use cases, use-case diagrams, and class models that describe the various subdomains and the relationships between them.

enterprise modeling The act of modeling an organization and its external environment from a business, not an information system, viewpoint.

guideline A description, ideally with an example provided, of how something should be done. It is recommended, but not required, that you follow guidelines—unlike standards, which are mandatory.

infrastructure artifact An item, such as your organization's software process, a standard, a guideline, or a chosen tool, that is common between project teams to build applications to support your organization.

infrastructure management A cross-project effort that includes your organization's architectural and enterprise modeling efforts, as well as the definition and support of your organization's processes, standards, guidelines, and chosen toolsets.

process A series of actions in which one or more inputs are used to produce one or more outputs.

standard A description, ideally with an example provided, of how something must be done. It is required that you follow standards (unlike guidelines which are optional).

technical architecture A set of models and documents that describes the technical components of an application, including but not limited to the hardware, software, middleware, persistence mechanisms, and operating systems to be deployed.

with infrastructure financing strategies such as having projects pay for reusable components. My advice is to simply treat infrastructure management as an investment, and then do what it takes to maximize the return on your investment. Yes, complex funding schemes are academically interesting for your accountants, but your really goal is to develop software, not financing nightmares.

3. **Use external sources.** You do not need to build your infrastructure from scratch; in fact, the vast majority of it can be purchased off the shelf. There are mature industry standards and guidelines for many of the tasks that you perform, a wide selection of tools available to you, and many libraries of reusable components and documentation templates.
4. **Work closely with reuse and quality assurance efforts.** Your organization's infrastructure, reuse, and quality assurance efforts are closely linked to each other. In many ways, your infrastructure is simply a collection of standards, guidelines, processes, and tools that are of proven quality and are reusable.
5. **Train everyone in your infrastructure.** People must understand your organization's chosen tools, standards, guidelines, and processes if they are to use them effectively. It is not enough to simply put your architectural models on the wall or your standards on a Web site somewhere.
6. **Recognize that each project may need to tailor the infrastructure.** This is what the Define Infrastructure stage is all about.

10.10 What You Have Learned in This Chapter

In this chapter you have discovered how the project and cross-project tasks—Project Management, People Management, Training And Education, Quality Assurance, Risk Management, Reuse Management, Metrics Management, Deliverable Management, and Infrastructure Management—of the OOSP work. This discussion included how the project and cross-project tasks support your software development efforts, the issues surrounding their management, and many tips and techniques.

10.11 References and Suggested Reading

Ambler, S.W. 1995. *The Object Primer: The Application Developer's Guide To Object Orientation*. NY: SIGS Books.

Ambler, S. W. 1998a. *Building Object Applications That Work—Your Step-By-Step Handbook for Developing Robust Systems with Object Technology*. New York: SIGS Books.

Ambler, S. W. 1998b. *Process Patterns—Building Large-Scale Systems Using Object Technology.* New York: SIGS Books/Cambridge University Press.

Barbour, D. 1996. What Makes a Good Project Fail? *Object Magazine* 6 (September), 60–62.

Bassett, P. G. 1997. *Framing Software Reuse: Lessons From the Real World.* Upper Saddle River, New Jersey: Prentice-Hall, Inc.

Booch, G. 1995. Practical Objects: Documenting Object-Oriented Systems. *Object Magazine* 5(June), 87–88.

Booch, G. 1996. *Object Solutions—Managing the Object-Oriented Project.* Menlo Park, California: Addison Wesley Publishing Company, Inc.

Brown, W., Malveau, R, McCormick, H., Mowbray, T. (1998). *AntiPatterns: Refactoring Software, Architectures, and Projects in Crisis.* New York:John Wiley & Sons.

Compton, S. B. and Conner, G. R. 1994. *Configuration Management for Software.* New York: Van Nostrand Reinhold.

Constantine, L. L. 1995. *Constantine on Peopleware.* Englewood Cliffs, New Jersey: Yourdon Press.

Coplien, J.O. (1995). *A Generative Development-Process Pattern Language.* Pattern Languages of Program Design, Addison Wesley Longman, Inc., pp. 183-237.

DeMarco, T. 1997. *The Deadline: A Novel About Project Management.* New York: Dorset House Publishing.

Goldberg, A. and Rubin, K. S. 1995. *Succeeding With Objects: Decision Frameworks for Project Management.* Reading, Massachusetts: Addison-Wesley Publishing Company Inc.

Grady, R. B. 1992. *Practical Software Metrics For Project Management and Process Improvement.* Englewood Cliffs, New Jersey: Prentice-Hall, Inc.

Harrison, N.B. (1996). *Organizational Patterns for Teams.* Pattern Languages of Program Design 2, Addison-Wesley Publishing Company., pp. 345-352.

Henderson-Sellers, B. 1995. The Goals of an OO Metrics Programme. *Object Magazine* 5(October), 73–79,95.

Humphrey, W. S. 1997. *Managing Technical People: Innovation, Teamwork, And The Software Process.* Reading, Massachusetts: Addison-Wesley Longman, Inc.

Jacobson, I., Griss, M., and Jonsson, P. 1997. *Software Reuse: Archi-*

tecture, Process, and Organization for Business Success. New York: ACM Press.

Karolak, D. W. 1996. *Software Engineering Risk Management*. Los Alimitos, California: IEEE Computer Society Press.

Korson, T. D. and Vaishnavi, V. K. 1995. The Object Technology Center. *Object Magazine* 5 (October), 31–38.

Korson, T. D. and Vaishnavi, V. K. 1996. *Object Technology Centers of Excellence*. Greenwich, Massachusetts: Manning Publications Co.

Landsbaum, J. B. and Glass, R. L. 1992. *Measuring and Motivating Maintenance Programmers*. Englewood Cliffs, New Jersey: Prentice-Hall Inc.

Lato, K. 1997. Learn to Learn: Training on New Technology. *Journal of Object-Oriented Programming* 10 (March–April), 24–29.

Lazar, B. 1998. IBM's San Francisco Project. *Software Development* 6(February), 40–46.

Lilly, S. 1995. The Top Ten Ways to Trash Your OT Training Program. *Object Magazine* 5 (March-April), 86–88.

Lorenz, M. 1995. Project Practicalities: Rules to Live By. *Smalltalk Report* 4 (July-August), 22–25.

Lorenz, M. and Kidd, J. 1994. *Object-Oriented Software Metrics*. Englewood Cliffs, New Jersey: Prentice-Hall.

Maguire, S. 1994. *Debugging the Development Process*. Redmond, Washington: Microsoft Press.

McClure, C. 1997. *Software Reuse Techniques: Adding Reuse to the Systems Development Process*. Upper Saddle River, New Jersey: Prentice-Hall, Inc.

Reifer, D. J. 1997. *Practical Software Reuse: Strategies for Introducing Reuse Concepts in Your Organization*. New York: John Wiley and Sons, Inc.

Schedlbauer, M. J. 1997. The Benefits of Mentoring. *Journal of Object-Oriented Programming* 10 (March-April), 28–29.

Steinman, J. and Yates, B. 1995. Managing Objects: Managing Project Documents. *Smalltalk Report* 4 (June), 22–25.

Strassmann, P. A. 1997. *The Squandered Computer: Evaluating the Business Alignment of Information Technologies*. New Canaan, Connecticut: The Information Economics Press.

Webster, B. F. 1995. *Pitfalls of Object-Oriented Development*. New York: M&T Books.

Whitaker, K. 1994. *Managing Software Maniacs: Finding, Managing, and Rewarding a Winning Development Team.* New York: John Wiley and Sons, Inc.

Whitenack, B. and Bounds, B. B. 1995. The Keys to a Truly Successful Smalltalk Project. *Object Magazine* 5 (June), 76–78.

Yourdon, E. 1997. *Death March: The Complete Software Developer's Guide to Surviving "Mission Impossible" Projects.* Upper Saddle River, New Jersey: Prentice-Hall , Inc.

Chapter 11

Introducing the OOSP into Your Organization

UP TO this point this book has concentrated on describing the Object-Oriented Software Process (OOSP), in the form of a collection of process patterns, that your organization can tailor for your specific needs. What I have not described until now is how you can do this. As Figure 11.1 shows, the OOSP is complex, composed of four serial project phases, fourteen iterative project stages, and nine project/cross-project tasks. The process patterns presented in this book have been proven to work in practice; your goal is to make them work within your organization.

Your goal is to successfully introduce the appropriate process patterns into your organization.

The reality of process improvement is that you cannot make all of the changes that you want to immediately; it is simply too great a change for your organization to absorb at once. This is why we have efforts such as the Software Engineering Institute's (SEI's) Capability Maturity Model (CMM) efforts (SEI, 1995) and the Software Process Improvement Capability Determination (SPICE) efforts (Emam, Drouin, and Melo, 1998) of the International Standards Organization (ISO). Both of these organizations suggest that you prioritize the process improvements that your organization needs to make, expect that it will take several years to make the needed changes, and expect that you will experience difficulties while doing so. Experience shows that organizations that try to make immediate, large-scale process changes are likely to fail doing so. This chapter provides proven advice for introducing the OOSP into your organization successfully.

Introducing the OOSP into your organization must be gradual to be successful.

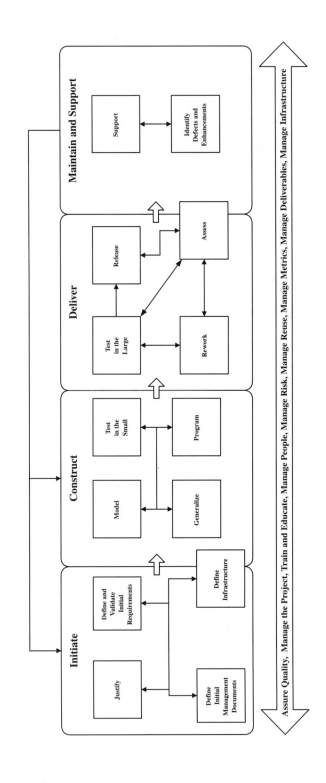

Figure 11.1.
The Object-Oriented Software Process (OOSP)

The good news is that competent technical workers will focus on process and process improvement whether you tell them to or not (DeMarco, 1997). In fact, many process improvement efforts are the result of a grass-roots uprising of developers who have grown tired of canceled projects, of endless months of overtime trying to meet an unrealistic schedule, of producing low-quality products because of a focus on coding too early in the life cycle of a project.

11.1 The Capability Maturity Model (CMM)

I would like to begin by reviewing the Capability Maturity Model (CMM), described in detail in *Process Patterns* (Ambler, 1998b), as it provides insight into the order in which you should consider introducing the process patterns described in this book. I begin this section by describing the five maturity levels of the CMM, then I

DEFINITIONS

Capability Maturity Model (CMM) A strategy, defined by the Software Engineering Institute (SEI), that describes the key elements of an effective software process.

Object-Oriented Software Process (OOSP) A collection of process patterns that together describe a complete process for developing, maintaining, and supporting software.

pattern The description of a general solution to a common problem or issue from which a detailed solution to a specific problem may be determined. Software development patterns come in many flavors, including but not limited to analysis patterns, design patterns, and process patterns.

process pattern A pattern which describes a proven, successful approach and/or series of actions for developing software.

project phase The large components of the OOSP that are performed in a serial manner. The four project phases are Initiate, Construct, Deliver, and Maintain and Support. A project phase is depicted by a process pattern.

project stage The components of a project phase, performed in an iterative manner, that make up a project phase. For example, the project stages that make up the Construct phase are Model, Program, Generalize, and Test in the Small. A project stage is depicted by a process pattern.

Software Process Improvement and Capability dEtermination (SPICE) An ISO software process improvement project.

> **DEFINITIONS**
>
> **key process area (KPA)** An issue that must be addressed to achieve a specific Capability Maturity Model (CMM) maturity level.
>
> **maturity level** A well-defined evolutionary plateau toward achieving a mature software process. According to the Capability Maturity Model (CMM), for an organization to achieve a specific maturity level it must satisfy and institutionalize all of the key process areas (KPAs) for that level and the levels below.

describe the key process areas (KPAs) of each maturity level, and then show how the process patterns of the OOSP map to the key process areas of the CMM. This mapping is critical to your determination of the order in which you will introduce process patterns within your organization—the knowledge that you must start at the first maturity level and work your way up, and knowing which process patterns map to each maturity level, indicates the order in which you should introduce process patterns into your organization.

11.1.1 The Five CMM Maturity Levels

The CMM defines five maturity levels—evolutionary plateaus toward achieving a mature software process—that an organization can attain with respect to their software process. The five maturity levels of the CMM are shown in Figure 11.2 and described in Table 11.1. All organizations are at least at Level 1: Initial, the lowest level of software process maturity, by definition.

As you can see, each maturity level builds upon aspects and features of the previous levels. This implies that for your organization to achieve CMM Level 4 is must satisfy the requirements for

Figure 11.2.
The five CMM maturity levels[1]

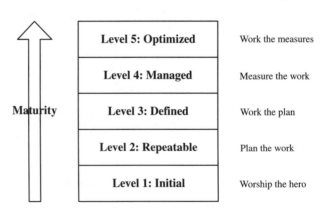

Level 5: Optimized	Work the measures
Level 4: Managed	Measure the work
Level 3: Defined	Work the plan
Level 2: Repeatable	Plan the work
Level 1: Initial	Worship the hero

Maturity

---

[1]The descriptions of the right side are taken from Whittington (1996).

TABLE 11.1. The Five CMM Maturity Levels

Level	Description	Characteristics
1. Initial	The software process is ad hoc, and occasionally even chaotic. Few processes are defined, and success depends on individual effort and heroics.	• Overcommitment is common. • During a crisis, planned procedures are abandoned and project teams revert to coding and testing. • Success depends on having an exceptional manager and a seasoned and effective software team. • The software process is effectively a black box to the user community. Resources go in and software potentially comes out.
2. Repeatable	Basic project management processes are established to track cost, schedule, and functionality. The necessary process discipline is in place to repeat earlier successes on projects with similar applications.	• The planning and management of new projects is based on experience with similar projects. • Process capability is enhanced at the project level by establishing basic process management techniques. • Software requirements and deliverables are baselined. • Processes often differ between projects, reducing opportunities for teamwork and reuse. • The user community is provided visibility into the project at defined occasions, typically via the review and acceptance of major project deliverables, allowing limited management control.

(continued)

TABLE 11.1. (continued)

Level	Description	Characteristics
3. Defined	The software process for both management and development activities is documented, standardized, and integrated into a standard software process for your entire organization. All projects use an approved, tailored version of the organization's standard software process for developing and maintaining software.	• A standard process is used on all projects, with possible tailoring. • Management has good insight into technical progress on the project. • Defined processes allow the user community greater visibility into the project and enable accurate and rapid status updates.
4. Managed	Detailed measures, called metrics, of the software process and product quality are collected. Both the software process and products are quantitatively understood and controlled.	• Productivity and quality are measured for important software process activities across all projects. • The user community can establish an accurate, quantitative understanding of the software process capability of your organization/team and the project risk before the project begins.
5. Optimized	Continuous process improvement is enabled by quantitative feedback from the software process and from piloting innovative ideas and technologies.	• Innovations that exploit the best software engineering practices are identified and shared throughout the organization. • The software process is improved by changing common causes of inefficiency. • Disciplined change is the norm, not the exception. • The user community and the software organization work together to establish a strong and successful relationship.

CMM Levels 2 and 3 as well as those for CMM Level 4. For our purposes the important thing is to identify the issues, called key process areas, for each maturity level so that you can determine which aspects of the software process you should concentrate on.

11.1.2 Understanding the Key Process Areas (KPAs)

Table 11.2 describes in detail the key process areas (KPAs) for each maturity level of the Capability Maturity Model (CMM).

11.1.3 Mapping the Key Process Areas to Our OOSP

In Chapter 1 of *Process Patterns* I claimed that the Capability Maturity Model (CMM) defines the requirements for a robust, mature, software process. Now is the time to put that claim to the test. Table 11.3 shows where the key process areas (KPAs) are implemented by our object-oriented software process (OOSP). Note that some KPAs are implemented by project stages, some by project phases, some by project tasks, and some by combinations of the three. The important thing to note is that the OOSP presented in this book supports, and often exceeds, the requirements defined by the CMM.

The process patterns presented in this book fully support, and often exceed, the requirements defined by the CMM.

11.1.4 A Potential Schedule for Introducing Process Patterns Into Your Organization

Now that you understand how the key process areas (KPAs) of the Capability Maturity Model (CMM) map to the process patterns of the OOSP you are now in a position for understanding the order in which you should improve your organization's software process. Table 11.4 presents a high-level schedule, organized by maturity level, for the process patterns that your organization should consider working on. The Software Engineering Institute (SEI, 1995) suggests that it takes between 18 and 24 months for an organization to progress between maturity levels, implying that an organization currently at level one will take between six and eight years to progress to level five.

Expect to take between six and eight years to evolve to a fully mature software organization.

11.2 Introducing Process Patterns into Your Organization

Humphrey (1997) describes the Software Engineering Institute's (SEI's) [SM]IDEAL (Initiating, Diagnosing, Establishing, Acting, and

---

[1] [SM]IDEAL is a service mark of Carnegie Mellon University.

Process improvement occurs on a continuing basis. Leveraging) model for process improvement. The experience of the SEI, and my experience, is that process improvement should be performed iteratively over a long period of time, often years, and that it is, in fact, a task that is never truly finished. In other words, you can always improve.

In this section I take the five iterative steps of the IDEAL model and use them for a basis from which to introduce, and then over

TABLE 11.2. The Key Process Areas (KPAs) of the Capability Maturity Model (CMM)

KPAs of CMM Level 2 (Repeatable): Focus is on establishing basic project management controls.	
KPA	**Description**
Requirements Management	The process of establishing and maintaining an agreement with the user community regarding the requirements for the project.
Software Configuration Management	The process of establishing and maintaining the integrity of the project deliverables throughout the entire life cycle.
Software Project Planning	The development and negotiation of estimates for work to be performed, establishing the necessary commitments, and defining the plan to perform the work.
Software Project Tracking and Oversight	The act of providing visibility into the actual progress of a project so that management can take effective actions whenever the performance on the project deviates from the plan.
Software Quality Assurance	The act of reviewing and auditing the project deliverables and activities to verify that they comply with the applicable standards, guidelines, and processes adopted by your organization.
Software Subcontract Management	The selection and effective management of qualified software subcontractors.

(continued)

TABLE 11.2. (continued)

KPAs of CMM Level 3 (Defined): Focus is on both project and organizational issues that establish an infrastructure to institutionalize effective software engineering and management processes across all projects.	
KPA	**Description**
Integrated Software Management	The integration of both software engineering and management activities into a coherent, defined process for each project that is tailored from the standard software process of your organization. This involves developing the project's defined software process and managing the software project based on this process.
Intergroup Coordination	The participation of a project team with other teams and groups throughout your organization to address the requirements, objectives, and issues that are applicable to your entire organization.
Organization Process Definition	The process of developing and maintaining your organization's standard software process, along with related process assets such as descriptions of software life cycles, process tailoring guidelines and criteria, your organization's software process database, and a library of software process-related documentation.
Organization Process Focus	The process of developing and maintaining an understanding of your organization's and project's software processes and coordinating the activities to assess, develop, maintain, and improve these processes. This responsibility should be assigned to a permanent team within your organization.
Peer Reviews	The methodical examination of deliverables by the developer's peers to identify potential defects and areas where changes are needed.
Software Product Engineering	The act of performing the engineering tasks to build and maintain the software in accordance with the project's defined software process and appropriate methods and tools.
Training Program	The identification of the training needed by your organization, projects, and individuals, and then developing or procuring training to address the identified needs.

(continued)

TABLE 11.2. (continued)

KPAs of CMM Level 4 (Managed):
Focus is on the establishment of a quantitative understanding of both the software process and the software products being built by your organization.

KPA	Description
Quantitative Process Management	The act of establishing goals for, and then measuring, the performance of a project's defined software process. It is critical that the performance of individuals are measured to aid in their professional development, but that the information not be used to their detriment.
Software Quality Management	The definition of quality goals for software products and the establishment of plans to achieve these goals. It also involves the monitoring and adjustment of the software plans, software work products, activities, and quality goals to satisfy the needs and desires of the user community for high-quality products.

KPAs of Level 5 (Optimized):
Focus is on this issues that your organization and projects must address to implement continuous and measurable software process improvement.

KPA	Description
Defect Prevention	The analysis of defects that were encountered in the past and taking specific actions to prevent the occurrence of those types of defects in the future.
Process Change Management	This involves defining process improvement goals and proactively and systematically identifying, evaluating, and implementing improvements to your organization's software process on a continuous basis.
Technology Change Management	This involves identifying, selecting, and evaluating new technologies and incorporating effective technologies into the organization.

time improve, a tailored version of the OOSP in your organization. My experience is that the most effective way to define and then introduce process patterns into your organization is to follow these steps:

Initiate	Get your process improvement program started.
Diagnose	Assess your situation and identify your goals.
Establish	Organize your process improvement program.
Act	Define processes for your organization.
Act	Implement processes.
Leverage	Assess and iterate.

11.2.1 Initiate—Getting Your Process Improvement Program Started

The first step is to identify a change agent—likely you, since you are reading this chapter—someone who is responsible for managing and supporting the implementation process. A good change agent will have strong views about both object-oriented development and following a defined process, although he or she will be willing to listen to and act on the views of others where appropriate. Change agents should be:

- Enthusiastic
- Knowledgeable
- Experienced
- Patient
- Technically competent
- Politically competent
- Respected

To ensure the success of your process improvement program Humphrey (1997) advises that you obtain the sponsorship of senior management and that you establish an environment receptive to process improvement. As with a software project, if you do not have the full, public support of senior management, then your process improvement efforts are likely to fail. Furthermore, you also need the support of the software professionals in your organization—if they are not receptive to your process improvement program, they are likely to thwart your efforts.

You need the support of senior management and the software professionals within your organization.

TABLE 11.3. Mapping the CMM Key Process Areas (KPAs) to the Process Patterns of the OOSP

Key Process Area	Level	OOSP Process Patterns/Tasks
Defect Prevention	5	Test in the Small stage Test in the Large stage Quality Assurance
Integrated Software Management	3	Define Infrastructure stage—Process Tailoring Project Management
Intergroup Coordination	3	Define Initial Management Documents stage—Management Define Infrastructure stage—Management Justify stage—Management Construct phase—Management Project Management
Organization Process Definition	3	Define Infrastructure stage—Process Tailoring Infrastructure Management
Organization Process Focus	3	Infrastructure Management
Peer Reviews	3	Define and Validate Initial Requirements stage—Walkthrough Requirements and Walkthrough prototypes Test in the Small stage—Validating Your Models, Code Inspections Quality Assurance
Process Change Management	5	Define Infrastructure stage—Creating a Group Memory Initiate phase—Exit Criteria Construct phase—Exit Criteria Test in the Large stage—Defect Source Metrics Assess stage Support stage—Escalation Assessments
Quantitative Process Management	4	Assess stage—Assessing Individuals Infrastructure Management
Requirements Management	2	Define and Validate Initial Requirements stage Rework stage Identify Defects and Enhancements stage

(continued)

TABLE 11.3. (continued)

Key Process Area	Level	OOSP Process Patterns/Tasks
Software Configuration Management	2	Construct phase Rework stage Release stage Identify Defects and Enhancements stage Deliverable Management
Software Product Engineering	3	Construct phase Rework stage
Software Project Planning	2	Define Initial Management Documents stage Construct phase Project Management
Software Project Tracking and Oversight	2	Project Management
Software Quality Assurance	2	Define and Validate Initial Requirements stage—Walkthrough Requirements and Walkthrough prototypes Quality Assurance Test in the Small stage—Validating Your Models, Code Inspections
Software Quality Management	4	Define Initial Management Documents stage Project Management Quality Assurance
Software Subcontract Management	2	Define Infrastructure—Define team
Technology Change Management	5	Model stage—Technical Architecture Modeling
Training Program	3	Define and Validate Initial Requirements stage Define Infrastructure stage Release stage

TABLE 11.4. A Schedule for Introducing Process Patterns into Your Organization

Maturity Level and Key Process Areas	OOSP Process Patterns/Tasks
Level 2: Repeatable **KPAs:** • Requirements Management • Software Configuration Management • Software Project Planning • Software Project Tracking and Oversight • Software Quality Assurance • Software Subcontract Management	• Construct phase • Define and Validate Initial Requirements stage • Define and Validate Initial Requirements stage— Walkthrough Requirements and Walkthrough Prototypes • Define Infrastructure stage— Define Team • Define Initial Management Documents stage • Deliverable Management • Identify Defects and Enhancements stage • Project Management • Quality Assurance • Release stage • Rework stage • Test in the Small stage—Validating Your Models, Code Inspections
Level 3: Defined **KPAs:** • Integrated Software Management • Intergroup Coordination • Organization Process Definition • Organization Process Focus • Peer reviews • Software Product Engineering • Training Program	• Construct phase • Construct phase—Management • Define and Validate Initial Requirements stage • Define and Validate Initial Requirements stage— Walkthrough Requirements and Walkthrough Prototypes • Define Infrastructure stage • Define Infrastructure stage—Management • Define Infrastructure stage—Process Tailoring • Define Initial Management Documents stage— Management • Infrastructure Management • Justify stage—Management • Project Management • Quality Assurance • Release stage • Rework stage • Test in the Small stage—Validating Your Models, Code Inspections

(continued)

TABLE 11.4. (continued)

Maturity Level and Key Process Areas	OOSP Process Patterns/Tasks
Level 4: Managed KPAs: • Quantitative Process Management • Software Quality Management	• Assess stage—Assessing Individuals • Define Initial Management Documents stage • Infrastructure Management • Project Management • Quality Assurance
Level 5: Optimized KPAs: • Defect Prevention • Process Change Management • Technology Change Management	• Assess stage • Construct phase—Exit Criteria • Define Infrastructure stage—Creating a Group Memory • Initiate phase—Exit Criteria • Model stage—Technical Architecture Modeling • Quality Assurance • Support stage—Escalation Assessments • Test in the Large stage • Test in the Large stage—Defect Source Metrics • Test in the Small stage

Very often the only way that you are going to obtain the support needed to improve your organization's software process is to have a crisis. In the preface to this book I indicated that I first became interested in software process improvement after my first experience on a failed project; for your organization to become sufficiently motivated to begin a process improvement program, it likely needs a similar experience. Perhaps your organization has suffered a failed project, like I did, or even a string of failed projects. Perhaps your organization is courting a new client that insists that you follow a mature software process, or perhaps your experiences with the Year 2000 (Y2K) problem have made you rethink the way that you develop software.

Humphrey (1997) points out that it can often be difficult for people to understand that there is a problem with your existing software process. When people see problems only one at a time—a common occurrence in large organizations where work is finely

It is often difficult for people to see the big picture.

subdivided—each problem seems fairly trivial, and it is hard to grasp their combined impact to the overall organization. The implication is that you may have a hard time convincing people that there is in fact a problem with the way that your organization develops software.

The point to be made is that if your organization is perfectly happy with your existing software process, then there is little motivation to improve it. This is an incredibly frustrating situation for you to be in if you recognize that your organization's software process is flawed. You may find that you need to spend several months, and sometimes several years, explaining the situation and garnering support for a process improvement program. If you perceive a crisis that others do not, you must begin by helping others to see the problems that you do.

Organizations, and people, are usually motivated to change only when they perceive a crisis.

Once you have obtained support for a process improvement program you must form a team, at first only two or three people but potentially growing to ten or more, whose responsibility is to plan and organize your efforts. This group must have a project charter, which defines its resources and responsibilities. Once a project charter is in place you must diagnose your organization's current situation.

11.2.2 Diagnose—Assess Your Situation and Identify Your Goals

The first thing that your process improvement team should do is assess the current environment, possibly by inviting professional

---

DEFINITIONS

change agent A person responsible for defining, implementing, and supporting change within your organization. This is a key role during software process improvement.

project charter A document issued by senior management that provides the project manager with the authority to apply organizational resources to project activities.

Year 2000 (Y2K) problem A common problem where dates within software, and databases, have been recorded with a two-digit year, for example 05, instead of a four-digit year, for example 2005. This problem results in software not recognizing dates on or after January 1st, 2000, believing that they represent dates on or after January 1st, 1900 instead.

process assessors to evaluate your organization, so that you have the information that you need to formulate a plan of action. The aim of this step is to appraise and characterize your existing software practices, and to determine your organization's goals with respect to software development.

Humphrey (1997) suggests that the people performing the assessment be knowledgeable in the key process areas (KPAs) of the Capability Maturity Model (CMM), assuming of course that your organization wishes to become CMM compliant (more on this later). I would add that the assessors also need to be experienced with OO development methods, techniques, and processes, and ideally have been actively involved with the development of several large, mission-critical applications built using object technology.

The people performing the process assessment should understand the software process and should have hands-on experience with object technology.

A key question to ask is why do you wish to improve your software process. Do you need to conform to the process requirements of a specific client? Do you want to improve the quality of the software that you develop? Do you want to reduce your time to market for the software that you develop? Do want to reduce your development costs? Do you need to develop software following a big-bang release strategy, or is an incremental approach to development more appropriate for your organization? Do you wish to develop software that is easy to enhance and extend so that you are able to react quickly to market opportunities? Understanding the goals and priorities of your organization is key to diagnosing your current situation.

Understand your organization's goals and priorities.

If your organization already has a documented software process in place (perhaps your organization is already following some of the process patterns presented in this book), then your assessment

---

TIP

Beware the Motivations of Professional Process Assessors

Strassmann (1997) warns that consultants hired to assess the CMM ratings have a vested interest in giving your organization a low initial rating, because it will be easier to persuade senior management to hire them to guide further improvements. To avoid this potential problem, I suggest a two-phase approach to working with consultants. The secret is to bring in consultants from one organization to perform an initial assessment of your current software process, and bring in a second set from another organization to help you to improve your process.

The issues that you need to address will be different depending on whether your organization already has an existing software process and whether it currently follows the object paradigm.

team will need to understand and summarize it. This is important because it is a completely different thing to introduce a tailored version of the OOSP into an organization with an existing process than it is to introduce it into one without an existing process. Table 11.5 describes the issues associated with each common situation that you may find yourself in.

TABLE 11.5. Common Organizational Situations and the Issues Involved with Introducing the OOSP

Situation	Potential Issues with Introducing the OOSP
No existing process; structured development	• Management and developers need to understand the need for a software process. • Management and developers need to understand the need to move to object-orientation (OO). • First perform two or three pilot projects in OO to gain experience in the technology before introducing a tailored version of the OOSP.
No existing process; OO development	• Management and developers need to understand the need for a software process.
Existing process; structured development	• Entrenched structured developers may be unwilling to move to OO. • If your existing process is effective it will be difficult to convince others to move to OO.
Existing process; OO development	• If your existing process is effective it will be difficult to convince others to improve it. • You may be better off not attempting to improve it—if it ain't broke do not fix it.

The goal of your diagnosis is to document the results of your efforts and to develop recommendations for proceeding with the improvement of your organization's software process.

11.2.3 Establish—Organizing Your Process Improvement Program

My experience is that a process improvement program should be treated exactly like a project. As you have seen in this book, the first phase of any project is the Initiate phase, in which you plan the project, put together the project team, and define the infrastructure for your project. Sounds like the type of things you need to do, doesn't it? To establish your process improvement program, perform the following, iterative tasks:

- Define your requirements.
- Define process action teams.
- Choose a general approach.
- Plan your process improvement program.
- Define your process improvement infrastructure.

11.2.3.1 Define Your Requirements
To establish your process improvement program effectively, one of the things that you must do is define your organization's requirements for a process. The best way to do so is to hold a joint

---

SCOTT'S SOAPBOX

The Writing Is on the Wall for the Structured Paradigm

With the scarcity of new releases of development tools which support structured development I am often surprised at people and organizations fighting the inevitable move to the object-oriented paradigm. It has been a long time since I have seen a development tool that did not involve the word "object" or the term "object-oriented" somewhere in its description. Personally, I would not feel comfortable betting my career on technology based on a structured, procedural, or data paradigm. Would you?

<table>
<tr><td>

DEFINITIONS

Capability Maturity Model (CMM) A strategy, defined by the Software Engineering Institute (SEI), that describes the key elements of an effective software process.

ISO 9001 A standard defined by the International Standards Organization (ISO) that defines how organizations should manage their quality-assurance programs.

ISO 9003 The standards defining how organizations should manage their software-quality assurance programs.

joint application development (JAD) A structured, facilitated meeting in which modeling is performed by both users and developers together. JADs are often held for gathering user requirements.

Software Process Improvement and Capability dEtermination (SPICE) An ISO software process improvement project.

</td></tr>
</table>

application development (JAD) session, defined in detail in *Process Patterns* (Ambler, 1998b). Some of the questions that the JAD should address include:

> *A pattern only works, fully, when it deals with all the forces that are actually present in the situation.*
> *—Christopher Alexander*

- Do you have to work with other organizations to develop software?
- Do you have to meet the quality assurance requirements defined by programs such as ISO 9001 or ISO 9003?
- Is your organization required to become CMM compliant? SPICE compliant?
- Do your processes need to support both structured and object-oriented development?
- How are your project efforts funded?
- What are your reporting requirements to senior management? To your users? To your customers? To the government?
- What internal organizations, such as operations and support, need to be involved?

11.2.3.2 Define Process Action Teams

Humphrey (1997) suggests that this is the point at which you want to establish process action teams (PATs), groups of software professionals responsible for identifying and defining applicable process patterns for your organization. As you will see in the next section, you will likely start with a single PAT whose responsibility is to develop a high-level software process for your organization. I hope that they will choose to modify the OOSP. Once your high-level software process is accepted, you may choose to have several PATs working in parallel to define detailed process patterns, based on those presented in this book.

When choosing the members for your PAT(s), you need to decide between taking an inclusive approach in which many people are involved in the definition of your processes, or an exclusive approach in which a small/core group of people are responsible for this work. The inclusive approach results in processes that are more likely to be accepted by your staff, but will take a long time to do so because of the inefficiencies of large groups. To counteract this difficulty, you must set rules and guidelines that your PAT must follow and have a strong leader that is able to manage the team effectively. The exclusive approach typi-

You need to establish process action teams (PATs) to identify and define process patterns tailored for your organization.

Do you wish to take an inclusive approach using large PATs or an exclusive one using small PATs?

TIP

How to Form Successful Process Action Teams (PATs)

I would like to take a moment to share with you tips that I have picked up over the years regarding the establishment of effective PATs:

- You need at least one person, although ideally everyone, on the team who is experienced with object-oriented development practices.

- You need at least one person familiar with identifying and developing software processes.

- You need at least one customer/user of the products that you produce (your customers often have intimate knowledge of what you are currently doing wrong).

- Everyone needs training in object-oriented technology.

- Everyone needs training in the fundamentals of process patterns.

- Everyone needs to understand, and agree with, the goals of your software process improvement efforts.

- PAT members should be dedicated to the effort on a full-time basis.

- PAT members should expect, and be willing to, argue among themselves during this effort.

- PAT members should understand that a paradigm shift is involved, that they will need to consider and accept new ways of doing things.

cally results in processes being developed much faster, but the processes are less likely to be accepted by others because they were not consulted in their development. To counteract this problem, your PATs must communicate their work to their coworkers and ask for their input, likely by posting their efforts on an internal web site or by printing and posting their work in a public place. Presentations are also an effective means of communicating the efforts of your PATs, and for obtaining feedback.

11.2.3.3 *Choose a General Approach*

There are two common approaches to process improvement, a breadth-first approach and a depth-first approach.

In addition to establishing process action teams you must also decide on a general approach to identifying and defining process patterns for your organization. There are two general approaches to choose from. The first is what I call a breadth-first approach, the one that I prefer, in which you begin by understanding the entire OOSP at a high-level and then define detailed process patterns based on the initial high-level pattern. This approach basically follows the Top-Down Modeling process pattern presented in (Ambler, 1998b). The second approach is to take a depth-first approach in which you start by defining detailed process patterns and then finish by deriving a high-level software process. It is my opinion that the depth-first approach is akin to hacking, although as indicated in Table 11.6, both approaches have their advantages and disadvantages. The rest of this chapter will be written from the point of view of a breadth-first approach.

11.2.3.4 *Plan Your Process Improvement Program*

Develop a plan.

One of the recommendations of the International Standards Organization's (ISO's) Software Process Improvement and Capability dEtermination (SPICE) effort is to develop a process improvement project plan. Like traditional software project plans, this plan should indicate the scope of your efforts, provide an outline of the steps that you will take, identify the key people and roles for the effort, indicate an allocation of adequate resources, and establish the appropriate milestones and review points.

You should also consider developing a risk assessment. This assessment should indicate the potential risks associated with improving your software process, such as short-term inefficiencies as your organization makes the transition. It should also describe the potential risks associated with not improving your software

TABLE 11.6. Comparing the Depth-First and Breadth-First Approaches

Approach	Advantages	Disadvantages
depth-first	• You are able to define specific, detailed process patterns just in time (JIT) to meet the schedules of existing projects. • You can work with a small subset of the overall process at a single time. • Specialized PATs can be used, albeit with difficulty, to describe the process patterns for your organization.	• Not having a high-level vision of the overall software process results in rework of processes defined early on in your efforts. • If your process improvement program is canceled at mid-point, you may completely miss key process patterns. • It is very difficult to manage parallel PAT efforts, as there is no common vision. • The overall time and effort to define a tailored software process is increased due to rework and the additional management overhead required for parallel efforts. • Your tailored OOSP is delivered in piecemeal fashion, potentially increasing the confusion of outsiders who are not involved with the PAT(s).
breadth-first	• You quickly define the context in which multiple PATs may work together. • You are in a position to communicate the overall OOSP to your organization and determine potential impacts to your organizational structure. • You minimize the overall time to develop process patterns. • The tailored OOSP is delivered as a consistent whole.	• Your PAT(s) need to understand the entire OOSP, requiring a wide range of knowledge and skills. • The tailored OOSP is delivered as a whole, negating your ability to deliver JIT processes.

DEFINITIONS

hacking A development approach where little or no effort is spent on analysis and design before coding begins.

process action team (PAT) A group of software professionals, often from different parts of your organization, who are given the responsibility to identify and define applicable process patterns for your organization.

project phase The large components of the OOSP which are performed in a serial manner. The four project phases are Initiate, Construct, Deliver, and Maintain and Support. A project phase is depicted by a process pattern.

project plan A project plan is a collection of several project management deliverables, including but not limited to a project overview, a project schedule, a project estimate, a team definition, and a risk assessment. Project plans are a deliverable of the Initiate phase and are updated regularly throughout a project.

project stage One of the components of a project phase, performed in an iterative manner, that make up a project phase. For example, the project stages that make up the Construct phase are Model, Program, Generalize, and Test in the Small. A project stage is depicted by a process pattern.

risk assessment A document indicating potential factors, called risks, that if they were to occur would harm the project. A risk assessment is used to identify risks so that they may be dealt with appropriately. Risk assessments are a deliverable of the Initiate phase and are updated regularly throughout a project.

Develop a risk assessment. process, such as continued project failures, continued low quality of delivered software, and continued cost and schedule overruns.

11.2.3.5 Define Your Process Improvement Infrastructure

Part of the Initiate phase is to define the infrastructure for your project, including the tools, standards, and techniques that you intend to use. Before your PATs get to work, you should:

1. **Choose your tools.** At a minimum you will need a word processor and a drawing tool to document your processes, or you may even choose to use a full-fledged CASE tool.
2. **Define documentation conventions.** You should initially invest some time to define a documentation template for processes and a set of visual drawing standards for process patterns. One of the things that you may have noticed about this book is that the process patterns are depicted consis-

---

DEFINITIONS

computer-aided software engineering (CASE) tool A tool that supports the creation of software.

groupware A form of software which allows several users to work together on common information, often simultaneously from different physical locations.

---

tently and that the descriptions of those patterns, in chapters, are documented consistently. That is because I decided on documentation conventions before writing this book. Processes typically have entrance and exit criteria (known in the patterns community as the initial context and resulting context respectively), a diagram depicting the tasks to be accomplished, and a description of how the work is to be performed. Process patterns, as you have seen in this book, can be depicted visually, indicating the inputs and outputs of the process as well as the main tasks to be undertaken.

3. **Setup a working area for your PATs.** You will need both a physical working area, such as one or more meeting rooms, and a virtual working area such as a common directory, database, and/or groupware tool.

11.2.4 Act—Defining Processes for Your Organization

Once a project plan is in place, your process action team (PAT) is ready to start by identifying and defining the process patterns for your organization. If you decide to taking a breadth-first approach, as suggested above, you will want to follow these steps in order:

1. Develop a high-level software process.
2. Determine potential impacts to your organization.
3. Develop detailed processes.
4. Determine exact impacts to your organization.

11.2.4.1 Develop a High-Level Software Process

When taking a breadth-first approach, you begin by defining a high-level software process for your organization, and a good place to start is with the OOSP in Figure 11.3. Your software process describes the phases and stages that a project moves through for a single release, showing the general order in which work must be performed. In addition to defining your software process, you should also describe, perhaps only in a paragraph or two, each project phase and stage as well as the deliverables that they produce. Luckily, this work has already been done for you in this book; you merely need to modify the material presented here to meet the specific needs of your organization.

The repetition of patterns is quite a different thing than the repetition of parts. Indeed, the different parts will be unique because the patterns are the same.
—Christopher Alexander

Considering the level at which you are currently working, it is likely that you will be able to reuse the OOSP presented in Figure 11.3 as it is. Some people will worry about this, at first believing that your organization is different from every other (and in many ways it undoubtedly is), but the OOSP really does describe the fundamentals of large-scale development, and the fundamentals should be the same across all organizations. Yes, your organization will likely implement the details of the OOSP differently than other organizations, but the general software process will remain the same.

11.2.4.2 Determine Potential Impacts to Your Organization

Your organization structure and the roles taken by individuals within your organization will likely change.

In addition to identifying the high-level software process that your organization will follow to develop software, you should also consider the impact that your new software process will have on your organization. For example, the OOSP calls out a Define Infrastructure stage and a Manage Infrastructure task, processes that will need to be worked by a group of professionals within your organization. You will also need to define the roles and positions that people will take within this group as they work their assigned processes. Potential roles and positions for large-scale object-oriented development have been described throughout this book.

Develop a rough outline of your new organization structure based on your high-level software process.

Although I strongly believe that organizational issues should be addressed after you have defined your software process, the reality is that your process action teams (PATs) are likely to get bogged down into "who does what" and "who owns what" issues. My experience has been that before you develop detailed process patterns, you should develop a rough outline of a potential organization structure (a topic covered in detail in Section 11.3) that is based on your high-level software process.

11.2.4.3 Develop Detailed Processes

The third step is to develop detailed processes that your organization will follow, including the supporting documentation for those processes. It is at this point that you may choose to have several process action teams (PATs) working in parallel, assigning

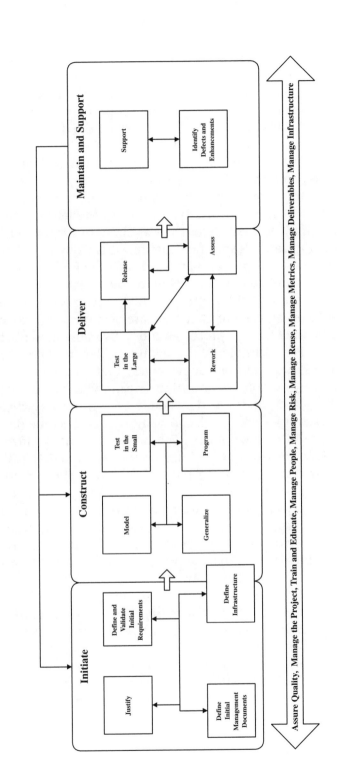

Figure 11.3.
The Object-Oriented Software Process (OOSP)

You may choose to have several process action teams (PATs) work in parallel to define detailed process patterns.

one or more project phases or stages to each PAT. The PATs would be managed in a similar way as you would manage parallel development teams, requiring regular communication between the teams to ensure effective coordination of their efforts.

Your PAT(s) should begin by modifying the detailed process patterns presented in this book for each project phase and stage. For example, the Release process pattern shown in Figure 11.4 is a good start for the tailored Release stage for your organization. If your organization doesn't have a support department, and has no intention of forming one (yikes!), the PAT defining this process pattern may decide to modify it as shown in Figure 11.5 to meet your organization's specific situation. It is likely that you will find that many of the process patterns presented for the process phases and stages are directly applicable to your organization.

Once your PAT(s) have the detailed processes defined, and have come to an agreement that they are accurate, they then need to describe in detail the processes and deliverables described by each pattern. For example, the diagram in Figure 11.5 shows nine processes and several deliverables that should be described. Depending on your organization's needs, you may decide to document each process and deliverable by writing anywhere from a few descriptive paragraphs to a multipage document describing each one in detail. Table 11.7 describes potential information to include in the documentation for processes and deliverables.

Your PATs should strive to define process patterns to the best of their ability, but should not expect to get them perfect.

An important thing to remember during the development of detailed processes is that you do not need to get it perfect the first time (and you probably won't anyway). This is why the Assess stage process pattern exists, to provide an explicit mechanism for improving your software process by learning from your experiences. Having said that, your PATs should still strive to define process patterns as best they can.

11.2.4.4 Determine the Exact Impacts to Your Organization

Once your PATs have developed the detailed processes for your organization, they need to revisit the initial organization structure they developed based on your high-level software process. The roles and positions will also need to be revisited, and documented appropriately. Section 11.3 describes the issues involved with redefining your organization.

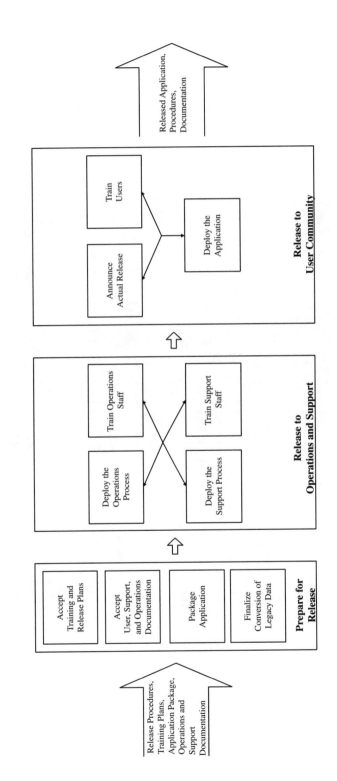

Figure 11.4.
The Release
process pattern

Figure 11.5.
A tailored version
of the Release
process pattern

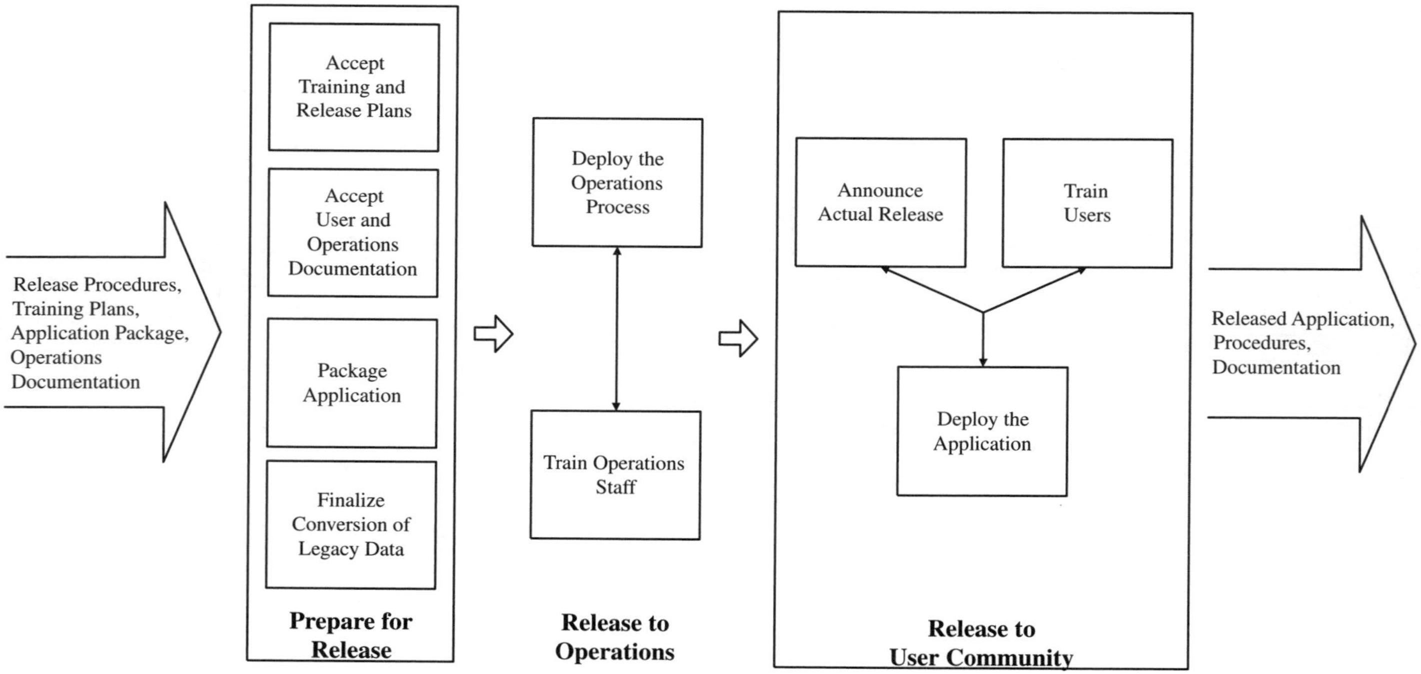

Prepare for Release

- Accept Training and Release Plans
- Accept User and Operations Documentation
- Package Application
- Finalize Conversion of Legacy Data

Release Procedures, Training Plans, Application Package, Operations Documentation

Release to Operations

- Deploy the Operations Process
- Train Operations Staff

Release to User Community

- Announce Actual Release
- Train Users
- Deploy the Application

Released Application, Procedures, Documentation

TABLE 11.7. Potential Information to Document About Processes and Deliverables

Process Documentation	Deliverable Documentation
• Description • Entry conditions for the process • Inputs into the process • Steps to perform the process • Exit conditions from the process • Outputs of the process • Personnel roles to work the process • Description of needed skills to work the process • References for further reading	• Description • Suggested tool(s) • Peer review criteria • Suggested standards and guidelines • Configuration management concerns • Example of the deliverable • A template, if applicable • References for further reading

11.2.5 Act—Implementing Processes

The easy part with process improvement, although it does not seem like it at the time, is the definition of the processes. The hard part is getting people to actually use them. Many people are perfectly happy doing things the way that they currently do them, and are rarely willing to modify their current behaviors. Myself, I love changing things but I am not that enthralled with being changed.

The hard part of process improvement is implementing the necessary changes.

The second step is to unfreeze the current situation within your organization; in other words, to convince everyone that they need to improve the way that they are working. My experience is that you can accomplish this by first identifying a long-term problem with their approach—for example, the process they are currently following will likely result in software that is difficult to maintain or extend—and asking them to work through common scenarios in which their software will need to be updated. My favorite scenarios include porting the software to another operating system or database, adding new functionality to support a new line of business, and increasing the usage/transactions that the software needs to support. By exploring these issues in detail, and then pre-

It is hard to give up preconceptions of what things "ought to be," and recognize things as they really are.
—Christopher Alexander

Run a trailblazer project to validate your new processes.

senting solutions to how the software could have been built to fulfill these scenarios, people begin to see that there are better ways to develop software.

Once you have unfrozen the current situation in your organization, the best way to implement your new processes is to choose a project to work the new processes. Remember, it is likely that you are not going to get your processes right the first time; therefore, you want to invest in a project that is responsible for finding and identifying fixes for any obvious problems with the new processes. You have likely read a lot about pilot projects, small-scale projects whose purpose is to prove the viability of object technology. Trailblazer projects are different—their purpose is to prove the viability of, and often to prototype, an object-oriented software process (OOSP).

Ideally, a trailblazer project should develop software that is important to your organization and is of a significant size. Typical trailblazer projects will involve twenty to fifty developers building software over a six- to nine-month period. The trailblazer team must understand that there will be problems with the defined processes, and be willing to fix the processes or at least suggest potential improvements to be considered at a later date. Furthermore, the trailblazer team should also expect that they may take longer than usual to work the new processes because they will both lose time being trained in them and then lose time struggling while they gain experience working them for the first time.

11.2.6 Leverage—Assess and Iterate

At the end of the trailblazer project it is critical that an assessment be performed, a topic covered in detail by the Assess stage (Chap-

---

TIP

Expect People to Resist Change

Why do people resist change? DeMarco (1997) points out that people will not embrace change if they do not feel safe—if their job or self-esteem is at risk, they are less likely to willingly accept new processes. Humphrey (1997) believes that people resist change when they do not understand why the change is needed, implying that the greater their inclusion in the definition of the new process patterns the greater their acceptance of the patterns.

DEFINITIONS

pilot project A small project whose purpose is to prove the viability of a new technology.

trailblazer project A medium-sized project whose purpose is to prove the viability of a software process by developing software while following the given process.

---

ter 6), so that your organization learns from its experiences. Assuming that your trailblazer was a success, or at least not a failure, then you should publicly acknowledge this fact, along with your lessons learned, so that everyone recognizes that your new processes work. When people see that the new processes are effective, they are much more willing to follow them.

Assess the trailblazer project and publicly acknowledge that the new processes work.

The final step of implementing process patterns within your organization is to freeze the changes in place to make your new processes permanent. This point in your process improvement program presents the greatest risk: after the initial impetus to improve your software process, your priorities often change, the original reasons why you made the changes are forgotten, people fall back into their former habits, and the new processes fall by the wayside. To prevent this from happening, you need to educate your entire staff in the new processes and to start using the processes on all of your projects. Furthermore, as change agent, your role has now evolved from being the implementer of new processes to being the supporter of the new processes, the person responsible for growing and nurturing them within your organization.

Humphrey (1997) reports that many organizations have introduced Software Engineering Process Groups (SEPG) whose sole responsibility is to support the improvement of your organization's software process. The change agent responsible for defining and implementing your organization's software process is usually a member of the SEPG, and is often the leader. The SEPG should be kept small—as a rule of thumb, I suggest one SEPG member for every one hundred developers in your organization—and should be a full-time job. The SEPG will assist in the efforts of the Assess stage (Chapter 6), SEPG members often taking on the role of Auditor; and will assist during the Define Infrastructure stage (Ambler, 1998b) in the role of Infrastructure Engineer to tailor your organization's processes to meet the specific needs of an individual project.

> ## DEFINITIONS
>
> **infrastructure engineer** A person who is responsible for defining and supporting the project infrastructure (processes, guidelines, standards, and tools). The role is applicable to the Define Infrastructure stage and all stages of the Construct phase.
>
> **project auditor** A professional who specializes in the review and assessment of projects. This is a key role during the Assess stage.
>
> **Software Engineering Process Group (SEPG)** A group of dedicated professionals whose sole responsibility is to support the improvement of your organization's software process.

11.3 Rethinking Your Organizational Structure

Your software process and your Information Technology (IT) department's organization structure go hand-in-hand. Having a perfect object-oriented software process (OOSP) is not going to do you any good if you do not have an organization capable of working the process. Your process should drive your organization structure, including definitions of the roles and responsibilities taken by people (covered in detail in Chapter 10) and of the groups/teams that they work in. Because you have redefined your software process, you now need to redefine your organization structure.

*The OOSP will
require the
redefinition of your
IT organization.*

Section 11.2 indicated that to define the processes for your organization you begin by defining a high-level software process, then define an initial organization structure, then define detailed process patterns, and then finalize the definition of your new organization structure. In this section I will suggest a collection of potential groups, based on the OOSP of Figure 11.6, to give you a good start at an initial organization structure.

First, I would like to start by identifying the groups that you are likely to have in your organization already, described in Table 11.8 and shown in Figure 11.7. The people in these existing groups will require extensive training and education in your new processes, and are likely to require significant mentoring because they are more likely to have your organization's existing processes ingrained.

*Begin defining
your organization
by analyzing the
OOSP.*

Second, there are several new groups that your organization will need as it transitions to object-oriented processes. These new groups, described in Table 11.8 and shown in Figure 11.7, have the advantage that they are starting fresh and do not have any

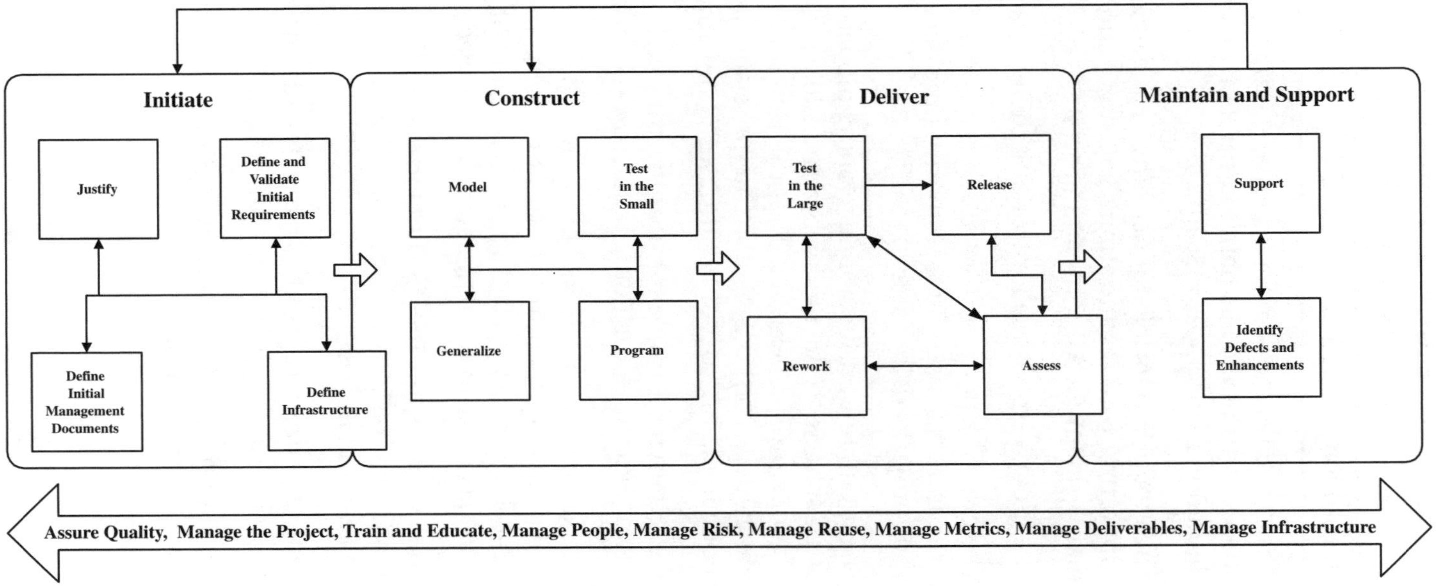
Initiate
Justify
Define and Validate Initial Requirements
Define Initial Management Documents
Define Infrastructure
Construct
Model
Test in the Small
Generalize
Program
Deliver
Test in the Large
Release
Rework
Assess
Maintain and Support
Support
Identify Defects and Enhancements
Assure Quality, Manage the Project, Train and Educate, Manage People, Manage Risk, Manage Reuse, Manage Metrics, Manage Deliverables, Manage Infrastructure

Figure 11.6. The Object-Oriented Software Process (OOSP)

TABLE 11.8. Groups that Likely Exist in Your Current Organization and Have a Role in the OOSP

Group	Description
Configuration Control Board	The group responsible for approving proposed software changes. Also called a change control board or software configuration review board (SCRB).
Configuration Management	The group responsible for defining, managing, and supporting your organization's software configuration management (SCM) tools and processes.
Development	The group responsible for working the Program stage.
Documentation/ Technical Writing	The group responsible for writing the documentation for your applications and for supporting the development of your project's deliverables.
Modeling	The group responsible for developing models. This group is often split, with the modelers responsible for detailed modeling for a project being a part of the Development group, and the modelers responsible for enterprise and architectural modeling being part of the Infrastructure group.
Operations	The group responsible for running your organization's computing resources, including both hardware and software.
Project Management	The group responsible for supporting your organization's project management processes, and who manage individual projects. In many ways this group is a pool of professionals who specialize in the management of projects.
Quality Assurance	The group responsible for supporting your organization's quality assurance processes, including the facilitation of peer reviews and inspections.
Requirements Analysis	Your organization's pool of requirements analysts. The group may be a subgroup of your Modeling or Development groups.
Support	The group responsible for supporting your users in their use of your organization's computing environment.

(continued)

TABLE 11.8. (continued)

Group	Description
Test	The group responsible for supporting your Development group test their work during the Test in the Small stage and for working the Test in the Large stage. Your Test and Quality Assurance groups will likely work closely together, and may in fact be a single group.
Training and Education	The group responsible for supporting your organization's training and education efforts, potentially including both your information technology (IT) professionals and your user community.

baggage from the past, but have the disadvantage that they need to define how they will fit into your organization.

Figure 11.7 depicts a potential organization structure for your Information Technology (IT) department. The first thing that you'll notice is that there is no formal reporting structure to the organization structure, there are, however, five groups—Operation Management, Strategic Management, Project Development, Project Support, and Post Delivery—that you may decide to implement. The reason why I have chosen not to show any form of reporting structure in Figure 11.7 is because you have a wide range of choices: a hierarchical organizational structure wherein each person reports to a single superior; a matrix organizational structure wherein individual potentially report to several managers (for example, a reuse engineer may report to a reuse group manager and to the project manager of the specific project to which they are assigned); or a virtual organizational structure wherein professionals collaborate as equals to perform specific tasks.

Coplien (1995) describes several organizational patterns that provide advice for determining your organization structure, and I would like to share several of them with you to give you an appreciation of the wealth of Coplien's work. First is Conway's Law, which states that your organization structure and architecture should reflect one another. Coplien points out that it is more likely that your architecture will drive your organization than vice versa. Second is the Aesthetic Pattern, which advises you to

TABLE 11.9. Groups that May Not Exist in Your Current Organization that Have a Role in the OOSP

Group	Description
Infrastructure	The group responsible for defining and supporting your organization's infrastructure, including the development/identification of standards, guidelines, and tools. Common names for these groups include Object Technology Centers (Korson and Vaishnavi, 1996) and Domain Engineering.
Metrics Management	The group responsible for defining, supporting, and managing your organization's measurement program.
Project Planners	The group responsible for supporting the planning of projects, often included in your organization's Project Management group.
Reuse Engineering	The group responsible for supporting and managing your organization's reuse efforts, often working closely with your architectural modelers to support systematic reuse and with your developers to support opportunistic reuse. This group may be part of your Infrastructure group.
Software Engineering Process Group (SEPG)	The group for supporting the definition and improvement of your organization's software process.
System Auditing	The group responsible for support the assessment of projects as well as performing formal audits/inspections within your organization. System Auditing will often work closely with your Quality Assurance group.

DEFINITIONS

hierarchical organization A organization with a reporting structure wherein each person reports to a single manager.

matrix organization An organization with a reporting structure wherein individuals potentially report to several managers - often, to the manager for the project to which they are currently assigned, and to the manager of a specialized group such as Modeling.

mentor An experienced developer who transfers her or his skills to less experienced developers to aid in their education experience. This is a key role during all phases, but specifically during the Construct phase.

organizational pattern A pattern that describes a common management technique or a structure appropriate to a software organization.

reuse engineer A senior, experienced developer who is responsible for supporting and enhancing the reuse process within your organization. This person works closely with component engineers and infrastructure engineers, and is a key role in all stages of the Construct phase.

virtual organization An organization with a reporting structure where professionals collaborate as equals to perform specific tasks.

develop groups that can grow into departments in their own right as your organization thrives and grows. The third organizational pattern is Shaping Circulation Realms, a pattern that suggests you should give people titles that create a hierarchy or pecking order, while at the same time assigning job responsibilities that suggest the appropriate interactions between positions/roles.

11.4 Secrets of Success

I would like to take the time to share a few tips and techniques for introducing process patterns into your organization.

1. **Remember the KISS rule.** KISS stands for "keep it simple, silly"—a concept that is directly applicable to your process improvement efforts. A common mistake that organizations make is to overspecify the processes that they intend to follow, a perfect example of a process that has gotten out of hand is shown in Figure 11.8. Never forget that your goal is to product software that meets the needs of your user community.

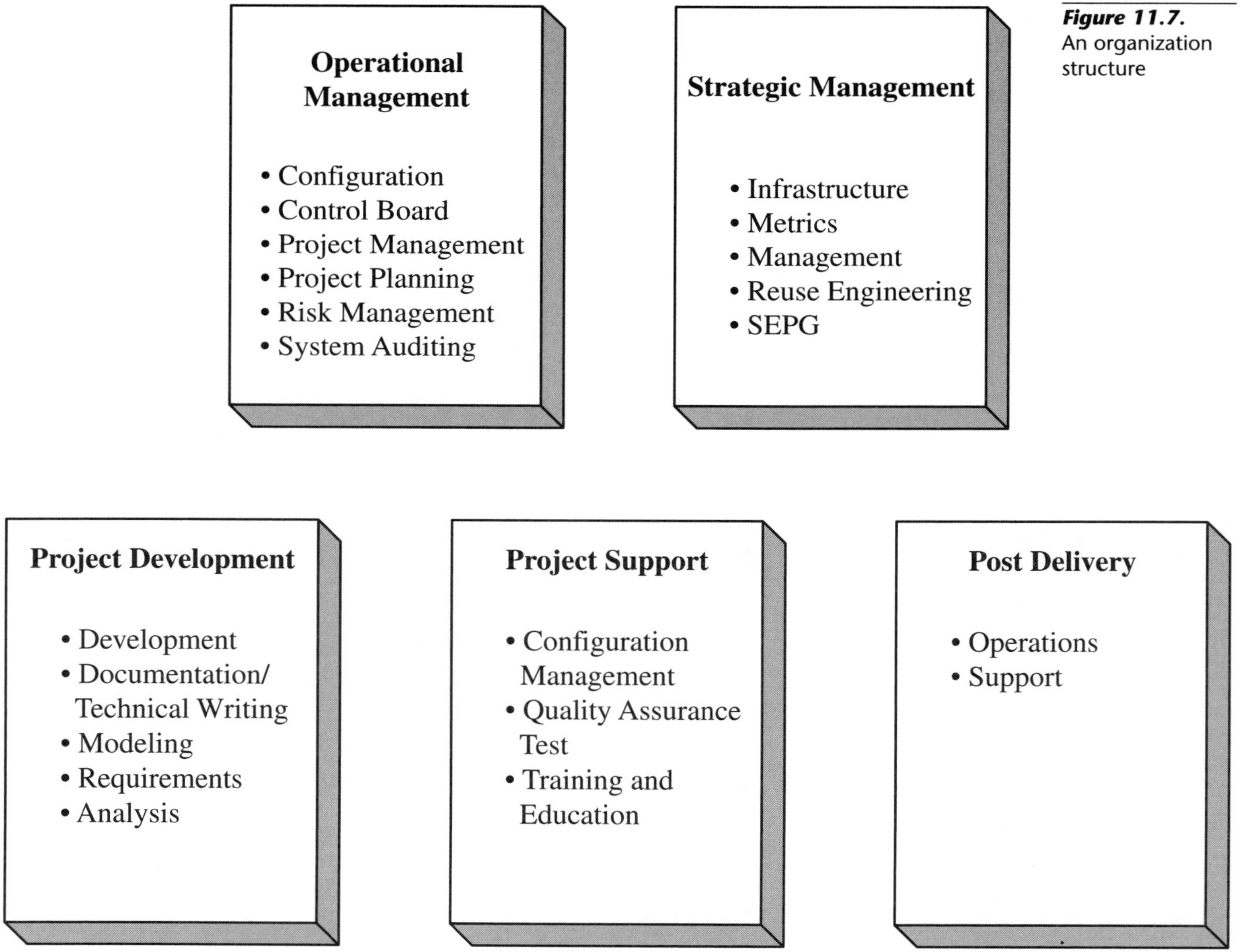

Figure 11.7.
An organization
structure

Strategic Management

- Infrastructure
- Metrics
- Management
- Reuse Engineering
- SEPG

Operational Management

- Configuration
- Control Board
- Project Management
- Project Planning
- Risk Management
- System Auditing

Post Delivery

- Operations
- Support

Project Support

- Configuration Management
- Quality Assurance
- Test
- Training and Education

Project Development

- Development
- Documentation/ Technical Writing
- Modeling
- Requirements
- Analysis

2. **Keep the real goal in mind.** My experience has been that process patterns, when applied intelligently, increase the productivity of developers. My experience has also been that when process patterns are applied less than intelligently, or when the paper pushers have too much influence within an organization, process patterns can also decrease your productivity. The process patterns presented in the book have been proven to work in practice; how you choose to implement them will determine the level of your success. Organizations that keep the end goal in mind—that of developing, maintaining, and supporting software that fulfills the needs of their user community—will be successful with process patterns. Those that follow processes simply for the sake of following processes are likely to fail.

3. **Realize that productivity improvement comes from long-term investment.** It takes time, often several years, to permanently improve the productivity of your software development efforts. There is not a simple, quick fix to your problems.

4. **Be aware of your organization's current culture.** Emam, Drouin, and Melo (1998) point out that organizations with cultures that are positive toward process improvement are likely to want to supply a quality product with reasonable business returns, have middle managers that are willing to set and work to targets to meeting your organization's needs and business goals, and have senior management leadership that is willing to launch and sustain a long-term change effort.

5. **Treat process improvement like a project.** Have an experienced project manager, ideally someone with both process and object-oriented development experience. Define the requirements for your processes, model them, implement them, and then test them with a trailblazer project.

6. **Document processes to the appropriate level.** My experience is that you should describe your architectural modeling efforts lightly and your project development efforts in greater detail. The reason for this is simple: your architecture group is likely to be a small team of highly experienced people, the type of people who do not need to refer to a documented process to do their jobs. Your project teams, however, are likely to be composed of larger groups of people who may not have worked together before and who are likely to be less experienced.

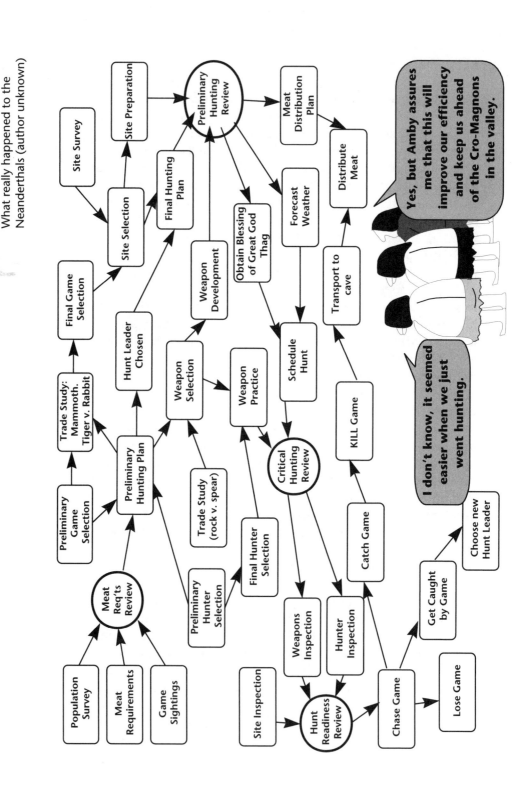

Figure 11.8.
What really happened to the Neanderthals (author unknown)

7. **Avoid "fire hazard processes."** A common mistake is to produce volumes of documentation describing your processes. Your goal is simply to describe your process patterns to such a level that they can be given to a professional skilled in the techniques of that process so they can work the processes appropriately.

8. **Understand that your organization is the same but different.** The process patterns presented in this book are fairly fundamental and should hold true for every organization. Your implementation of the process patterns is where you will differ from other organizations. Every organization is unique, but the fundamentals still apply to every single one.

9. **Verify that the processes work for you.** Run a trailblazer project to validate the processes before implementing them across your organization. By doing so, you will ensure that your new processes are, in fact, relevant to your organization

10. **Adopt process patterns because they make sense.** Review each of the process patterns presented in this book. If they make sense to you, then adopt them; otherwise, do not. Some organizations will choose to adopt the process pattern of the Generalize stage, which supports opportunistic reuse, whereas others will decide that systematic reuse supported by the Top-Down Modeling process pattern (Ambler, 1998b) is sufficient for their needs.

11. **Do not forget the deliverables.** When defining processes, always remember that the deliverables that are used as inputs into them must have come from somewhere, perhaps another process, and that the deliverables produced by a process should be used somewhere else.

12. **Hold everyone responsible for process improvement.** Senior management must be willing to actively support and sustain process improvement, project managers must be held responsible for ensuring that their teams follow the defined processes, and developers must be held responsible for learning and then following the processes. This is often a difficult task because senior management often demands immediate results, whereas process improvement often takes years. Project managers resent diverting scarce resources from their projects, and developers often resent being told how to do their jobs.

13. **Bring in an expert to advise you.** Process improvement is a complex and difficult endeavor, one for which you are likely to need help to accomplish. You can increase your chance of success by bringing in a consultant who has both a process background and an OO development background—someone who has been actively involved in a process improvement program and who has worked on large-scale, mission-critical software development projects using OO technology. My experience is that a consultant, or consultants, should be brought in as an advisor or as a process action team (PAT) member, but should not be the leader of your process improvement efforts. The reason for this is simple: your organization owns your software process; therefore, someone from your organization should be in charge.

14. **Do not think that everyone is on board.** There is likely to be a small core of people within your organization who do not want to use object technology for large, mission-critical projects, and these people will actively undermine your efforts. You need to identify these dissenters and work together with them to see the advantages of working with object technology and of following a set of defined process patterns to help you to develop OO software.

15. **A fool with a process pattern is still a fool.** For your organization to be successful with process patterns, your software professionals will need to understand the processes, the concepts, the techniques, and the problem domain. Implementing the OOSP in your organization involves more than going out and purchasing a couple of new books and development tools.

16. **Develop a user guide for your process.** You can make it easy for your staff to learn your chosen processes by providing a well-written handbook (I have seen good ones written in less than ten pages) that provides an overview of the OOSP as it is to be implemented in your organization.

17. **Concentrate on the Construct phase.** It is in the Construct phase that most of the differences between object-oriented and structured techniques exist. Yes, the Initiate, Delivery, and Maintain and Support phases are all affected by the OO paradigm, but none nearly as much as the Construct phase.

18. **Have patience.** Progress will be slow at first, slower than you

DEFINITIONS

opportunistic reuse A reuse approach where reusable items are harvested from project deliverables after the fact.

systematic reuse An approach to reuse which involves modeling techniques whose purpose is to define high-leverage, reusable components.

hoped or expected. Introducing the OOSP into an organization via the use of process patterns takes time—the required culture shift often takes years to complete.

19. **Everyone must understand the required paradigm shift.** Your entire development organization needs to make the shift to object orientation if you are to be able to develop large-scale, mission-critical software. This includes all of the major groups presented in Figure 11.8: Operation Management, Strategic Management, Project Development, Project Support, and Post Delivery.

The fact that these rules are simple does not mean that they are easy to observe, or easy to invent.

—Christopher Alexander

11.5 What You Have Learned in This Chapter

In this chapter you have discovered the issues surrounding the successful introduction of the Object-Oriented Software Process (OOSP) into your organization. I began by describing the Software Engineering Institute's (SEI's) Capability Maturity Model (CMM), showing how it maps to the process patterns of the OOSP and how it can be used to define a potential schedule for your process improvement efforts. You then saw that the SEI's [SM]IDEAL (Initiating, Diagnosing, Establishing, Acting, and Leveraging) model for process improvement can be used to guide your efforts to tailor the OOSP to your needs. Finally, you saw that you will need to rework the organization structure of your Information Technology (IT) department to meet the new demands placed on it by the OOSP.

11.6 References and Recommended Reading

Ambler, S. W. 1998a. *Building Object Applications That Work—Your Step-By-Step Handbook for Developing Robust Systems with Object Technology*. New York: SIGS Books.

Ambler, S. W. 1998b. *Process Patterns—Building Large-Scale Systems Using Object Technology.* New York: SIGS Books/Cambridge University Press.

Booch, G. 1996. *Object Solutions—Managing the Object-Oriented Project.* Menlo Park, California: Addison Wesley Publishing Company, Inc.

Coplien, J.O. (1995). *A Generative Development-Process Pattern Language.* Pattern Languages of Program Design, Addison Wesley Longman, Inc., pp. 183–237.

DeMarco, T. 1997. *The Deadline: A Novel About Project Management.* New York: Dorset House Publishing.

Emam, K. E., Drouin J., and Melo, W. 1998. *SPICE: The Theory and Practice of Software Process Improvement and Capability Determination.* Los Alamitos, California: IEEE Computer Society Press.

Grady, R. B. 1992. *Practical Software Metrics For Project Management and Process Improvement.* Englewood Cliffs, New Jersey: Prentice-Hall, Inc.

Graham, I., Henderson-Sellers, B. and Younessi, H. 1997. *The OPEN Process Specification.* New York: ACM Press Books.

Goldberg, A. and Rubin, K. S. 1995. *Succeeding With Objects: Decision Frameworks for Project Management.* Reading, Massachusetts: Addison-Wesley Publishing Company Inc.

Humphrey, W. S. 1997. *Managing Technical People: Innovation, Teamwork, And The Software Process.* Reading, Massachusetts: Addison-Wesley Longman, Inc.

Korson, T. D. and Vaishnavi, V. K. 1996. *Object Technology Centers of Excellence.* Greenwich, Connecticut: Manning Publications Co.

Lorenz, M. 1995. Project Practicalities: Rules to Live By. *Smalltalk Report* 4 (July–August), 22–25.

Software Engineering Institute 1995. *The Capability Maturity Model: Guidelines for Improving the Software Process.* Reading Massachusetts: Addison-Wesley Publishing Company.

Strassmann, P. A. 1997. *The Squandered Computer: Evaluating the Business Alignment of Information Technologies.* New Canaan, Connecticut: The Information Economics Press.

Webster, B. F. 1995. *Pitfalls of Object-Oriented Development.* New York: M&T Books.

Whittington, L. W. 1996. *The SEI Software Capability Maturity Model.* Http://home.earthlink.net/~rpr-online/LW-CMM.htm

Chapter 12

Parting Words

■■■■■■■■■■■■

Mind what you have learned.

Save you it can.

—Yoda

Visit The Process Patterns Resource Page:
http://www.AmbySoft.com/processPatternsPage.html

Glossary

A

abstract class A class from which objects are not instantiated, but are instead used to implement common behavior inherited by other classes.

accessor method A method that is used to either modify or retrieve a single attribute.

ActiveX An approach to developing reusable components defined by Microsoft.

activity diagram A UML diagram that can be used to model a high-level business process or the transitions between states of a class (in this respect, activity diagrams are effectively specializations of statechart diagrams).

actor A role played by any person, organization, or system that interacts with an application but is external to it. Actors are modeled on use-case diagrams.

ad-hoc reporting Reporting performed for the specific purposes of a small group of users, in which it is common that the report(s) are written by the users themselves.

aggregation A structure that represents *is-part-of* relationships between objects.

allocated baseline A baseline in which all requirements defined by the functional baseline are assigned/ mapped to classes within your design.

alpha testing A testing period in which pre-release versions of software products, products that are often buggy, are released to users who need access to the product before it is to be officially deployed. In return these users are willing to report back to the software developers any defects that they uncover. Alpha testing is typically followed by a period of beta testing.

analysis An approach to modeling in

which the goal is understanding the problem domain.

analysis error When a user requirement is missed or misunderstood.

analysis paralysis A derogatory term used by system professionals to describe the actions of a development team that spends too much time when modeling in trying to document every minute detail.

analysis pattern A modeling pattern that describes a solution to a business/domain problem.

analysis testing The testing of your analysis modeling efforts.

analyst A person responsible for defining and validating the initial requirements for the application via working closely with subject matter experts. This is a key role during the Define and Validate Initial Requirements stage and the Model stage.

antipattern The description of an approach to solving a common problem, an approach that in time proves to be wrong or highly ineffective.

application package The software and supporting documentation that is deployed to your user community.

application release A software release that delivers an application containing new, improved, and/or fixed functionality.

application release schedule A schedule indicating the dates of the incremental releases of your application.

application server A server on which

business logic is deployed. Application servers are key to an *n*-tier client/server architecture.

application-specific class Any class that is used in a single application.

approach process pattern A process pattern that depicts a general approach to development; for example, serial development or parallel development.

architectural modeler A person who is involved in understanding and modeling the enterprise, business architecture, and/or technical architecture for your organization. This is a key role during the Model stage.

architectural modeling High-level modeling, either of the business or technical domain, whose goal is to provide a common, overall vision of your domain. Architectural models provide a base from which detailed modeling will begin.

artifact reuse The reuse of previously created development artifacts: use cases, standards documents, domain-specific models, procedures and guidelines, and other applications.

association A relationship between two or more objects or classes. For example, students TAKE courses.

audit trail A complete record of changes to a deliverable, also called a modification log or revision history.

automatic call distribution (ACD) system A phone system that distributes calls to support engineers in an efficient manner.

B

back end *See* Server

baseline A tested and certified version of a deliverable representing a conceptual milestone that thereafter serves as the basis for further development, and that can be modified only through formal change control procedures. A particular version becomes a baseline when a responsible group decides to designate it as such.

beta testing Similar to alpha testing, except that the software should be less buggy. This is typically used by software development companies who want to ensure that they meet as many of their client needs as possible.

big-bang development An approach to development in which an application is released all at once in one, single project.

black-box tests Test cases that verify that given input A, the component/ system being tested gives you expected results B.

boundary-value test A test that checks unusual or extreme situations that your code should be able to handle.

bug *See* Defect

build The process by which a software product is created from its base source code. This is the act of compiling and linking source code in compiled languages such as Java and C++, or packaging code in languages like Smalltalk.

builder A tool that developers use to build software, such as a compiler, a linker, or a packager.

business-domain expert (BDE) Someone with intimate knowledge of all or a portion of a problem domain. Often referred to as a subject matter expert (SME).

C

calendar time The overall time that it takes to complete a project, measured from the start of a project to its end. A project that starts on May 1st which then ends on May 24th of the same year has a calendar time of twenty-four days.

Capability Maturity Model (CMM) A strategy, defined by the Software Engineering Institute (SEI), that describes the key elements of an effective software process.

cardinality An indication of how many.

change agent A person responsible for defining, implementing, and supporting change within your organization. This is a key role during software process improvement.

change request (CR) A formal document describing a potential modification to an application or system. Software problem reports (SPRs) and enhancement descriptions are specializations of change requests.

class A person, place, thing, event, concept, screen, or report.

class diagram Class diagrams show the classes of a system and the associations between them. Class diagrams are often mistakenly referred to as object models.

class library A collection of classes,

typically purchased off-the-shelf, which you can reuse and extend via inheritance.

class model A class diagram and its associated documentation.

Class Responsibility Collaborator (CRC) card A standard index card divided into three sections that show the name of the class, the responsibilities of the class, and the collaborators of the class.

Class Responsibility Collaborator (CRC) model A collection of CRC cards that describe the classes that make up an application or a component of an application.

class testing The act of ensuring that a class and its instances (objects) perform as defined.

class-integration testing The act of ensuring that the classes, and their instances, that form an application perform as defined.

client A single-user PC or workstation that provides presentation services and appropriate computing, connectivity, and interfaces relevant to the business need. A client is also commonly referred to as a *front end.*

client/server (C/S) architecture A computing environment that satisfies the business need by appropriately allocating the application processing between the client and the server processes.

code inspection A form of technical review in which the deliverable being reviewed is source code.

code reuse The reuse of source code within sections of an application and

potentially across multiple applications.

cohesion A measure of how much something makes sense. Cohesive items have a single purpose.

collaboration diagram A diagram that shows instances of classes, their interrelationships, and the message flow between them. The order of the messaging is not indicated.

collaborator On a CRC card, a collaborator of a class is another class that it interacts with to fulfill one or more or its responsibilities.

commercial-off-the-shelf (COTS) system A system produced by a third-party vendor that is available for commercial purchase.

Common Object Request Broker Architecture (CORBA) An OMG specification defining a distributed-object architecture. CORBA specifies how to develop OO applications that are able to connect and communicate with other CORBA-compliant (and potentially non-OO) applications.

component Small-scale, cohesive items such as user interface widgets that programmers reuse when building applications.

component diagram A diagram that shows the software components, their interrelationships, interactions, and their public interfaces that comprise an application, system, or enterprise.

component engineer A person who builds and then supports reusable components. Component engineers will often act as internal consultants to project teams to ensure that the teams are gaining the greatest benefits from reusable components. This is a key role for both the Program and Generalize stages.

component reuse The reuse of pre-built, fully encapsulated components in the development of your application.

computer-aided system engineering (CASE) tool A tool that supports the creation of software.

computer-based training (CBT) A program designed for the purpose of training users in a specific topic. CBT programs often use multimedia features such as animated graphics and sound.

concrete class A class from which objects are instantiated.

concurrency The issues involved with allowing multiple people simultaneous access to your persistence mechanism.

concurrency strategy The approach taken by the developer of a class to support concurrent access to instances of that class. Common concurrency strategies include the following: synchronized objects, balking objects, guarded objects, versioned objects, concurrency policy controllers, and acceptors.

configuration auditing The process of verifying and validating that a proposed configuration is complete and consistent.

configuration control The management of changes to configuration items.

configuration control board (CCB) The group responsible for approving

proposed software changes. Also called a change control board or software configuration review board (SCRB).

configuration control board (CCB) manager The person responsible for managing the CCB. This is a key role during the Identify Defects and Enhancements stage.

configuration identification The process of designating configuration items and their components.

configuration item (CI) Any deliverable, or portion of a deliverable, that is subject to SCM procedures.

configuration item owner The person or group responsible for developing and updating a given configuration item. This is a key role during the Identify Defects and Enhancements stage.

configuration status accounting The process of keeping records of the other three configuration management activities (configuration identification, configuration control, and configuration auditing) for use in the CM process.

cost/benefit breakpoint The point at which the investment you make in your project is exactly the same as its expected return.

coupling A measure of how connected two items are.

coverage testing The act of ensuring that all lines of code are exercised at least once.

critical path In a project network diagram, it is the series of activities that determines the earliest completion of a project. The critical path for a project will change from time to time as activities are completed ahead of or behind schedule.

CRUD Abbreviation for create, retrieve/read, update, delete. The basic functionality that a persistence mechanism must support.

customer The customer of an application is your user community, your operations department, and your support department.

D

data access map A depiction of a query into a database, made by an application or report, showing the tables accessed and the order in which they are accessed.

data conversion plan A plan describing how a legacy data schema will be reworked to meet the new needs of your organization. A data conversion plan will likely refer to data models for both the existing and new data schema as well as the data access maps associated with both models.

data diagram A diagram used to communicate the design of a (typically relational) database. Data diagrams are often referred to as entity-relationship (ER) diagrams.

data dictionary A repository of information about the layout of a database, the layout of a flat file, the layout of a class, and any mappings among the three.

data flow In a process model a data flow represents the movement of information, either physical or electronic, from one source to another.

data model A data diagram and its corresponding documentation.

data store In a process model, a place where information is stored, such as a database or filing cabinet.

data warehouse A large database, almost always relational, that is used to store data for reporting purposes.

database administrator (DBA) A person responsible for administering and maintaining the schema of a database.

database cursor A connection to a persistence mechanism, that was the result of a query, that allows you to traverse the result set of the query.

database proxy An object that represents a business object stored in a database. To every other object in the system, a database proxy appears to be the object that it represents. When other objects send a proxy a message, it immediately fetches the object from the database and replaces itself with the fetched object, passing the message on to it.

database server A server that has a database installed on it.

data-flow diagram (DFD) A diagram that shows the movement of data within a system among processes, entities, and data stores. Called a process diagram for OO development.

defect Anything that detracts from your application's ability to completely and effectively meet your user's needs. Also known as a bug, fault, or feature.

defensive programming An approach in which additional code is written to verify that the proper input to a method has been received and that, when a method was invoked, it worked properly.

degenerate pattern A pattern that has been described without the use of a pattern template.

deliverable Any document or system component that is produced during the development of a system. Some deliverables are used internally on a project, whereas others are produced specifically for users of the application. Examples of deliverables include user requirements, models, plans, assessments, or other documents.

deliverable management The process of organizing, monitoring, and directing the deliverables of a project.

deployment diagram A diagram showing the hardware, software, and middleware configuration for a given system.

design A style of modeling with the goal of describing how a system will be built based on the defined requirements.

design pattern A modeling pattern that describes a solution to a design problem.

detailed design A style of modeling which focuses on the design of a single piece of software.

developer Any person directly responsible for the creation of

software, including, but not limited to, modelers, programmers, and reuse engineers. This is a key role during the Construct and Deliver phases.

development/maintenance trade-off Development techniques that speed up the development process often have a negative impact on your maintenance efforts, whereas techniques that lead to greater maintainability will negatively impact your development efforts, at least in the short term.

developmental baseline This represents the incremental software builds needed to develop the application. Developmental baselines are major deliverables of the Program stage.

diagram A visual representation of a problem or solution to a problem.

distributed objects An object-oriented architecture in which objects running in separate memory spaces (such as in different computers) interact with one another transparently.

domain architecture A collection of high-level models that describe the problem domain. Domain architectures are typically documented by high-level use cases, use-case diagrams, and class models that describe the various sub domains and the relationships between them.

domain component A large-scale component that encapsulates cohesive portions of your business domain. Domain components are identified by architectural modeling.

domain modeler A person who is actively involved in modeling the problem domain for an application and/or for a reusable large-scale domain component. This is a key role during the Model stage.

domain programmer A developer who writes, documents, and tests program source code for an application. This is a key role in the Program stage.

domain/business classes Domain/business classes model the business domain. Business classes are usually found during analysis, examples of which include the classes Customer and Account.

domain-component reuse The reuse of prebuilt, large-scale domain components that encapsulate cohesive portions of your business domain.

dynamic SQL A structured query language (SQL) statement that is generated, often by a persistence layer, based on information describing the mapping between your objects and the schema of the persistence mechanisms in which they are stored.

E

economic feasibility An assessment of whether an application or system will pay for itself.

education The process by which people gain knowledge and understanding.

effort time The total time taken to develop an application, calculated by adding up all the time expended by each person contributing to development. A project that has two people working on it for four weeks each, and one person working on it for three, has an effort time of eleven weeks.

embedded SQL An SQL statement that is written directly in the code of your application. When the schema of your persistence mechanism changes, or the schema of your application, then this code will need to be updated to reflect those changes. Embedded SQL increases the coupling between your application and your persistence mechanisms.

engineering month *See* Work month

enhancement description A type of change request that specifies a new feature for an application or system.

enterprise modeling The act of modeling an organization and its external environment from a business, not an information system, viewpoint.

environmental requirement A nonfunctional requirement that deals with the environment in which the application will be used. This may be a politically motivated requirement, an ergonomic requirement, a requirement to follow specific standards or guidelines, or a requirement generated by the external business environment in which your firm operates.

escalation procedures The process by which difficult support calls are forwarded to people with greater expertise, within both your support organization and your development community.

estimator/planner This person(s) is responsible for activities such as initial project estimating, scheduling, and planning. This is a key role during the Define Initial Management Documents stage and Justify stage.

exception handling The act of identifying and acting on run-time problems (exceptions) in an application.

exit date The date that a person leaves, or is scheduled to leave, a project.

extensibility A measure of how easy it is to add new features to a system. The easier it is to add new features, the more extensible we say the system is.

external entity In a process model, the source or destination of data that is external to the system being modeled. In a class diagram we would call this an actor class.

F

facade class A class that provides the interface for a component or domain component. A facade class is composed of a collection of public methods that route messages to the other classes within a component. A component may have multiple facade classes to provide different versions of its interface.

fat-client A two-tiered client/server architecture in which client machines implement both the user interface and the business logic of an application. Typically, servers simply supply data to client machines with little or no processing done to it.

fault *See* Defect

feasibility study A document that addresses three main issues: can the system be built, can you afford to build the system, and, once the system is in place, can you maintain and support it? In other words, is the system technically feasible, is it economi-

cally feasible, and is it operationally feasible? Feasibility studies are a deliverable of the Justify stage.

feature *See* Defect

feature creep The addition, as development proceeds, of new features to an application that are above and beyond what the original specification called for. This is also called scope creep.

feature points A metric that is the superset of function points, adding a count of the algorithmic complexities within your software.

flow chart A diagram depicting the logic flow of a single process.

foreign key A column in a relational table that identifies a row within another relational table.

Fountain SDLC An iterative approach to application development first proposed by Brian Henderson-Sellers and Julian Edwards.

fourth-generation language (4GL) A category of computer languages in which the development environment includes tools that generate some or all of the source code for your application.

framework A reusable, almost-complete application that can be extended to produce custom applications.

framework reuse The reuse of collections of classes that together implement the basic functionality of a common technical or business domain.

front end *See* Client

Full Life Cycle Object-Oriented Testing (FLOOT) A testing methodology for object-oriented development that comprises testing techniques that taken together provide methods to verify that your application works correctly at each stage of development.

function points A metric used for estimating software size that is calculated by counting five items: the inputs to the software, the outputs from it, inquiries by users, the data files that would be updated by the software, and the interfaces to other software.

function testing A part of systems testing in which development staff confirm that their application meets the user requirements specified during analysis.

functional baseline The application requirements, and related test criteria, that are defined in such a manner that software development can be performed. The requirements are typically in the form of a requirements document or System Requirements Specification (SRS).

functional requirement A feature that describes a behavioral aspect of the business/problem domain.

G

Gantt chart A graphic display of schedule-related information, listing the activities to be completed down the left-hand side of the diagram, dates shown across the top, and horizontal bars showing activity duration between given dates within the diagram. Resources (teams, positions/roles, individuals) allocated to the

activities are often shown on the bars, and dependencies between activities are shown as arrows connecting the horizontal bars. Relationships between tasks, for example task A must complete before task B starts, can also be indicated.

getter method An accessor method that retrieves the value of an attribute.

glossary A document that summarizes the business and technical terms being used by the development team. Glossaries help to facilitate communications and avoid misunderstandings.

graphical user interface (GUI) A style of user interface in which graphical components, as opposed to text-based components, are used.

group memory A record of what your project team accomplished, decisions made by your team and the reasoning behind them, deferred decisions, and the lessons learned on your project. A group memory provides a mechanism to record this information when it is first recognized so that it isn't lost.

groupware A form of software which allows several users to work together on common information, often simultaneously from different physical locations.

GUI testing *See* user interface testing

guideline A description, ideally with an example provided, of how something should be done. It is recommended, but not required, that you follow guidelines (unlike standards, which are mandatory).

H

hacking A development approach where little or no effort is spent on analysis and design before coding begins.

hierarchical organization A organization with a reporting structure where each person reports to a single manager.

human-factors engineer (HFE) A person who is expert at the analysis and design of the user interface for an application and/or work environment for your users. This is a key role during the Define and Validate Initial Requirements, Model, and Program stages.

I

ignored method An inherited method that is overridden to remove its functionality.

immature software organization A software organization that is reactionary, its managers usually focused on solving immediate crises. There is no objective basis for judging product quality or for solving product or process problems. There is little understanding of how the steps of the software process affect quality, and product quality is difficult to predict.

impact analysis A determination of how your application will be affected by a given change. Your analysis should describe the modifications that need to be made to your models, documentation, and source code and should provide an estimate of the work effort involved to make those changes.

incremental development An approach to development in which applications are released in several "mini-projects," each delivering a portion of the required functionality for the overall application.

infrastructure artifact An item, such as your organization's software process, a standard, a guideline, or a chosen tool, that is common between project teams to build applications to support your organization.

infrastructure engineer A person who is responsible for defining and supporting the project infrastructure (processes, guidelines, standards, and tools). The role is applicable to the Define Infrastructure stage and all stages of the Construct phase.

infrastructure management A cross-project effort that includes your organization's architectural and enterprise modeling efforts, as well as the definition and support of processes, standards, guidelines, and chosen toolsets.

inheritance The representation of an *is a*, *is like*, or *is kind of* relationship between two classes.

inheritance-regression testing The act of running the test cases of all the super classes, both direct and indirect, on a given subclass.

inheritance reuse The use of inheritance in your application to take advantage of behavior implemented in existing classes.

inheritance tree depth The maximum number of classes from the root of a class hierarchy to its lowest node, including the root class.

installation testing The act of ensuring that your application can be installed successfully.

instance Another word for *object*. We say that an object is an instance of a class.

integration testing A test that verifies that several portions of software work together.

integration plan A plan that describes the schedule, resources, and approach to integrating the elements of an application.

interaction diagram *See* Sequence diagram

interface-flow diagram A diagram that models the interface objects of your system and the relationships between them.

internal rate of return (IRR) The interest rate that equates the cost of an investment to the present value of the respected returns from the investment.

International Standards Organization (ISO) A non-profit organization promoting the development and support of internationally accepted standards.

invariant A set of assertions about an instance or class that must be true at all "stable" times, where a stable time is the period before a method is invoked on the object or class and immediately after a method is invoked.

ISO 9001 A standard, defined by the International Standards Organization (ISO), that defines how organizations should manage their quality-assurance programs.

ISO 9003 The standards defining how organizations should manage their software quality assurance programs.

iterative development An approach to development that occurs in a non-serial manner.

J

JAD/meeting facilitator This person(s) is responsible for organizing, running, and summarizing the results of joint application development (JAD) sessions in which requirement definition and validation is performed. This is a key role during the Define and Validate Initial Requirements stage.

Java An industry standard object-oriented programming language originally developed by Sun Microsystems.

Java applet A program written in Java that is commonly operated in a Web browser.

Java bean A well-defined approach to developing reusable components with the Java programming language.

joint application development (JAD) A structured, facilitated meeting in which modeling is performed by both users and developers together. JADs are often held for gathering user requirements.

K

key A column, or several columns when combined, within a relational database table whose value(s) uniquely identifies a row.

key process area (KPA) An issue that must be addressed to achieve a specific Capability Maturity Model (CMM) maturity level.

L

leaf class A class within an inheritance hierarchy that does not have other classes inheriting from it.

learning history A written narrative of an organization's recent critical experience; often, the experiences of a software development project team.

learning team A small group of people assigned the task of working together to learn a particular subject.

legacy application Any application or system currently in production. Legacy applications are often difficult, if not impossible, to maintain and enhance.

life cycle process pattern A process pattern that depicts a software life cycle process, often made up of a collection of phases, stages, and tasks.

maintenance The update of configuration items (CIs) based on prioritized software change requests (SCRs) allocated in such a way as to retain and/or enhance the reusability and robustness of said CIs.

maintenance change A description of a modification to be made to one or more existing configuration items (CIs).

maintenance release An application release that contains only bug fixes and does not contain new functionality.

man month *See* Work month

master test/quality assurance(QA) plan A document that describes both your testing and quality assurance policies and procedures, and the detailed test plans for each portion of your application.

matrix organization An organization with a reporting structure wherein individuals potentially report to several managers: often, one manager for the project to which they are currently assigned, and another manager of a specialized group such as Modeling.

mature software organization A software organization in which the managers monitor the quality of the software products and the process that produces them. There is an objective, quantitative basis for judging product quality and analyzing problems with the product and process.

maturity level A well-defined evolutionary plateau toward achieving a mature software process. According to the Capability Maturity Model (CMM), for an organization to achieve a specific maturity level it must satisfy and institutionalize all of the key process areas (KPAs) for that level and the levels below.

member function *See* Method

mental model An internal representation of a person's conceptualization and understanding of a system.

mentor An experienced developer who transfers their skills to less experienced developers to aid in their education experience. This is a key role during all phases, but specifically during the Construct phase.

method The object-oriented equivalent of a function or procedure, with the exception that a method is specific to the class, and subclasses thereof, for which it is defined.

method-invocation box One of the long, thin vertical boxes appearing on sequence diagrams that represent a method invocation in an object.

method response A count of the total number of messages that are sent as a result of a method being invoked.

method testing The act of ensuring that a method (member function) performs as defined.

methodology In the context of systems development, it is the collection of techniques and approaches that you take when creating systems.

metric A measurement.

metrics management The process of collecting, summarizing, and acting on measurements (metrics) to potentially improve both quality of the software that your organization develops and the actual software process of your organization.

middleware The technology that allows computer hardware to communicate with one another. This includes the network itself, its operating system, and anything needed to connect computers to the network.

milestone A significant event in a project, usually the completion of a major deliverable; a point where upper management is traditionally informed of the status of the project. Because the OOSP is serial in the large and iterative in the small, the only clear milestones occur at the completion of project phases.

model An abstraction describing a problem domain and/or a solution to a problem domain. Traditionally, models are thought of as diagrams plus their corresponding documentation, although non-diagrams such as interview results, requirement documents, and collections of CRC cards are also considered to be models.

model review A technical review in which a model is inspected.

modeling The act of creating or updating one or more models.

modeling pattern A pattern depicting a solution, typically in the form of a class model, to a common modeling problem.

N

notation The set of symbols that are used in the drawing of diagrams. The Unified Modeling Language (UML) defines a de facto industry-standard modeling notation.

not-invented-here (NIH) syndrome A common myth in the information technology (IT) industry that states that developers are unwilling to reuse the work of others. The reality is that developers will only reuse high-quality work of other developers.

n-**tier client/server** A client/server architecture in which client machines interact with application servers, which in turn interact with other application servers and/or database servers.

O

objectbase *See* Object-oriented database management system (OODBMS)

object database *See* Object-oriented database management system (OODBMS)

object identifier (OID) An attribute that uniquely identifies an object; the object-oriented equivalent of a key.

object-interaction diagram *See* Sequence diagram

OPEN modeling language (OML) A set of notations for OO modeling proposed by the OPEN Consortium.

object-oriented database management system (OODBMS) A persistence mechanism, also known as an objectbase or object database, that fully supports the storage and manipulation of objects.

Object-Oriented Software Process (OOSP) A collection of process patterns that together describe a complete process for developing, maintaining, and supporting software.

object-oriented test case A collection of: objects that are in states appropriate to what is being tested; message sends to those objects; and the expected results of those message sends that together verify that a specific feature within your application works properly.

object/relational impedance mismatch The difference resulting from the fact that relational theory is based on relationships between tuples that are queried, whereas the object paradigm is based on relationships between objects that are traversed.

object technology center (OTC) A technology transfer group that specializes in the rapid development and deployment of the infrastructure

necessary to use object-oriented software development techniques successfully on a corporate scale.

OPEN Object-oriented Process, Environment, and Notation; a standard development method developed by the OPEN Consortium.

OPEN Consortium A group of individuals and organizations promoting and enhancing the use of object-oriented technology.

OPEN Process An object-oriented software process promoted by the OPEN Consortium.

operational feasibility An assessment of whether your organization can maintain and support an application or system once it is deployed.

operations documentation The documentation deployed to your operations department, including backup procedures, batch job and printing requirements, data extraction/sharing requirements, installation procedures for your application, resource requirements for your application, and the version description document (VDD) describing the product baseline for your application.

operations engineer A person responsible for operating one or more applications once they are placed in production. This is a key role during the Maintain and Support phase.

operations manager A person responsible for managing your organization's operations department and operations engineers. This is a key role during the Maintain and Support phase.

operations testing The act of ensuring that the needs of operations personnel who have to support and/or operate the application are met.

opportunistic reuse A reuse approach where reusable items are harvested from project deliverables after the fact.

optionality An indication of whether something is required.

organizational pattern A pattern that describes a common management technique or a potential organization structure.

override The redefinition of a method or attribute in a subclass.

P

paradigm A way of thinking about a given subject.

parallel development An approach to developing applications in which work on various sub-applications proceeds simultaneously in parallel.

patch release A software release that contains one or more bug fixes, replacing only a portion of the total application.

path testing The act of ensuring that all logic paths within your code were exercised at least once. This is a superset of coverage testing.

pattern The description of a general solution to a common problem or issue from which a detailed solution to a specific problem may be determined. Software development patterns come in many flavors, including but not limited to analysis patterns, design patterns, and process patterns.

pattern language A collection, or catalog, of related patterns. A pattern language for processes enables you to create an infinite variety of combinations, each one of which would be considered a tailored software process.

pattern template A predefined format for describing a pattern. There is currently an effort within the patterns community to describe a standard template for process patterns, but at the time of this writing one has not been finalized.

pattern reuse The reuse of publicly documented approaches, called patterns, to solving common problems.

peer review A style of technical review in which a project deliverable, or portion thereof, is inspected by a small group of people with expertise in the product being reviewed.

people management The process of organizing, monitoring, coaching, and motivating people in such a manner to ensure that they work together effectively and contribute to a project/organization positively.

performance requirement A requirement defining the speed at which a software feature is to operate.

persistence The issue of how to store objects to permanent storage. Objects need to be persistent if they are to be available to you and/or to others the next time your application is run.

persistence classes Classes that provide the ability to permanently store objects. By encapsulating the storage and retrieval of objects via persistence classes, you are able to use various storage technologies interchangeably without affecting your applications.

persistence layer The collection of classes that provides business objects the ability to be persistent. A persistence layer effectively wraps access to your persistence mechanisms.

persistence mechanism The permanent storage facility used to make objects persistent. Examples include relational databases, object databases, flat files, and object/relational databases.

person month *See* Work month

PERT chart *See* Project network diagram

phase *See* Project phase

phase process pattern A process pattern that depicts the interactions between the stage process patterns for a single project phase.

pilot project A small project whose purpose is to prove the viability of a new technology.

pilot testing A testing process equivalent to beta testing that is used by organizations to test applications they have developed for their own internal use.

planned reuse *See* systematic reuse

pop-up menu A style of menu, often tailored depending on the context in which it is invoked, that is displayed when requested by a user. A common GUI design standard is to display a pop-up menu when the user clicks the secondary mouse button. Also called

a context-sensitive menu or hidden menu.

postcondition An expression of the properties of the state of an object after a method has been invoked successfully.

precondition An expression of the constraints under which a method will operate properly.

present-day value An amount of money into which inflation has been taken into account to determine its value in today's terms.

primary key The column(s) of a table that have been chosen as the primary means of uniquely identifying rows in that column.

private visibility An indication that a method or attribute is accessible only by instances of a class.

problem reproduction environment An environment in which a copy of your application runs in isolation. This environment is used by support engineers to simulate problems reported by your user community.

procedure A series of steps to be followed to perform a given task.

process A series of actions in which one or more inputs are used to produce one or more outputs.

process action team (PAT) A group of software professionals, often from different parts of your organization, who are given the responsibility to identify and define applicable process patterns for your organization.

process antipattern An antipattern

that describes an approach and/or series of actions for developing software that is proven to be ineffective and often detrimental to your organization.

process checklist An indication of the tasks that should be completed while working a defined process.

process diagram A diagram that shows the movement of data within a system. Similar in concept to a data-flow diagram (DFD) but not as rigid and documentation-heavy.

process improvement plan A plan identifying potential improvements to your existing object-oriented software process (OOSP), including an estimate, schedule, and staff assignments for making the improvements.

process pattern A pattern that describes a proven, successful approach and/or series of actions for developing software.

process specialist A person who is responsible for choosing and/or defining the development processes to be used on the project, and who may act as an infrastructure consultant during later phases. This is a key role during the Define Infrastructure stage.

product baseline The exact version of the software that is released to the user community.

programme A collection of projects or releases of one or more applications.

project assessment A two- or three-page document that summarizes what occurred on a project. This document is often used as introductory material

to your learning history for the given project, and for the process improvement plan that results from the lessons learned on the given project.

project auditor A professional who specializes in the review and assessment of projects. This is a key role during the Assess stage.

project charter A document issued by senior management that provides the project manager with the authority to apply organizational resources to project activities.

project-defined software process The process, tailored from your organization's standard software process, used for a given project.

project estimate An appraisal of how long a project will take and how much it will cost, given a specific environment and a specific team. Change the environment and/or change the team, and your estimate should change. Project estimates are a deliverable of the Initiate phase and are updated regularly throughout a project.

project funding The money and resources used to finance a project.

project infrastructure The team, tools, and processes that will be used on a given project.

project management The process of organizing, monitoring, and directing a project.

Project Management Institute (PMI) An organization dedicated to the research of, and dissemination of information about, project management techniques.

project manager A person who is responsible for obtaining funding and authorization for the project from upper management, as well as for day-to-day management of a project. This is a key role during all phases of the project.

project network diagram A schematic display of the logical relationships between project activities, always drawn left-to-right to reflect project chronology. Often incorrectly referred to as a PERT (Program Evaluation and Review Technique) chart.

project objectives A description of the criteria against which the success of a project will be measured. This potential includes clear, measurable definitions of goals for the cost of the project, desired delivery date, quality factors, and desires of the various project stakeholders.

project overview A description of the purpose of the project, the scope of the project, its advantages and disadvantages, the expected cost and delivery date(s), and the technical platform for which it will be developed. A project overview is effectively a summary of the other components the schedule, estimate, team definition, and risk assessment that comprise a project plan. Project overviews are a deliverable of the Initiate phase.

project phase The large components of the OOSP that are performed in a serial manner. The four project phases are Initiate, Construct, Deliver, and Maintain and Support. A project phase is depicted by a process pattern.

project plan A project plan is a collection of several project management deliverables, including, but not limited to, a project overview, a project schedule, a project estimate, a team definition, and a risk assessment. Project plans are a deliverable of the Initiate phase and are updated regularly throughout a project.

project schedule A project schedule indicates what will be done, when things will be done, and who will do them. A major component of a project schedule is a Gantt chart with its corresponding descriptions of tasks and resources. Project schedules are a deliverable of the Initiate phase and are updated regularly throughout a project.

project scope A definition of the functionality that will, and will not, be implemented by an application.

project skills matrix A chart that relates the skills needed on a project to the skills of the people (potentially) on a project team.

project sponsor A person who takes responsibility for supporting, nurturing, and protecting the project throughout its life, and who is crucial for starting the project successfully. This is a key role during the Justify stage.

project stage The components of a project phase, performed in an iterative manner, that make up a project phase. For example, the project stages that make up the Construct phase are Model, , Program, Generalize, and Test in the Small. A project stage is depicted by a process pattern.

project stakeholder Any individual or organization that may be affected by project activities.

proof-of-concept prototype Software written to prove or test the viability of a technology, language, or environment. Also called a technical prototype.

protected visibility An indication that an attribute or method is accessible only to the instances of the class, and all subclasses of, that the method/attribute is defined in.

prototype A mock-up of all or a portion of your application.

prototype walkthrough A process by which your users work through a collection of use cases using a prototype as if it was the real thing. The main goal is to test whether or not the prototype design meets their needs.

prototyping An iterative analysis technique in which users are actively involved in the mocking up of the user interface for an application.

proxy object An object that is used to represent another object. A common responsibility of a proxy object is to pass messages that it receives to the object for which it is a proxy.

public interface The collection of public methods and attributes of a class or component.

public visibility An indication that a method, attribute, or class is accessible to all objects within your application.

pure inheritance When a subclass inherits everything from its superclass(es).

Q

qualitative factor A cost or benefit that is subjective in nature, against which it is very difficult to identify a monetary value.

quality assurance (QA) The process of ensuring that the efforts of a project meet or exceed the standards expected of them.

quality assurance (QA) engineer A person responsible for validating that the deliverables produced by the development team meet or exceed the agreed-to standards and guidelines for the project. This is a key role during all stages of the Construct phase, the Define and Validate Initial Requirements stage, and the Rework stage.

quality gate An objectively identifiable point in a project at which a review is performed to validate one or more project deliverables. To meet a milestone, your project will usually need to "pass through" a quality gate successfully.

quantitative factor A cost or benefit against which a monetary value can easily be identified.

R

R&D/proof-of-concept engineer A developer who creates technical prototypes, also called proof-of-concept prototypes, to determine how to solve a given technical issue. This role is applicable to the Model stage to verify decisions made during technical architectural modeling and detailed design.

refactoring The act of reorganizing OO development efforts. For source code and models, refactoring will often comprise the renaming of methods, attributes, or classes; the redefinition of methods, attributes, or classes; or the complete rework or methods, attributes, or classes. For other project deliverables refactoring may simply be the renaming or reorganization of sections of the deliverable.

reference manual A document, either paper or electronic, aimed at experts who need quick access to information.

regression testing The act of ensuring that previously tested behaviors still work as expected after changes have been made to an application.

regulatory requirement A requirement that you must fulfill by law. Regulatory requirements include the need to provide specific information to the government, perhaps for taxation or environmental reasons, or the use of a specific programming language or technique in the case of government contracts.

relational database (RDB) A type of persistence mechanism, based on relational theory, that stores data in tables. The rows of data within tables are related to one another; hence the term *relational database*.

release A version of an application or component that has been made available for use by its developers.

release plan A plan that describes when your release procedures will be applied, and by whom, to release your application.

release procedures A description of the tasks, and the order in which to take them, to release an application. Release procedures will refer to your data conversion plan and your training plan for your release.

repository A centralized database into/from which you can check in and check out versions of your development work, including documentation, models, and source code.

requirement Something that is essential, or perceived to be essential.

requirements allocation matrix (RAM) A mapping of requirements, defined in your requirements document, to the portions of your model(s) that implement them.

requirements document A document, also called a System Requirements Specification (SRS), that describes the user, technical, and environmental requirements for an application. This document potentially contains the major use cases for the application, detailed use-case scenarios for the application, and traditional requirements for the application as well. Requirements documents are a deliverable of the Initiate phase and are updated regularly during modeling. Requirements documents are also updated during the Maintain and Support phase as bugs and enhancements are identified.

requirements engineering The identification and validation of requirements.

requirements instability A metric calculated by taking the number of changed requirements in a given time frame by the total number of requirements.

requirements triage The act of prioritizing requirements, for example, "must have," "nice to have," and "nonessential" to aid in the definition of an application that can be delivered with resources at hand.

requirement-verification matrix A document that is used to relate use cases to the portions of your application that implement the requirements addressed by those use cases. For OO applications, the names of classes are listed across the top of the matrix, the use cases are listed along the left-hand axis of the matrix, and in the squares are listed the main method(s) involved in fulfilling each use case.

responsibility Behavior that a class is expected to be able to perform, either for its own use or in response to a request from another class. A responsibility may be for a class to know something, to have data, or to do something (to perform a function).

Reuse Capability Model (RCM) A model which describes five maturity levels at which your organization may operate with respect to reuse.

reuse consumer A developer that reuses the work of other developers.

reuse engineer A senior, experienced developer who is responsible for supporting and enhancing the reuse process within your organization. This person works closely with component engineers and infrastructure engineers, and plays a key role in all stages of the Construct phase.

reuseless An item that has been promoted as reusable but in practice is found to be too specific or of low quality.

reuse management The process of organizing, monitoring, and directing the efforts of a project team that lead to reuse on a project, either of existing or of purchased items.

reuse producer A developer that creates reusable items.

reuse repository A tool used to store reusable items.

revision A change to a deliverable.

risk assessment A document indicating potential factors, called risks, that if they were to occur would harm the project. A risk assessment is used to identify risks so they may be dealt with appropriately. Risk assessments are a deliverable of the Initiate phase and are updated regularly throughout a project.

risk assessor A person who is responsible for identifying and potentially addressing the initial risks associated with your project. This is a key role during the Define Initial Management Documents stage and Justify stage.

risk management The process of identifying, monitoring, and mitigating the risks faced by a project team. These risks may typically be strategic, technical, and/or political.

risk officer Someone in your organization who is responsible for supporting and overseeing risk management.

robustness A measure of the quality of a product. Robust software products continue to operate once an error occurs and are relatively easy to maintain and enhance.

root class The top class in an inheritance hierarchy.

S

schema The design of something.

scope creep *See* Feature creep

sequence diagram A diagram that shows the types of objects involved in a use-case scenario, including the messages they send to one another and the values that they return. Also referred to as an event trace diagram or simply an interaction diagram.

serial development An approach to development in which a series of tasks are performed in a defined, sequential order.

server One or more multiuser processors (with shared memory) that provide computing connectivity, database services, and interfaces relevant to the business need. A server is also commonly referred to as a "back end."

setter method An accessor method that modifies the value of an attribute.

silver bullet Any product or technique that (unrealistically) promises order-of-magnitude improvements in your development productivity.

singleton A class that will have at most one instance.

skills assessment (deliverable) A summary of the proficiencies of an individual, used for the purpose of developing a training plan for the individual and for identifying projects where their skills are needed.

skills assessment (process) A process in which the skills, both technical skills such as C++ programming and people skills such as eliciting requirements from users, of an individual are determined and measured.

skills database A database that records the skills and experiences of people within your organization. This information is both the input and the output of a skills assessment.

software change request (SCR) A description of a potential improvement to a software deliverable, often identified by users of that deliverable.

software configuration management (SCM) A set of engineering procedures for tracking and documenting software and its related deliverables throughout their life cycles to ensure that all changes are recorded and the current state of the software is known and reproducible.

software configuration manager A person responsible for ensuring that software and its related deliverables are managed appropriately under configuration control, as well as to communicate all SCM policies and procedures to developers. The greater the complexity of the software being developed, the greater the need for a software configuration manager. This is a key role throughout the Construct, Deliver, and Maintain and Support phases.

Software Engineering Institute (SEI) An organization within Carnegie Mellon University whose goal is to provide leadership in advancing the state of the practice of software engineering to improve the quality of systems that depend on software.

Software Engineering Process Group (SEPG) A group of dedicated professionals whose sole responsibility is to support the improvement of your organization's software process.

software maintenance The update of existing configuration items based on change requests allocated in such a way as to retain and/or enhance the reusability and robustness of said configuration items.

software problem report (SPR) A description of a potential software defect identified by someone who is not directly responsible for a given software deliverable.

software process A set of project phases, stages, methods, techniques, and practices that people employ to develop and maintain software and its associated products (plans, documents, models, code, test cases, and manuals).

software Process Improvement and Capability dEtermination (SPICE) An ISO software process improvement project.

software quality assurance (SQA) The process and techniques by which the development of software is verified, tested, and ensured to be of sufficient levels of excellence for your organization.

software unit An identifiable portion of software potentially an application, a file that is a portion of an application, a domain component, or a service supported by your technical architecture. Software units are one type of configuration item (CI).

Spiral SDLC An iterative approach to application development first proposed by Barry Boehm.

staff assessment A summary of the performance with your organization of a single staff member. An assessment of the staff member's skills is included, as is a training plan for maintaining and improving those skills.

staff month *See* Work month

stage *See* Project stage

stage process pattern A process pattern that depicts the steps, often performed iteratively, of a single project stage.

standard A description, ideally with an example provided, of how something must be done. You are required to follow standards (unlike guidelines, which are optional).

standards specialist A person responsible for choosing and/or defining the development standards to be used on a project, and who may act as an infrastructure engineer/consultant during later phases. This is a key role during the Define Infrastructure stage.

state A representation of a stage in the behavior pattern of an object. A state can also be said to represent a condition of an object to which a defined set of policies, regulations, and physical laws apply. On statechart diagrams a state is shown as a horizontal rectangle.

state diagram *See* Statechart diagram

statechart diagram A diagram that describes the states that an object may be in, as well as the transitions between states. Also called a "state diagram" or "state-transition diagram."

state-transition diagram *See* Statechart diagram

status report A two- or three-page document briefly summarizing the work performed on a project over a given period of time and any change in status of the project, including updates to your risk assessment.

stored procedure A function implemented within a relational database.

strategic reuse plan Your organization's plan for implementing its reuse management approach, including a description of its reuse goals, its schedule, and its commitment to supporting reuse management.

stress testing The act of ensuring that the system performs as expected under high volumes of transactions, high numbers of users, and so on.

stress-test plan The test plan that describes how you intend to go about stress-testing your application.

string of message sends A series of messages sent to the same object.

Structured Query Language (SQL) A standard mechanism used to CRUD records in a relational database.

subject matter expert (SME) A person who is responsible for providing pertinent information about the problem and/or technical domain either from personal knowledge or from research. This is a key role during the

Define and Validate Initial Requirements stage and the Model stage.

support center A group of support engineers and their support tools.

support documentation The documentation deployed to your support department, including your support call recording process, applicable call escalation procedures, relevant points of contact within your development and operations departments, and all user documentation for your application.

support engineer A person whose job is to collaborate with users needing help to use your software. This is a key role during the Support stage and Test in the Large stage.

support flow The process through which support requests are received by support engineers from users, solutions are found, and answers are returned to the user.

support manager The person responsible for managing your organization's support center and support engineers. This is a key role during the Support stage.

support request A request for aid using an application made by a user. This may be in the form of a phone call, an electronic mail (e-mail) message, a fax, or an entry into a support request database (likely via a Web page).

support request database An application built for the specific purpose of recording support requests. This database may be accessible to your users to allow them to submit support requests, perhaps via a Web page data entry screen.

support request escalation A process in which a support request is passed from the support engineer who initially responded to it to another person, potentially a more senior support engineer or developer, to be resolved.

support testing The act of ensuring that the needs of support personnel who have to support the application are met.

support user's guide A brief document, usually a single page, that describes the support services for your application that are available to your user community. This guide will include support phone numbers, fax numbers, and Web site locations as well as hours of operations and tips for obtaining the best services.

system analysis The process of determining what projects will be undertaken, the order in which they will be undertaken, how they will be developed, and the scope of each project.

system classes System classes provide operating-system-specific functionality for your applications, or they wrap functionality provided by other tool/application vendors. System classes isolate you from the operating system, making your application portable between environments, by wrapping OS-specific features.

system development life cycle (SDLC) The process by which software is developed. An SDLC is comprised of interrelated techniques that are used to define, build, implement, support, and maintain software.

system layer The collection of classes that provide operating-system-specific

functionality for your applications, or that wrap functionality provided by non-OO applications, hardware devices, and/or non-OO code libraries.

system requirement specification (SRS) *See* Requirements document

system testing A testing process in which you find and fix any known problems to prepare your application for user testing.

systematic reuse An approach to reuse that involves modeling techniques whose purpose is to define high-leverage, reusable components.

T

table join A relational database concept in which information from two or more tables are accessed. Tables are joined by selecting rows from each table that contain identical values in one or more common columns.

tailored software process A software process that has been modified to meet the needs of a specific project.

task list A list of activities that an individual or team is to perform in a defined period of time. Task lists are often defined to manage the creation of a project deliverable.

task process pattern A process pattern that depicts the detailed steps to perform a specific task, such as detailed modeling or performing a technical review.

team definition A document describing who will be involved with a project, what their roles on the project will be, and when they will be involved. This document should also provide a reporting structure, or organization chart, for the team.

team lead The developer who is responsible for ensuring the overall technical integrity of the project and for working together with the project manager to aid and support the other developers on the team. A main responsibility of team leads is to ruthlessly eliminate any obstacles that keep the developers away from working to improve the application. This is a key role during all stages of the Construct phase.

technical architecture A set of models and documents that describe the technical components of an application, including but not limited to the hardware, software, middleware, persistence mechanisms, and operating systems to be deployed.

technical feasibility An assessment of whether an application or system can be built with a defined set of tools and technologies.

technical prototype *See* Proof-of-concept prototype

technical requirement A description of a nonbehavioral feature, such as the required time for something to run in or the operating system that an application must work in.

technical review A testing technique in which the design of your application is examined critically by a group of your peers. A review will typically focus on accuracy, quality, usability, and completeness. This process is often referred to as a walkthrough or a peer review.

technical-review plan A document that describes the goal of a technical review, who is to attend and why, the information that the reviewers require before the review, and the records and documentation that will be produced by the review.

technical writer The person responsible for writing, updating, and/or improving the technical documentation produced on the project, potentially including the requirements, models, standards, guidelines, and project plans. This is a key role throughout all project phases.

template reuse The reuse of a common set of layouts for key development artifacts documents, models, and source code within your organization.

templated pattern A pattern that has been documented using a pattern template.

test case A description, often documented as a series of steps, of a situation that a software item must support.

test engineer This person is responsible for verifying that the application works as defined by the requirements for the application. This is a key role during all stages of the Construct phase and the Test in the Large stage.

test log A chronological tracking of your testing activities.

test manager The person responsible for managing the testing engineers and testing process within your organization. This person works closely with your organization's project managers to ensure that the testing of applications is being performed in an effective manner. This is a key role during all stages of the Construct phase and the Test in the Large stage.

test plan A document that prescribes the approach to be taken during the testing process.

test script The steps to be performed to run a test case. Test scripts will be implemented using a variety of techniques, from source code for code tests to written steps for function testing.

test suite A collection of test scripts.

testability The measure of ease of which a product may be tested.

testing The act of verifying that the "right" thing, as defined by its requirements, was built.

testing release A software release in which your application is released for alpha/beta/pilot testing.

test-procedure scripts The description of the steps that must be carried out to perform all or part of a test plan.

thin client A two-tiered client/server architecture in which client machines implement only the user interface of an application.

timebox A defined period of time, from several days to several months, in which a team of developers is assigned to produced a given deliverable. With a timebox the end date is actually a fixed deadline; if the team needs to, it will cut features out of the deliverable rather than extend the delivery date.

tools specialist A person who is responsible for evaluating and selecting the development tools to be used on the project, and who may act as an infrastructure engineer/consultant during later phases. This is a key role during the Define Infrastructure stage.

traceability The ease with which the features of one deliverable a document, model, or source code can be related or traced to the features of another.

trailblazer project A medium-sized project whose purpose is to prove the viability of a software process by developing software while following the given process.

trainer A person responsible for the delivery, and possibly development, of training courses. This is a key role during the Release stage.

training The process by which people gain tangible skills.

training manager The person responsible for managing your organization's training department. This person oversees your organization's internal trainers, if any, and is responsible for hiring outside training firms to deliver courses to your organization's employees. This is a key role during the Release stage.

training plan A plan that describes the training to be delivered, to whom it will be delivered, how it will be delivered, when it will be delivered, and where it will be delivered.

transition A transition is a progression from one state to another. A transition will be triggered by an event (either internal or external to the object). A transition is shown on a statechart diagram as an arrow leading from one state to another.

tutorial manual A document, either paper or electronic, aimed at novice users who need to learn the fundamentals of an application.

two-tiered client/server An approach to client/server architectures in which client machines directly interact with server machines.

U

Unified Modeling Language (UML) The industry-standard OO modeling notation proposed by Rational Corporation of Santa Clara, California. The UML has been accepted by the Object Management Group (OMG) to make it the industry standard.

unit testing The act of testing small components of a system to ensure that they work. In the object world this is both method and class testing.

usability testing The verification, typically performed by human-factors engineers, that an application or system is as easy to use as it needs to be for its user community.

use case A description of a high-level business process that an application may or may not be expected to support.

use-case diagram A diagram that shows the use cases and actors for the application you are developing.

use-case scenario A description of a specific, detailed user requirement that an application may or may not

be expected to handle. A use-case scenario is a detailed example of a use case.

use-case scenario testing A testing process in which users work through use cases with the aid of a facilitator to verify that the user requirements are accurate.

user acceptance testing (UAT) A testing technique in which users verify that an application meets their needs.

user documentation The documentation deployed to the user community, potentially including a user manual, tutorial manual, reference manual, and support user's guide.

user interface (UI) The portion of an application with which the user directly interacts, including the screens, reports, documentation, and software support (via telephone, electronic mail, and so on).

user interface classes User interface classes provide the ability for users to interact with the system. User interface classes typically define a graphical user interface for an application, although other interface styles, such as voice command or handwritten input, are also implemented via user-interface classes.

user interface event An occurrence (often) initiated by a user, such as keyboard input, a mouse action, or spoken input captured by a microphone, that causes action within your application.

user interface object An object displayed as part of the user interface for an application. This includes simple objects such as buttons and list boxes, icons, screens, and reports as well as complex objects such as editing screens and reports.

user interface testing The testing of the user interface (UI) to ensure that it follows accepted UI standards and meets the requirements defined for it. This is often referred to as graphical user interface (GUI) testing.

user manual A document, either paper or electronic, aimed at intermediate users who understand the basics of an application but may not know how to perform all applicable work tasks with the application.

user requirement A behavioral requirement for an application that describes the needs of all or part of the user community, and whose source either directly or indirectly came from the user community.

user requirement review A testing process in which a facilitated group of users verify and prioritize the user requirements gathered by a development team.

user testing Testing processes in which the user community, as opposed to developers, performs the tests. User testing techniques include user acceptance testing, alpha testing, beta testing, and pilot testing.

V

version One or more revisions to a deliverable results in a new version.

version control tool A software tool used to check in/out, define, and manage versions of project deliverables.

version description document (VDD) A complete list of all items included in a product baseline release of software, including all configuration items and supporting deliverables. The VDD includes an indication of all changes made to the software from the previous version and a list of all applicable SPRs and SCRs implemented in the current version.

virtual organization An organization with a reporting structure wherein professionals collaborate as equals to perform specific tasks.

visibility An indication of the level of access to a class, method, or attribute.

volume testing A subset of stress testing that deals specifically with determining how many transactions or database accesses an application can handle during a defined period of time.

W

waterfall SDLC An approach to building applications in which development efforts proceed in a serial manner from one project stage to another.

white-box test A test that verifies that specific lines of code work as defined. This is also referred to as a clear-box test.

widget A user interface component such as a list, button, or window.

work breakdown structure (WBS) A deliverable-oriented grouping of project elements which organizes and defines the total scope of the project. Each descending level represents an increasingly detailed definition of a project component.

work day A standard amount of time, measured in hours, which your organization considers a day. Most organizations define a standard work day as being seven, seven-and-a-half, or eight hours.

work month A standard amount of time corresponding to the average number of work days in an average month. Also known as a man month, person month, staff month, or engineering month.

wrapper A collection of one or more classes that encapsulates access to non-OO technology to make it appear as if it is OO.

wrapper class Any class that is part of a wrapper.

wrapping The act of encapsulating non-OO functionality within a class, making it look and feel like any other object within the system.

Y

year 2000 (Y2K) problem A common problem where dates within software, and databases, have been recorded with a two-digit year (for example 05), instead of a four-digit year (for example 2005). This problem results in software not recognizing dates on or after January 1st, 2000, believing that they represent dates on or after January 1st, 1900 instead.

Index